LAW IN SPORT: CONCEPTS AND CASES

Fifth Edition

Titles in the Sport Management Library

Case Studies in Sport Business Marketing, 3rd Edition

Developing Successful Social Media Plans in Sport Organizations

Developing Successful Sport Marketing Plans, 5th Edition

Developing Successful Sport Sponsorship Plans, 5th Edition

Economics of Sport, 2nd Edition

Foundations of Sport Management, 4th Edition

Fundamentals of Sport Business Marketing, 5th Edition

Law in Sport: Concepts and Cases, 5th Edition

Media Relations in Sport, 5th Edition

Sponsorship for Sport Managers

Sport Facility Management: Organizing Events and Mitigating Risks, 3rd Edition

Sport Governance in the Global Community

Ticket Operations and Sales Management in Sport

For a current list of Sport Management Library titles visit
www.fitpublishing.com

LAW IN SPORT: CONCEPTS AND CASES

Fifth Edition

John Grady, JD, PhD
University of South Carolina

FiT PUBLISHING

FiT Publishing
A Division of the International Center for Performance Excellence
375 Birch Street, WVU-CPASS
PO Box 6116
Morgantown, WV 26506-6116
www.fitpublishing.com

Library of Congress Card Catalog Number: 2022940010

ISBN Print: 9781940067735
ISBN eBook: 9781940067742

Cover Design: 40 West Studios
Cover Photos: University of South Carolina Football Game photo, Allen Wallace, University of South Carolina, 2021.
ID 93247863 © Piotr Adamowicz | Dreamstime.com
Project Editor: Kassandra Roberts
Copyeditor: Brittany Murray

10 9 8 7 6 5 4 3 2 1

FiT Publishing
A Division of the International Center for Performance Excellence
West Virginia University
375 Birch Street, WVU-CPASS
PO Box 6116
Morgantown, WV 26506-6116
800.477.4348 (toll free)
304.293.6888 (phone)
304.293.6658 (fax)
Email: fitcustomerservice@mail.wvu.edu
Website: www.fitpublishing.com

Table of Contents

Dedication

To my family and friends, whose support means the world to me.

To my South Carolina "family" who I see more often, your daily encouragement helps me to thrive.

To Annie Clement, with whom a professional relationship and personal friendship flourished at Florida State University and whose work on the previous four editions provides much inspiration to those studying law in sport today.

To my Gamecock faculty colleagues, where dedication to student success makes teaching a joy!

To my FSU professors, mentors, and fellow PhD classmates, who taught a young lawyer about sports.

To Rebekah Griggs, for your careful and dedicated research assistance and sharp insight on legal trends.

To Spenser Burns, for your helpful comments and research assistance, as well as your keen insights into sports business and law.

To Kassi Roberts, Eileen Harvey, Brittany Murray, and Barb Dalton for your support and unwavering commitment to preparing the 5th edition.

And finally, to my USC current and former students, who bring the cases and examples in this book to life in our classroom each day.

-JG

Dedication

Preface

The fifth edition of *Law in Sport* is designed to make introductory legal concepts and their application to sport and physical activity easy to understand. The new edition explores the diversity of legal issues facing the contemporary sport manager, and helps them to become aware of frequent legal issues they may face in their early careers. This text is recommended for use in courses that cover legal aspects of sport, and is intended for both undergraduate and graduate student audiences. By viewing legal issues impacting sport through the lens of a sport manager, the student can connect legal theory to practical application in an engaging way. Students using this text will develop a deeper appreciation of the context in which these legal issues may arise and will be able to proactively manage potential liability and legal risks.

This text explains the law to students who have begun to understand how sport organizations function in a user-friendly way. Special focus is placed on the role of recent cases in exploring the unique application of law in sport. As with previous editions, students using this text will appreciate the role they play in making decisions that affect the success of their organization. For the sport management student, identifying areas of potential legal exposure they frequently may experience and recognizing situations when more advanced legal advice is needed are critical skills necessary to effectively manage sport organizations.

Introduction:
The Study of Law in Sport

"Law in Sport" Or "Sport Law"?

A historical debate exists over the use of the terms "law in sport" and "sport law" (Davis, 2001). "Law in sport" is the wide range of legal concepts faced in the day-to-day decisions in the sport industry. These concepts have been taken from the laws of negligence, intentional torts, product liability, contracts, constitution, labor, agency, intellectual property, and others. They are applied to sport and physical activity just as they are applied to non-sport situations.

Sport law, on the other hand, refers only to the basic law and court decisions that are unique to sport. A body of law, including case law and law reviews, unique to sport continues to develop. Specialized courses dedicated only to the law unique to sport now exist in several law schools, as well as in most graduate and undergraduate programs in sport management.

An example of one of the many unique aspects of law in sport is the draft system found in professional team sports. The draft involves the rating of athletes and the opportunity of teams to select and employ individual athletes according to an inverse relationship, which is based on the win/loss record of the league's teams the previous year. If this were a general business practice, we would find each year's MBA graduates rated by grades or some other formula, waiting to be picked by industries according to the previous year's profits of the industries. Those industries with the lowest profits would select first. No MBA student would have a choice of location or company.

In addition to the example listed above, the following items are just a few of the myriad unique aspects of law that exist because sport differs from traditional business practices:

- antitrust issues as a result of lockouts by major professional sport leagues in the United States
- the dual union/representation combination found in professional team sport contracts
- free agency
- drug testing of professional and amateur athletes
- high levels of assumption of risk far beyond what is expected in traditional business operations
- intellectual property cases involving fantasy sports
- sex of the team rather than sex of the coach used as a factor in discrimination

- stadium accessibility requirements under the Americans with Disabilities Act
- restructuring naming rights deals during an economic downturn (e.g., COVID-19 pandemic)
- legal issues resulting from revenue sharing among professional teams and leagues

Status of Law in Sport

The study of law in sport, physical activity, and related areas began in the 1980s. In response to negligence suits occurring in physical activity and the dedicated interest in risk management practices, sport specialists began to look to the legal profession for help. Communication was difficult, as lawyers saw "sport" as mainly professional sport and viewed the legal needs of professional teams and leagues as focusing on contract, labor, and agency law. Sport professionals, however, viewed law as personal injury and civil rights issues. While there were very few sport specialists who served the legal industry as expert witnesses at the time, these individuals are credited for forming the connection between law and sport that exists today. As sport management grew as an academic field of study, the need for the business components of law that had originally been championed by the legal profession became increasingly important to sport professionals at all levels (professional, collegiate, Olympic).

Law in sport and physical activity continues to grow and evolve. Current legal trends that developed and were shaped in the context of sport have become part of the mainstream in the popular press and are now discussed on sport law blogs, demonstrating interest by a far wider audience than ever before. Moreover, the separate area of risk management and compliance in sport exemplifies the return to the originally identified need for negligence and civil rights law. The chapter on risk management (Chapter 11) reflects best practices in stadium management and provides students with an introduction to the risk management process, especially in light of the COVID-19 pandemic.

Today, sport law is a popular required course in many sport management and physical activity undergraduate and graduate programs and is of special interest in law school curricula. Yet, even the top sports law scholars, such as Tulane Law School's Professor Gabe Feldman acknowledged in 2015 "that there is no defined area of law called 'sports law.' Rather, a sports lawyer is simply an attorney who represents clients in matters involving one or more legal areas that are implicated in the context of the sport industry (Tulane University Law School, 2015, p. 5).

Components of a Lawsuit

Anyone can be sued. A lawsuit can be brought against any person or agency. A suit is brought when a person believes that he/she has been wronged and decides to place liability for that wrong on another person or agency. Court records verify that persons in nearly every profession have been forced by a court of law to defend their employment practices, programs, supervision, and management. All professionals should assume they can be sued, think through what a suit would mean emotionally, physically, and financially, and plan strategies that will provide a good chance of prevailing in a court of law.

Monetary damages are nearly always the goal in tort situations; in recent years, civil rights decisions have also resulted in monetary damages. In a court of law, the object of a damage award is to return the injured party to his/her condition prior to the incident. This is often called making the person "whole." Therefore, a specific sum of money is agreed upon by the court as making the injured person/plaintiff whole again. Personal injury litigation usually results when a victim has sustained a substantial financial loss. The loss may be a result of medical bills, lost wages, or rehabilitation fees. In addition, the loss may include future losses for persons who will require continuous assistance and rehabilitation. The expense of a catastrophic injury or death is high.

Selection of an Attorney

When an individual determines that he/she has been harmed, the next step is usually to select an attorney. The attorney must understand the circumstances of the incident, become conversant with accepted professional standards of care both in sport and physical activity, and be aware of any civil rights issues or concerns. Once the attorney understands the incident and the appropriate standard of care, the attorney is ready to advise the client. Among the client's choices is to bring a cause of action (lawsuit) against the party (or parties) that caused the harm. Every effort is made by the attorney and client to settle the differences among the parties; a lawsuit is considered a last resort. If one of the parties refuses to negotiate or there is a significant difference of opinion about the facts of the case, a formal complaint is filed.

Stages of a Lawsuit

A suit is divided into four stages: complaint, discovery, trial, and appeal.

Complaint

The complaint is a written statement alleging the cause of action, rights of the injured parties, legal theories, and award sought. The court issues a summons that is served on the defendant—the person or agency alleged to have caused the harm. An answer to the court is filed by the defendant in a specified period of time (usually 30 or 45 days). Once an individual receives a summons, legal counsel should be obtained. The ideal approach is for the defendant to have retained legal counsel that has been involved in risk and business decisions, and thus understand the environment in which the alleged injury occurred.

Discovery

Once a formal complaint is filed, both parties are in a favorable position to obtain information about the incident. This period of time is referred to as the discovery period. During the discovery period, parties learn as much as possible about the incident in which the alleged injury occurred, and value the injury in the context of similar incidents. Information is obtained by subpoena of records and by interviewing persons involved in the incident. The results of these discussions are made permanent as affidavits and depositions (statements of persons, under oath) of parties directly involved. Furthermore, the depositions of experts can assist the lawyers, the court, and ultimately the jury, in establishing standards of care and best business practices.

A case can be settled at any time during the discovery period. Members of the court stay in touch with the lawyers and their clients throughout the discovery period. The majority of court claims are settled during this period. The discovery period has a starting and finishing date. If the dispute is not resolved on the final date of discovery, the parties move into the motion phase and prepare for trial. Motions are requests to the court, controlled by the rules of the court, and assist the parties in resolving disputes. Motions for settlement may be made prior to and during trial.

Trial

The trial is either bench or jury. In a bench trial, a group of judges makes the decision. In a jury trial, people selected by the lawyers and the judge make the decision. The decision is based on the testimony at trial and the documents produced. Once the jury is selected, the attorneys for the plaintiff and defendant make opening statements to the court summarizing their case. After the opening statements, the plaintiff presents his/her case. The defendants are permitted to cross-examine each witness provided by the plaintiff. When the plaintiff has completed the presentation, the defendant presents his/her case. Again, the opposing counsel is permitted to cross-examine all witnesses.

At any time—but usually at the completion of either the plaintiff's presentation or the defendant's presentation—a motion can be made to the court to settle the case. If no motion is made or if the motions are not granted, the attorneys request that the court moves to closing arguments. Following closing arguments, the judge instructs the jury. The jury deliberates and returns a verdict to the judge. The verdict determines who wins and who loses. The judge typically accepts the jury's verdict and announces the decision.

Appeal

If the party that loses believes that there has been error, or that new information about the facts of the case are available, he/she will usually appeal the trial court's decision to a higher court (the court of appeals for the state or the state supreme court). The appellate court (consisting of a panel of judges) reviews the record of the trial. Attorneys for both sides file briefs and/or summaries. The appellate court may affirm, reverse, or remand the case for further study.

The Legal System

To work effectively with legal concepts, it is helpful to possess knowledge of both how law is created and the role of the courts in the interpretation of law. Understanding sources of law and the structure and role of federal and state courts will provide such foundational information.

Sources of Law

Law in the United States is derived from federal and state constitutions, legislative enactments, and the results of decisions rendered by federal and state courts. The United States Constitution and the constitutions of each state create the federal and state judicial systems, respectively. Federal government powers are limited to those identified in the U.S. Constitution. The Tenth Amendment to the U.S. Constitution provides that all powers not specifically granted to the federal government in the U.S. Constitution be made available to the states.

Federal and state statutes, executive orders, and city ordinances form the basis for statutory law. Congress, state legislatures, city councils, and county boards of commissions have authority to enact laws dealing with a wide range of topics. Their powers are limited only by federal and state constitutions. For example, states, communities, and local municipalities have the power to regulate—within their jurisdiction—resources and human activity for the promotion of health, safety, and welfare. Compliance with an occupancy limit at a stadium, for instance, would be used by a city to promote public safety, particularly during emergencies.

Administrative law covers the rules, regulations, and directives issued by the executive branch of government within the scope of the acts of Congress. Specific administrative agencies, such as the Office of Civil Rights, are charged with the responsibility of overseeing the execution of the rules, regulations, and directives of the executive branch.

Case law forms the basis for common law in the United States. Under common law or judge-made law, the results of court decisions in state and federal courts establish legal precedent, which is then used by courts as a guide in deciding future cases under stare decisis. Stare decisis is the legal principle by which courts must honor past precedent. As noted by Moorman and Grady (2020), determining the precedential value of a court decision involves first identifying the level of court deciding the case, then analyzing legal sources to put the court decision in the context of case law that existed before the current decision was made. As a result of the use of precedent, laws may differ from one state to another, from one court to another, or from one federal jurisdiction to another. This means that a particular legal decision may be used in Minnesota, while a slightly different precedent or decision may be used in Florida.

Determining whether the precedent is binding or persuasive is also important. "A decision rendered by the U.S. Supreme Court is binding on all lower federal courts and carries the highest precedential value, whereas a state court decision has limited impact only to the one state and represents the opinion of just one court" (Moorman & Grady, 2020, p. 191). In cases involving sport and physical activity, these differences are not extreme. Laws discussed throughout the text will relate to the general principles of law and will avoid unique regional decisions.

This textbook facilitates future sport professionals' acquisition of knowledge related to the legal decisions appropriate to their professional needs. The student will acquire knowledge of the United States Constitution and skill in locating the constitution and case law in the student's respective state. Furthermore, the student will become acquainted with federal, state, and local statutes, executive orders, and city ordinances. All of these sources of legal knowledge are pertinent to the student's future role in managing sport and physical activity.

Courts

The United States has two judicial systems: one at the federal level and one in each state. Though certain aspects of their responsibilities interrelate, these systems are largely independent. Each state is governed by its own state constitution and the U.S. Constitution. Jurisdiction of the federal court system extends to all cases and controversies arising under the U.S. Constitution and all statutes and treaties pursuant to the U.S. Constitution. State and local courts are responsible for controversies arising under the constitutions for each state and the laws of cities and counties.

Local courts also hear the cases of citizens, unless the issue relates to a citizen's right that has been proscribed or limited by the Constitution. When such rights have been affected, the cases are under the jurisdiction of the federal courts. Should the laws of a county, city, or state conflict with the Constitution, the controversy will be brought to the federal courts. In some situations, the state court will be the court of last resort. In other circumstances, the federal court will be the final court. Sometimes, the state and federal court systems will have concurrent jurisdiction or joint responsibility for law enforcement.

Federal Courts

The federal courts are structured in three tiers: the District Court at the lowest level, the Courts of Appeals at the intermediate level, and the Supreme Court at the highest level (see Figure 1). Other courts established by the U.S. Constitution include the Court of Claims, Court of Military Appeals, and Customs Court. The national judiciary also includes legislative and administrative agencies created by Congress. These agencies perform judicial functions subject to review by the courts. it should be noted that the word "review" refers to the power of a court to examine decisions made by administrative units. Such examinations ascertain the validity of the rulings in light of applicable statutes, regulations, previous opinions, and findings of fact.

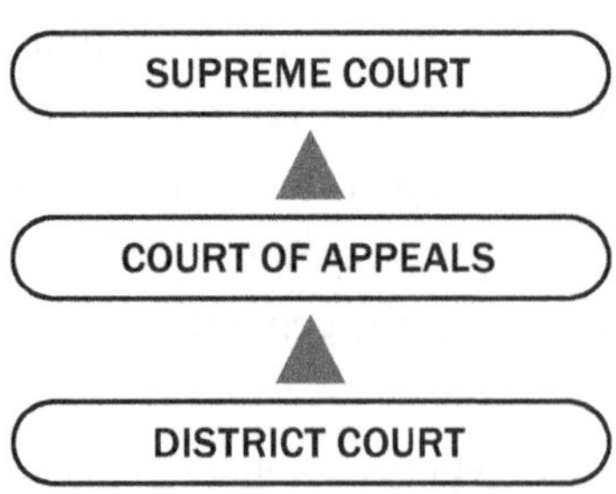

FIGURE 1. FEDERAL COURT TIERS

Federal courts deal with certain kinds of cases (often referred to as federal questions) and with certain parties to a dispute from different states. The phrase "federal question" means the case involved an interpretation and application of the U.S. Constitution, Acts of Congress, or treaties. Diversity of citizenship refers to a case between parties who reside or do business in different states; a citizen of the United States and an alien; or a United States citizen and a foreign government.

Article III of the U.S. Constitution extends federal jurisdiction to all cases involving the Constitution, as well as all statutes and treaties that may be made in pursuance of it. Admiralty and maritime law, whether statutory and international in character, fall under the exclusive jurisdiction of the federal courts. Controversies involving persons such as ambassadors, public ministers, and consuls also fall under the jurisdiction of the national judiciary, as do controversies involving two or more states.

District Courts

The district courts are the basic civil and criminal trial courts in the federal system. Most cases in federal law originate here, and no case is appealed to a district court. There are 94 district courts in the 50 states, the District of Columbia, Puerto Rico, the Virgin Islands, the Canal Zone, and Guam. Each court is presided over by a single judge who has been appointed by the President of the United States. District courts usually establish the record used to determine the guilt or innocence of the defendant in criminal matters and the determination of legal responsibility in civil issues. The report containing the facts of the controversy is usually established in the district court.

Courts of Appeals

The courts of appeals are the intermediate courts. They take cases only on appeal from a federal district court or from a regulatory commission, such as the Securities and Exchange Commission. The United States is presently divided into 11 courts of appeals districts, each having a group of three to nine judges. Cases are heard (and decisions rendered) by as few as two judges; however, three is a more standard number. Appeals courts review the proceedings of the original trial court to ascertain whether the substantive and procedural rights of the parties involved have been honored. The court also decides whether the statute or regulation under which the indictment was brought is constitutional.

Supreme Court

The Supreme Court, the highest court of the United States, is presided over by one chief justice and eight associate justices (28 USC, Section 1). The justices are appointed by the President of the United States subject to the approval of the Senate. "The judges serve during 'good Behaviour' which has generally meant a life term" (Supreme Court, n.d.). The U.S. Constitution gives the Supreme Court original jurisdiction—or the capacity to create the record—only for cases involving ambassadors, public ministers, and consuls and for proceedings in which a state is a party. Its appellate jurisdiction is more flexible, as it can be altered by an act of Congress. It should be noted that the phrase "appellate jurisdiction" means the record is reviewed to ascertain that the substantive and procedural rights of the parties involved have been honored and that the statute or regulation under consideration is constitutional.

At present, the Supreme Court may review cases that originate in the state courts, in the lower federal courts, or in the federal regulatory boards and commissions. The Supreme Court is required to take an appeal from the highest state court, from a United States court of appeals in a case in which a federal statute or treaty has been declared invalid, or when a state constitutional provision or statute appears to violate the U.S. Constitution or an act of Congress. It should be noted that the route of appeal from the highest state court is directly to the Supreme Court and not through the lower federal structures.

Many of the cases that go to the Supreme Court are by a writ of *certiorari* and not by the appeals route. A writ is an order issued by the court calling up an important case for review because the case is constitutionally significant. The Supreme Court makes its decision to take cases on certiorari and on appeal. The refusal of the Supreme Court to hear an appeal or to accept a petition for certiorari generally means that the members have decided to accept as valid the decision of the highest state court or the lower federal court.

State Courts

Court systems differ from state to state. It should be noted that effort has been made to make generalizations with reference to the state courts. Therefore, the discussion within this textbook may not mirror the exact judicial form in every state. For example, state judges are either appointed by the governor or elected by popular ballot.

Courts are classified by the types of cases presented: juvenile courts meeting the needs of youth, criminal courts hearing offenses against society, and civil courts adjudicating issues involving the rights of the private sector. Although courts may differ from state to state, all states have trial and supreme courts. A minority of states have courts of appeals (see Figure 2). All states have administrative agencies that perform judicial functions and are subject to judicial review.

State Trial Courts

When parties decide to resort to the judicial system to settle a dispute, their initial contact will be with a trial court. Civil and criminal cases are usually tried in different courts at this level. Trial courts decide disputes of fact. Detailed findings of fact based upon the evidence provided are then subjected to rules of law. Therefore, the judge and jury (or the judge standing alone) renders a decision.

State Courts of Appeals

A party wishing to appeal a judgment made by the trial court can take the case to a court of appeals. With the exception of a few states, both civil and criminal cases generally go to the same court of appeals. Courts of appeals make decisions both by using the record of facts obtained in the trial court and by reviewing the questions of law. If one of the parties is not satisfied with the decision of the state court of appeals, the issue may be taken to the state supreme court.

State Supreme Court

The state supreme court is the highest appellate court and the court of last resort on matters of state law. As a court of appeals, the state supreme court will examine the record to be sure the substantive and procedural rights of the parties have been properly adjudicated and that the constitution, statutes, and regulations of the state have been adequately interpreted. When appropriate, a state supreme court decision can be appealed directly to the U.S. Supreme Court.

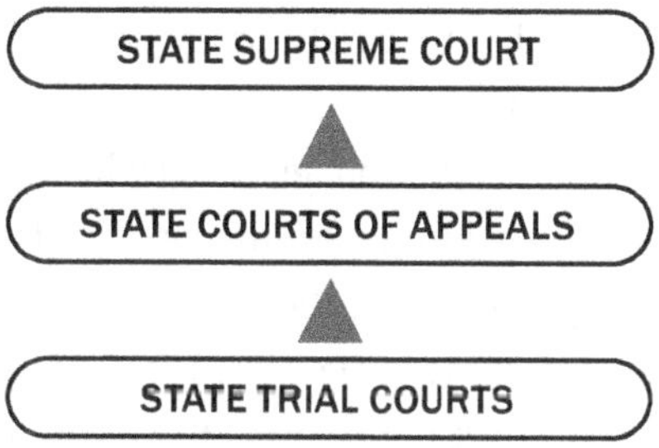

FIGURE 2. STATE COURT TIERS

The Legal Research Process

The legal research process is fundamentally different from other research paradigms with which the reader may be familiar. A goal of conducting qualitative research may be to seek an in-depth understanding of a phenomenon affecting sport management practice, such as interviews with executives from companies sponsoring the Olympics about perceptions of ambush marketing. A goal of quantitative research, on the other hand, may be to observe variables in the sport environment to come to a conclusion about a hypothesis, such as predicting factors impacting spectator motivations to attend wheelchair basketball events. While sharing some of these same goals, the goal in conducting legal research is distinct: to develop a comprehensive understanding of a legal topic, including analyzing all sides of a legal issue. The legal researcher must utilize a combination of legal and non-legal sources to ensure a comprehensive research approach (Moorman & Grady, 2020).

In searching for and analyzing applicable sources of authority, the legal researcher uses a nonlinear process to begin the research process with a broad legal topic in mind and continues to refine it by going back and forth between sources as relevant sources continue to be located (Moorman & Grady, 2020). The researcher continually narrows his/her focus on a specific legal issue. For example, a researcher may want to investigate the constitutionality of pat-down searches at NFL stadiums. In order to understand the "big picture" of this legal issue, the researcher could start by searching for published cases involving pat downs at similar public places where large numbers of people gather similar to stadiums, such as at airports. She could then narrow her search to cases specifically involving pat-down searches at sporting events. Unexpected perhaps in the legal search results, this would likely lead her to cases about drug testing of athletes, which also constitutes a search, yet is factually dissimilar from the topic of searches of spectators. The value of finding these seemingly off-target search results is the possibility for analogous fact patterns to what is being studied and of ultimate value to the researcher's questions. This initial "road block" may require searching for additional sources more directly on point, such as for cases involving pat downs of spectators at high school athletic contests. The legal sources will often identify and provide guidance about subtle changes in the legal landscape over time that may impact the narrow legal topic that a beginning researcher may not be able to identify from merely reading a handful of seemingly similar cases.

The legal researcher uses both primary and secondary legal sources to integrate or synthesize the information instead of providing a summary of each source (Moorman & Grady, 2020). This process of continually narrowing the focus of the research has been described as an inverted pyramid analytical approach (Dernbach et al., 2007). This approach has been adapted for use in legal research in sport management (Moorman & Grady, 2020).

Once a legal concept is clearly understood through use of the research process described above, the researcher can then research additional legal materials as well as find additional support in articles relating to sport management in order to better grasp the application of the legal concept to the management and practice of sport and physical activity. For example, once the concept of negligence in sport is generally understood through analyzing primary sources like court cases, a researcher may want to analyze how negligence has been applied by the courts specifically in crowd management situations at sport facilities. Another person may be interested in the impact of negligence on lifeguards, while yet another may be interested in how negligence will impact his/her personal training business. Each of these issues can be further studied using secondary sources of legal materials, such as law review articles and legal or trade journals. This remainder of this introduction guides student researchers through the legal research process described above using cases, law review articles, journals, and books related to the application of law to sport and physical activity. It also enables individuals to locate statutes and case law cited in this text and in legal periodicals and to utilize various sources of legal materials in preparing presentations and publications.

Legal publications can be found in courthouses, public libraries, public and private institutions that offer law-based courses, and university and college law schools. Numerous private law firm libraries—while at times more difficult to access—also exist and contain numerous research collections. With advances in technology and growth of the internet and digital content, there is now more widespread access to legal research materials than ever before, and everyone from legal scholars to undergraduate sport management students can learn to conduct legal research.

Nexis Uni

A commonly available legal research retrieval system created for general university use is called Nexis Uni (formerly LexisNexis Academic). It allows students enrolled in subscribing academic institutions an opportunity to electronically search for many sources of legal information, including court decisions, statutes, and constitutions, as well as news articles in the popular Law360 news series.

Nexis Uni can commonly be found under the electronic library databases of subscribing university websites. The search process is similar to conducting an internet search with the option to narrowly search for specific legal topics. For example, a student may decide to search for "negligence" involving "soccer" in the student's home state or in all of the United States. Cases identified through the search (e.g., negligence) and soccer will appear in the search results using case titles. The student can scan each case to ascertain its value to his/her research interest and then read in detail only those valuable cases. To gain familiarity with Nexis Uni, a recommended strategy is to find a case of interest in any chapter of this textbook and perform a search using Nexis Uni to identify subsequent cases in which the original case has been cited or discussed (also referred to as Shepardizing).

Nexis Uni also allows students to search for law review articles. Many of the law review articles specifically devoted to the study of law and sport are written to educate lawyers about the context and nuances of sport as well as how to apply legal theory uniquely to situations involving sport. These articles are often very valuable to sport management students in courses in law but also in finance, governance, and management. Nexis Uni has a tutorial to assist the user in acquiring a range of legal search strategies.

Sources of Legal Information

Legal materials can be separated into two categories: primary and secondary sources. Primary sources are actual statements of the law and include legislative statutes, court decisions, executive decrees and orders, and administrative regulations and rulings. Federal and state statutes and appellate court decisions are the primary documents most often used in legal research. Primary sources can be relied upon to determine what the law is and what the law requires (Moorman & Grady, 2020). Secondary sources explain, interpret, and comment on the law or its application (Moorman & Grady, 2020) and include textbooks, law review articles, treatises, practice manuals, commentaries, restatements, and periodicals.

Case Law

Case law plays an important role in sport and physical activity, as many legal theories have evolved as a result of case decisions. Cases can be located through researching topical areas in case digests and citations from textbooks and periodicals. Results of case law are published according to the organization of the courts with reporters for the U.S. Supreme Court, the federal appellate courts, and all state appellate and supreme courts. All of these materials can be found on an electronic retrieval system.

Statutes and Codes

A systematic compilation of statutes and regulations is usually identified as a Code. The regulations of federal agencies are first published in the Federal Register and later codified into the Code of Federal Regulations. The United States Code Annotated (USCA) contains federal, legislative, and congressional statutes. Each state has a similar code. Putnam (2003) noted that "the body of law represented by statutory law has expanded greatly. Many matters once governed by common law are now governed by statutory law" (p. 49). Through statutory analysis, a lawyer, researcher, or student can determine whether a statute, such as an "open records" statute, applies to communications generated by a state university's athletic compliance department, how it applies, and the effect of that application (Putnam, 2003).

Annotated Reports

Annotated reports are legal references reported according to subject matter. For example, American Law Institute Reports include past developments and current laws in most states and future trends.

Legislative History Reports

Researchers often will trace the history of a law to locate documents that will reveal the intent of Congress or a state legislature. Statutory research will include pre-enactment history of earlier statutes and the current status of law under consideration. Legislative historical documents include presidential messages, congressional bills, reports of hearings, committee reports, debates, House and Senate hearings, and Senate executive reports.

Administrative Documents

Administrative materials are located under the title of the agency. Therefore, knowledge of the agency is important to the researcher. Such information also can be located in the United States Government Manual, Federal Register, Code of Federal Regulations, and Administrative Rules and Decisions.

Periodicals

Many periodicals address issues of law in sport and physical activity on a single-article basis, while others dedicate an entire volume or publish only in the area of sport. The indexes of legal periodicals and their electronic databases will identify these articles.

System for Case Analysis

After a judge renders a decision in a case, an explanation of the reasoning behind the decision is written. The explanation and a summary of the presentation to the court are published as an opinion. When several judges have participated in the decision and agreement does not exist among the judges, one judge writes the opinion of the majority of the judges. Disagreeing judges are free to write their dissenting opinions either as a group or as individuals. A case opinion will usually contain the following general categories: title, facts, issues, decision or holding, and the reasoning of the court.

Summary

A difference exists between the phrases "law in sport" and "sport law." "Law in sport" is the selection of a wide range of legal concepts that are relevant to the day-to-day decisions made in the sport industry. These concepts have been taken from the laws of negligence, intentional tort, product liability, contract, constitution, labor, agency, intellectual property, and others. By contrast, "sport law" refers only to the basic law and court decisions unique to sport.

The constitutions, statutes, administrative decisions, and the results of court cases constitute the law used in the United States. Congress, through the Senate and House of Representatives, has the power to create new law. Court systems are organized for the federal government and within each state. Each system consists of a lower court, in which the facts are ascertained for the record prior to judicial decision; and a series of higher order courts of appeals, in which the record is examined for procedural or substantive errors.

Case analysis is used to learn details of litigation and the topics that could become the subject of litigation. That knowledge can be used to create and implement risk management programs or to prepare research reports. It is significant to ascertain whether the results of the case establish new law or utilize existing law from other jurisdictions. Case analysis can identify patterns of litigation, where the litigation is occurring, and what specific conduct and activities in sport and physical activity appear to have been called into court.

References

Davis, T. (2001). What is Sports Law? *Marquette Sports Law Review, 11*(2). 211.

Dernbach, J. C., Singleton, R. V., Wharton, C. S., & Ruhtenberg, J. M. (2007). *A practical guide to legal writing and legal method* (3rd ed.). Aspen.

Moorman, A. M. M., & Grady, J. (2020). Legal Research. In D. P. S. Andrew, P. M. Pedersen, & C. D. McEvoy. *Research methods and design in sport management* (2nd ed., pp. 185–207). Human Kinetics.

Putnam, W. H. (2010). *Legal research, analysis, and writing* (3rd ed.). Delmar Cengage Learning.

Supreme Court of the United States. (n.d.). The Court as an institution. http://www.supremecourt.gov/about/institution.aspx

Tulane University Law School. (2015). Sports & Society. https://law.tulane.edu/sites/law.tulane.edu/files/Files/2015SportsAndSociety.pdf

Recommended Reading

Andrew, D. P. S., Pederson, P. M., & McEvoy, C. D. (2019). *Research methods and design in sport management* (2nd ed.). Human Kinetics.

Mitten, M. J., Davis, T., Smith, R. K., Shropshire, K. L. (2019). *Sports law and regulation: Cases, materials, and problems* (5th ed.) Wolters Kluwer.

Part I: Tort Law

A tort is an injury or a civil wrong that has caused harm to a person or a person's property for which the courts will provide a remedy. Broad categories of tort found in sport and physical activity are negligence, intentional tort, and product liability. The American Law Institute tracks changes in the law of tort and periodically publishes these changes in a Restatement. Each of the Restatements presents a contemporary structure of the discipline of tort. Numerous writers, judges, and practicing lawyers were involved in the creation of the Restatements to present the current state of the law.

Negligence is covered in Chapter 1. A person acts negligently when they do not exercise reasonable care under the circumstances. Historically, negligence has been the legal theory most often encountered in sport and physical activity. Intentional torts, explained in Chapter 2, are torts caused by a deliberate act. Product liability, discussed in Chapter 3, is the accountability of the manufacturer, retailer, and seller of a dangerous or defective product to those people injured by the product.

1

Negligence

OBJECTIVES

Upon completing this chapter, you will,

- understand the elements of negligence and apply them to sport contexts;
- recognize the relationship between duty and foreseeability;
- articulate the defenses to negligence and give examples of each defense;
- identify and define the particular types of assumption of risk;
- explain how comparative negligence is allocated;
- recognize the types of premise liability and research local and state law in the area; and
- describe the various kinds of immunity.

Introduction

A person acts negligently if the person does not exercise reasonable care under all circumstances. "Primary factors to consider in ascertaining whether the person's conduct lacks reasonable care are the foreseeable likelihood that the person's conduct will result in harm, the foreseeable severity of any harm that may ensue, and the burden of precautions to eliminate or reduce the risk of harm" (*Restatement Third, Torts: Liability for Physical and Emotional Harm,* Section 3). It is the person's acts and the person's omissions, or failure to act. Negligence also includes a balancing of risks and benefits or a cost benefit test. The "risk is the overall level of the foreseeable risk created by the actor's conduct and the benefit is the advantages that the actor or others gain if the actor refrains from taking precautions" (*Restatement Third, Torts: Liability for Physical and Emotional Harm,* Section 3[e]).

Elements of Negligence

The following five elements must exist for a court to find a person or agency negligent:

- Duty
- Breach of Duty
- Factual Cause
- Scope of liability including foreseeability
- Damage

Duty

"An actor ordinarily has a duty to exercise reasonable care when the actor's conduct creates a risk of physical harm. In exceptional cases, when an articulated countervailing principle or policy warrants denying or limiting liability in a particular class of cases, a court may decide that the defendant has no duty or that the ordinary duty or reasonable care requires modification" (*Restatement, Third, Torts: Liability for Physical and Emotional Harm,* Section 7). A relationship sufficient to create a legal duty may arise by statute, ordinance, administrative rule, contract, voluntary assumption, or judicial decision. Three different standards of care (explained later) are reasonable person, special relationship, and professional standard. A reasonable person duty is the standard applicable to society in general. Parents are among those with special relationships. Coach-athlete, teacher-student, trainer-client, therapist-client, employer-employee, and principal-agent are relationships that establish a professional legal duty of care. The standards of the profession or industry generally dictate the duty elements of negligence.

Breach of Duty

Once the legal duty or standard of care is established, proof must be provided to the court by the plaintiff (injured person) that the duty was breached. Professional sport and physical activity specialists have specific duties. These legal duties are sometimes in writing for some professionals, which are also known as standards of care. For other sport industry professionals, they are unwritten standards commonly accepted by members of the profession. Among a number of sport and physical activity professionals, one common legal duty is providing emergency care. Although professionals do not have to provide emergency care personally, they must make provisions for such care. Failure to make provisions for emergency care is an example of a breach of legal duty. Instructors, teachers, therapists, and exercise specialists are obligated to provide learning experiences that are challenging but not so difficult or so far beyond the capacity of the learner that injury is likely to occur. When clients or students are injured as a result of being allowed to participate in risk activities far beyond their physical capacity, professionals breach of their duty of care. If sport facilities are not maintained according to industry standards, professionals will also breach the duty of care.

Factual Cause

When it has been determined that the defendant breached the duty of care, the court identifies the relationship between the breach and the injury. A breach can be an act or omission. Was the breach the cause of the injury? For liability to be found, the breach must be the cause of the injury. The plaintiff must show a direct relationship between the breach of the duty and the injury or damage. For example, was the defendant's negligent act the cause of the injury? Would the same harm have resulted had the negligent act never occurred? Reasonable care is

> The balance between the magnitude of the foreseeable risk and the burden of precaution that can eliminate the risk. The "magnitude" of risk includes the likelihood of a harm-causing incident and the severity of the harm that may occur. If the burden is greater than the magnitude of the risk, the actor who declines to adopt the precaution is generally not negligent. But if the risk is somewhat greater than the burden, the actor is negligent for failing to adopt the precaution. (*Restatement, Third, Torts: Liability for Physical and Emotional Harm,* Section 2 [d])

Scope of Liability, Including Foreseeability

After establishing factual cause, scope of liability-foreseeability is ascertained. Foreseeability is the capacity of the defendant to anticipate an accident or incident. Was the harm to the plaintiff a reasonable, foreseeable consequence of the defendant's actions? Was the defendant responsible? At trial, the court will ask if the accident or incident in which the plaintiff sustained injuries was an event that could or should have been predicted as one that might cause injury. To what extent could it have been predicted that participation in the activity would result in injury? Was the occurrence of the injury foreseeable? The harm must have been foreseeable before the event; decisions about foreseeability are not to be made after the injury has been sustained. Sufficient foresight must exist to enable professionals to prevent or alter actions in an effort to avoid injury. A remote possibility is not sufficient; substantial damage must be probable, not just possible. In sport and physical activity settings, risk management processes can be used to establish foreseeability.

Damage

For the court to find negligence, substantial damage must exist. Cuts and bruises are not sufficient; the person must be seriously damaged physically or mentally. If the question exists as to whether the damages are substantial, the question of damages will go to the jury to determine an amount.

Standards of Care

There are three standards of care: reasonable person, special relationship, and professional.

Reasonable Person

Reasonable person is a hypothetical scenario that asks what an average adult would have done in a similar situation. For example, the court will ask what care an ordinary person would have provided under the circumstances of the incident to avoid injuries to others. Did the defendant behave as a reasonable, prudent adult? Would a reasonable person have recognized the risk and taken steps to avoid it?

There is no duty to act affirmatively on behalf of all other people or "no duty to rescue." A person walking past a playground and observing an injured child has no obligation or responsibility to provide immediate and temporary care for the injured child. Duty exists only when a special relationship has been formed. If the person walking past a playground decides to provide help to the child, the person is obligated to continue the help until professional emergency medical assistance is on the scene. Once a rescuer begins to give assistance, a special relationship is created. Assistance must continue until emergency help arrives. Children are held to the standard of care expected of a child of similar age, education, intelligence, and experience. Children under five or those engaging in a dangerous activity that is characteristically undertaken by adults do not possess the capacity to be negligent.

Special Relationship

Parents and schools are examples of people and agencies with special relationships that dictate a distinct standard of care. An exception to the "no duty to rescue" rule exists for parents. Parents do have an obligation to rescue their child when the child is in danger. The special relationship that exists between spouses and between parents and children is a duty to rescue within the context of skill, knowledge, and ability. Therefore, a parent who does not know how to swim would not have a duty to jump into the water to rescue his/her drowning child but would have a duty to call for help.

Among a school's responsibilities to children is a duty to be prepared to render emergency medical assistance when it is needed. In *Kleinknecht v. Gettysburg* (1991), the court held that the college had a duty to be prepared for a medical emergency resulting from collegiate athletics. In this case, an athlete suffered a cardiac arrest and died during practice. Also, schools are expected to provide protection for children through age-appropriate supervision.

Professional

A professional standard is established when a body of professional knowledge exists and a recognized level of performance is adhered to by members of that profession. This is the level most relevant to sport and physical activity professionals. The level of duty owed is higher than the level expected of a reasonable person. A person is found negligent under a professional standard for failing to perform at the level expected of a person with the training, knowledge, and skill of a member of the profession. In turn, the public can rely on receiving a predictable level of performance from a professional because of the person's training, knowledge, and skill. The professional's legal duty of care to another is satisfied when unreasonable risks of harm are eliminated. To successfully eliminate unreasonable risks of harm, the professional must recognize and know the dangers of harm inherent in the activities in use.

Among the many professional standards in sport and physical activity are facility inspection, proper use of equipment, supervision, instructional protocols, rescue procedures, and emergency care. The standard of care is the written statement or standard accepted by the profession. To satisfy the standard, it may require specific courses or learning experiences, industry-specific training, attainment of proficiency in competency tests, and periodic renewal of professional certifications. When a standard does not exist, the legal duty of care is that of a reasonable professional or a reasonable person under similar circumstances.

A legal duty of care may exist even though the professional is not on the payroll. Technical expertise, not job status or wage, is the basis upon which one's duty of care is judged. It is anticipated that certain expertise will accompany specific jobs. A professional will be held to the level of expertise recognized in a job even if the professional does not hold the appropriate credentials for the job. Professionals are held to the same duty of care when they serve as a volunteer as when they are a paid employee working in a professional capacity.

Defenses

The defenses against claims of negligence:

- Contributory Negligence
- Assumption of Risk
- Comparative Fault or Comparative Negligence

Contributory negligence uses the objective standard of a "reasonable person," the standard used in ordinary negligence cases. The defense of assumption of risk uses a subjective standard based on the victim's knowledge of the risk and willingness to assume the risk. In most states, contributory negligence and assumption of risk are merged into comparative fault.

Contributory Negligence

Contributory negligence means that the plaintiff, or injured person, is responsible in part for his/her injuries. One has a duty to protect one's self from injury. The plaintiff's conduct has somehow contributed, as a legal cause, to the harm the plaintiff has suffered (*Restatement, Third, Torts: Liability for Physical and Emotional Harm,* Section 3 [k]).

The standard of conduct used in negligence is that of a reasonable person under ordinary circumstances. It is also the standard applied in contributory negligence. In contributory negligence, however, the defendant is not relieved of a duty toward the plaintiff. Contributory negligence becomes a part of the formula in allocating damages between the plaintiff and defendant. It is also a defense to negligence. It is not, however, a defense to an intentional tort.

Assumption of Risk

Assumption of risk occurs when the victim becomes responsible for some portion of the risk of an activity and, as a result of assuming the risk, assumes liability for that portion of damages. In complete assumption of risk, the victim has contracted away his/her right to a cause of action through a signed written agreement, which is considered a contract. Only adults, not minors, can create contracts. Therefore, minors cannot waive their right to sue. Also, in many states, a minor may sue over an injury sustained while a minor, after he/she becomes an adult.

Warnings, risk education, and signed forms may not bar recovery for all adults but will serve to inform participants of the dangers inherent in the activity. Even though a court may not accept an assumption of risk statement as a contract or a complete bar to recovery, the document will demonstrate that the victim had knowledge of the risk involved in the activity.

Knowledge and Appreciation of the Risk

When a participant encounters a dangerous situation, the participant must have adequate knowledge to appreciate the danger. Knowledge and appreciation of danger is not based on a reasonable person standard but on a standard tailored for the individual involved. Persons using equipment or taking instructions for the first time are not expected to possess the same level of knowledge and appreciation of danger as persons with considerable experience in the activity. Once the person understands the danger, he/she is able to make informed decisions about taking the risk of participating in the activity.

In many court decisions, knowledge and appreciation of a danger is a question for the jury. An industry professional's method of demonstrating that patrons or clients had knowledge and appreciation of the risks in the activity in which they were participating involves the use of instructional protocols, progress records, and other documents. Assumption of risk involves either express or implied consent. There are two types of assumption of risk: primary and secondary assumption of risk. These will be discussed after the types of consent.

Express Consent

Express consent is usually a signed agreement between the participant and the service provider that meets the standard of a contract and can relieve the provider of a lawsuit for negligence. The plaintiff expressly assumes the risk and agrees, prior to the time of the injury-causing event, to hold the defendant blameless. Some states and courts may refuse to honor these contractual agreements, stating that public policy prohibits injured parties from signing away their rights.

When a person who fully understands the risk of an activity voluntarily agrees to take part and to relieve the defendant of any duty, they are said to have given express consent. Under this agreement the plaintiff:

- knows that the risk exists;
- understands the nature of the risk; and
- freely chooses to incur the risk.

The decision to assume the risk must be free and voluntary; some sign or manifestation of consent must be present to relieve the defendant of his/her obligation. Should the plaintiff be placed in a position where the consent was forced, the plaintiff cannot be said to have assumed the risk. Age, experience, and knowledge of information pertinent to the activity are critical factors in determining a plaintiff's ability to comprehend and appreciate a risk.

Implied Consent

In sport and physical activity, persons who understand the risk of an activity can, as a result of participating in the activity, agree to the inherent risks without signing a contract. In implied consent, the defendant is not relieved of a responsibility. Implied consent becomes a part of the comparative fault percentage. The following explanation of the two types of assumption of risk, primary and secondary, is somewhat unique to sport and physical activity.

Primary Assumption of Risk

Primary assumption of risk occurs when a party or potential plaintiff voluntarily participates in a sporting event or activity involving inherent risk and the defendant is under no duty to protect the plaintiff from the inherent risks of the activity. It should be noted that the defendant is liable for injury when his/her behavior becomes reckless. This heightened reckless standard was found in decisions in California, Kentucky, Louisiana, Michigan, Nebraska, Ohio, and Texas and is becoming more frequent across the United States. To recover in court, an injured athlete plaintiff must show that the injuries sustained in sport and physical activity did not flow from the normal course of participation or competition. In other words, that the injuries were not normally expected or assumed by the participants in that particular sport. For example, in lacrosse, knee injuries are common, expected, and assumed by athletes as part of playing the sport. However, if a knee injury resulted from a defect in the field or playing surface, this would not be considered an assumed risk that the participant agreed to undertake while participating in the sport. Athletes should expect a playing surface free from defects where the practice or athletic competition will take place.

Secondary Assumption of Risk

Secondary assumption of risk occurs when a party voluntarily participates in a risky activity and has not consented to relieve the defendant of his/her duty of care, and the defendant breaches a duty of care owed the plaintiff. Secondary assumption of risk is not a bar to recovery; it becomes part of the comparative fault formula. In summary, primary and secondary assumption of risk are similar to express and implied consent. Primary assumption of risk is essentially consent and relieves the defendant of fault. Secondary assumption of risk does not involve consent and thus may only reduce, not remove, the plaintiff's liability for the harm.

Comparative Negligence/Comparative Fault

Comparative negligence is a system in which the percentage of responsibility of the injured party and the percentage of responsibility of the persons or agency that contributed to or caused the harm are balanced in a formula. The contributory negligence of the injured party is used to reduce the recovery for the injured party. Recovery is allocated in proportion to the relative fault of each party. For example, the injured party may be found to be 30 percent at fault (contributory negligence and assumption of risk) and the person causing the injury at 70 percent fault. Table 1.1 shows the allocation of a $100,000 judgment.

Comparative fault, in contrast, is the apportionment of damages among the joint defendants according to the percentage attributed to each. Table 1.2 explains the above situation involving three—rather than one—defendants. The three defendants are responsible for 70% of the damage award with Defendant 1 responsible for 30%, Defendant 2 for 25%, and Defendant 3 for 15%.

A modified system of fault allocation used in some states denies the injured party recovery if the injured party's negligence was as great as 50% or 51% of the fault. Other states have a system called "joint and several liability" for the damage award. Thus, if only Responsible Party 1 was able to pay, she would be responsible for the total or $70,000. If only Responsible Parties 2 and 3 could pay, each would be responsible for 50% of $70,000, or $35,000.

TABLE 1.1. COMPARATIVE NEGLIGENCE

PARTY	FAULT	JUDGMENT SUM
Plaintiff	30%	Assumes $30,000 of expenses
Defendant	70%	Pays $70,000 to plaintiff

Waiver of Liability

A range of educational tools and agreements are used in sport and physical activity to educate and inform participants about risks. These risk and/or informed consent documents will be used by the court to demonstrate that the parties were informed of the risks, understood the risks (provided the forms withstand the scrutiny of the court), agreed to encounter the risks, and signed a statement acknowledging their understanding of the risks. Statements are to be so specific that the participant has an estimate of the probability of

TABLE 1.2. COMPARATIVE FAULT

PARTY	FAULT	JUDGMENT SUM
Injured party	30%	Assumes $30,000 of expenses
Defendant 1	30%	Pays $30,000 to injured party
Defendant 2	25%	Pays $25,000 to injured party
Defendant 3	15%	Pays $15,000 to injured party

sustaining a loss and what the loss might be. Courts have found defendants not guilty of negligence when the plaintiff had signed a waiver of liability that fully conformed with the legal requirements of a contract. The release must be clear, unambiguous, explicit, and concise. On occasion, waivers of liability may be considered by the courts to be so offensive to society that parties are not permitted to sign away those rights. Signed statements of release are often misinterpreted to mean that the participant has agreed not to sue.

In addition to the contract requirements, it should be noted that only adults can enter into a contract; parents cannot sign away the rights of their children, but parents can sign away their own rights to a cause of action for their children. This means that they can agree to the knowledge of a full disclosure of the risks including probability, extent, and magnitude of the harm that could occur to their child while he/she participates in the activity. In the event of a lawsuit, such an agreement will be examined by the court to determine its validity as a defense. Injured children reaching the age of majority have the benefit of their state's statute of limitations to bring a cause of action for a harm that occurred while they were a minor. All documents used as educational tools and waivers of liability are to be drafted by legal counsel and are to conform to relevant local and state statutes.

Owners and Occupiers of Land

Premises liability is a theory of property liability currently being incorporated into negligence in many states. An understanding of this area is essential for reviewing cases where it remains the law and for the examination of older cases. Historically, in the United States, persons owning large tracts of land were encouraged to allow others to use their land for hunting, fishing, and recreation. To protect the owners of these lands from liability, property laws were created in various states. Premises liability defined the duty of care of the owner or person in possession of land to individuals injured on their property. Persons entering the land are classified as one of three types of entrants on the land: invitees, licensees, and trespassers.

Invitees have the greatest protection, while licensees are given less care. Trespassers are owed the lowest duty, sometimes referred to as zero duty. Tennessee, Maine, Connecticut, Florida, and Illinois were the first to abolish premises liability. Other states have followed their direction. As states reject the categories of invitee, licensee, and trespasser, they are moving toward a reasonable person standard for the liability of the landowner or person in possession of the land.

Invitee

An invitee is a person who has either expressly or impliedly been invited onto the land of another for an economic benefit to the person in possession of the land (known as a business invitee), or one who enters land open to the public (known as a public invitee). Stadium patrons are business invitees. Thus, the owner or operator of the stadium is responsible for providing a reasonably safe environment. In state and federal recreation areas and parks, the public has been impliedly invited onto the land. Even though no economic motive may influence the invitation to the public, the person or organization in possession of the land is responsible at an invitee level.

Common duties owed by the facility owner or occupier to the invitee include keeping the premises in a reasonably safe condition and warning of known dangerous conditions. The possessor of land also has a duty to inspect for unknown dangers. The possessor of land is not only responsible for reasonable care and adequate warnings to invitees about known dangers, but also for care and warnings about those conditions of which the possessor/owner should have been aware.

Licensee

A licensee is a person who is on the land with the owner's consent but does not have a business purpose for being on the land. In other words, there is no economic motive for their presence on the land, such as shopping at a retail store. The licensee is typically a social guest, an individual who goes onto someone's land and is not asked by the owner to leave. For example, a neighbor who has joined in a backyard game is a licensee. Duties owed to the licensee are the same as those owed to the invitee (reasonable care), with one important exception: the licensee is to be warned of or protected from only those harms of which the possessor of the land is aware. The owner must keep the property in a reasonably safe condition and warn or protect persons entering the land from harms of which the owner is aware. For licensees, there is no duty to inspect or discover dangerous conditions. There is also no duty to make the land safe for licensees. A licensee accepts the land in the same condition as the landowner, without any additional efforts to make the land safe.

Trespasser

A trespasser is a person who goes onto another person's land without permission and without the knowledge of the land owner. The owner of the land owes no duty of care to the trespasser. Land owners do not have a duty to inspect the premises, to make the land safe, to warn of dangers, or to use reasonable care in anticipating trespassers. However, when an owner or person in possession of land becomes aware that trespassers may be on their property or that trespassers frequent the property, their duties change. They must either remove the trespasser from the land or secure the land from the trespasser. Failure to do so entitles the trespasser to a licensee status or reasonable standard of care. Under a reasonable care standard, the owner is to exercise care and warn of known dangers.

Attractive Nuisance

When the trespasser is a minor, the reason that the trespasser is on the land becomes important. If the condition of the land or an object on the land is such that it entices someone to enter the land, an attractive nuisance may exist. In this situation, the possessor must foresee the potential attractiveness of the property and the fact that a child could be seriously harmed. Precautions must be taken when the owner or possessor knows or has reason to know that children will be attracted to the land. No defense is available in attractive nuisance, as children are considered too young to appreciate the danger.

Open and Obvious

Section 343A of the *Restatement of the Law of Torts (Second)* was the basis for the "open and obvious" application in tort. "A possessor of land is not liable to his invitee for physical harm caused to them by any activity or condition on the land whose danger is known or obvious to them, unless the possessor should anticipate the harm despite such knowledge of obviousness" (218). One area in sport and physical activity nearly always considered "open and obvious" is water. Thus, a person taking part in aquatic activities is to know and understand the potential harm water possesses. It is part of assumption of risk. In most states, open and obvious is a complete bar to liability, while in other states, it is a factor to be considered in determining liability in tort.

Violation of a Statute, Ordinance, or Regulation

On occasion, the defendant accused of negligence may be in violation of a statute, ordinance, or regulation. State statutes, for example, may define reasonable and prudent care, industry standards, or the application of negligence. Health codes for food preparation, swimming pool depths, and lifeguard-to-swimmer ratios are examples of state and local statutes. Federal statutes tend to influence watercraft and parks.

When negligence is based on the violation of a statute, the following questions are to be answered:

1) Was the statute designed to protect the type of conduct the actor violated?
2) Is the accident victim within the class of persons the statute was designed to protect? (*Restatement of the Law Third, Torts, Liability for Physical and Emotional Harm,* Section 14)

Sport professionals should become acquainted with local, state, and federal statutes, as well as ordinances and regulations that affect their position and profession. Also, professionals need to be aware of how violation of the laws will be enforced by public authorities. An example is exceeding the occupancy code of an arena, which is typically enforced by a city fire marshal.

Immunity

Immunity is freedom from liability or freedom from a lawsuit. This special status is found most often in government entities and is referred to as sovereign immunity. The Federal Tort Claims Act of 1946 played a major role in the evolution of immunity as we know it today. The Act states that when the government engages in activities in which private persons are also engaging, the government cannot be sued; the act gave the public consent to sue the federal government in tort. The Act provides "monetary recovery from the federal government where damages, loss of property, personal injury, or death are caused by the negligence or wrongful acts of federal employees acting within the scope of their employment, and where the United States, if a private person, would be liable in accordance with the law of the place where the tort occurred" (28 USCS 2675). Immunity statutes include federal, state, and local government, Good Samaritan, hazardous recreation activity, and volunteer laws.

Governmental Immunity

Sovereign or governmental immunity in the English common law was a system modified and adopted by the United States. An English subject could not sue the king, and America decided that the United States government could not be sued without its consent. Sovereign immunity protects the government against liability but doesn't protect all of the government employees against liability. Immunities and levels of immunity have been crafted for certain responsibilities. Those charged with making the most serious governmental decisions appear to have the greatest amount of immunity. Judges, legislators, and high executive officers usually have absolute immunity.

Immunity among public officials goes back to the statement of our founding leaders: that we cannot be sued without the consent of the federal government. As mentioned earlier, the Federal Torts Claims Act of 1946 generally provides, with exceptions, that when the government engages in activities in which private persons are also engaging, the government cannot be sued. Among the exceptions to the Federal Tort Claims Act are intentional torts, military personnel, contract interference, and torts committed in the conduct of government business. Thus, federal employees have immunity for discretionary decisions, but they do not have immunity for ministerial decisions. Discretionary functions are usually planning functions; the carrying out of the plan is ministerial and not covered by immunity (*Restatement, Second, Torts,* Section 895D [f, h]).

Immunity is governed by state and local laws, with state governments differing in the scope of immunity legislation. Schools and recreation agencies are among those provided a level of immunity by state and local governments. Laws generally encourage risk management and appropriate insurance coverage to mitigate potential or actual risks.

Good Samaritan Laws

Good Samaritan laws are state statutes that provide immunity from suit for negligence for persons who administer emergency care to others. In 1959, California was the first state to pass Good Samaritan legislation; the legislation was directed at medical doctors. Many states have enacted similar legislation to enable medical doctors to rescue and aid victims without fear of lawsuits. Some of these state statutes include nurses, paramedics, persons performing CPR, dentists, and others.

The majority of the state statutes grant immunity to anyone who renders emergency care. The rescuer is to work only at the scene of the accident, act in good faith, be a reasonable and prudent rescuer, follow the methods advocated by his/her license or certificate, and provide service gratuitously. California's Business and Professional Code No. 2398 (2010), Aid to Participants in Athletic Events and Contests, states that

> No licensee, who in good faith and without compensation renders voluntary emergency medical assistance to a participant in a community college or high school athletic event or contest, at the site of the event or contest, or during

> transportation to a health care facility, for an injury suffered in the course of such event or contest, shall be liable for any civil damages as a result of any acts or omissions by such person in rendering such voluntary medical assistance. The immunity granted by this section shall not apply to acts or omissions constituting gross negligence.

Some states have sport-specific Good Samaritan or emergency care statutes. Under these statutes, physicians and other emergency care personnel are exempt from negligence for assistance provided in practice and games. The Wisconsin Statute (895.48, 2011) states,

> Any physician or athletic trainer, ... chiropractor, dentist, ... emergency medical technician, first responder, ... physician assistant, ... registered nurse, ... or a massage therapist or bodyworker ... who renders voluntary health care to a participant in an athletic event or contest sponsored by a nonprofit or a school, ... is immune from civil liability for his or her acts or omissions in rendering that care if all of the following conditions exist:
>
> a) the health care is rendered at the site of the event or contest, during transportation to a health care facility from the event or contest, or in a locker room or similar facility immediately before, during, or immediately after the event or contest.
>
> b) the physician, athletic trainer, chiropractor, dentist, emergency medical technician, first responder, physical assistant or registered nurse, massage therapist, or bodyworker does not receive compensation for the health care, other than reimbursement for expenses.

The California Education Code No. 49409 (2011) immunity statutes for school districts grants civil immunity to physicians and surgeons who render voluntary emergency medical assistance to participants in school athletic events or contests. The state code reads as follows:

> Notwithstanding any provision of any law, no physician and surgeon who in good faith and without compensation renders voluntary emergency medical assistance to a participant in a school athletic event or contest at the site thereof, or during transportation to a health care facility, for an injury suffered in the course of the event or contest, shall be liable for any civil damages as a result of any acts or omissions by the physician and surgeon in rendering the emergency medical care. The immunity granted by this paragraph shall not apply in the event of an act or omission constituting gross negligence.

Recreational Use Statutes

Recreational use statutes and hazardous recreation sport statutes began to appear in the 1960s. Ski incidents may have prompted some of the early statutes; rights of skiers and rights of ski resort owners and operators are among the most detailed statutes. In most cases, the primary recreational activities of a state are reflected in its statutes. Colorado, for example, defines recreational purpose as including, but "not limited to, any sport or recreational activity of whatever nature undertaken by a person while using the land, including ponds, lakes, reservoirs, streams, paths, and trails ... and includes, but is not limited to, any hobby, diversion, or other sport or other recreational activity" (CRS 33-41-102, 2011).

The California Government Code Section 831.7 (2011) states the following:

> Neither a public entity nor a public employee is liable to any person who participates in a hazardous recreational activity, including any person who assists the participant, or to any spectator who knew or reasonably should have known that the hazardous recreational activity created a substantial risk of injury to himself or herself and was voluntarily in the place of risk, or having the ability to do so failed to leave, for any damage or injury to property or person arising out of that hazardous recreational activity.
>
> (a) As used in this section, "hazardous recreational activity" means a recreational activity conducted on property of a public entity that creates a substantial as distinguished from a minor, trivial, or insignificant risk of injury to a participant or a spectator.

The act goes on to say that this does not limit liability in situations where the facility should guard or warn of known dangerous conditions or where injury was caused by negligent failure to maintain a facility.

Volunteer Immunity

Immunity for volunteers has become an increasingly important legal issue to understand in sport contexts. Volunteer immunity is applicable only in negligence; it does not exist in recklessness. It merely transfers the responsibility for the incident from the nonpaid staff to the facility itself. It does not absolve the facility, agency, or organization from liability. The Volunteer Protection Act of 1997, the first federal statute, provides the following limitations on liability for volunteers. Section 14503 (2011) provides liability protection for volunteers ... no volunteer of a nonprofit organization or government entity shall be liable for harm caused by an act or omission of the volunteer on behalf of the organization or entity if

1) the volunteer was acting within the scope of the volunteer's responsibilities in the nonprofit organization or government entity at the time of the act or omission;

2) if appropriate or required, the volunteer was properly licensed, certified, or authorized by the appropriate authorities for the activities or practice in the State in which the harm occurred, where the activities were or practice was undertaken within the scope of the volunteer's responsibilities in the nonprofit organization or governmental entity;
3) the harm was not caused by willful or criminal misconduct, gross negligence, reckless misconduct, or a conscious, flagrant indifference to the rights or safety of the individual harmed by the volunteer; and
4) the harm was not caused by the volunteer operating a motor vehicle, vessel, aircraft, or other vehicle for which the State requires the operator or the owner of the vehicle, craft, or vessel to (A) possess an operator's license or (B) maintain insurance.

Remedies

In tort, damages are compensatory, occasionally punitive, and seldom injunctive. Compensatory damages are those fees paid for medical expenses, property repair, lost wages, pain or emotional suffering, loss of property, loss of bodily function, and any bills directly related to the incident. Compensatory damage is assessed to make the injured person whole or to pay for the damage done.

Punitive damages, seldom found in negligent actions, occur in intentional torts and product liability claims. They are assessed in an effort to punish a party for the damage done to society in general and to the plaintiff in particular. The purpose of a punitive damage award is to deter the person or agency from acting again in a similar manner. These damages are not in response to the bills the plaintiff has obtained as a result of the incident. Financial status and assets of the person or organization that caused the harm are used to arrive at a punitive damage award. The award is the amount of money essential to cause the wrongdoer sufficient financial loss such that they will avoid such harm in the future.

Injunctive relief, a request to the court to require the defendant to stop doing an offensive act, is discussed in Chapters 4 and 5, the civil rights chapters, and in civil rights cases where it is often used. While injunctive relief is often listed with damages, it is seldom awarded in tort decisions.

Litigation

The court decisions can be studied under a number of different categories. In this case, legal theories and sport and physical activity specifics will lead the discussion. Among the legal theories discussed are assumption of risk, open and obvious, spectators, statutes, waiver of liability, and risk management.

Decisions in Assumption of Risk

California took the lead in primary assumption of risk and in the theory of co-participant responsibilities in the classic decision of *Knight v. Jewett* (1992). Kendra Knight and Michael Jewett attended a Super Bowl party at the home of friends. During halftime, they were among a group who played touch football. No rules were agreed to prior to play, and at times during play, participants asked that roughness be eliminated. Michael Jewett jumped to catch a ball and collided with Kendra Knight, knocking her down and injuring her hand and finger as he returned to the ground. After three unsuccessful surgeries, one of Knight's fingers was amputated.

Knight filed suit against Jewett on theories of negligence, assault, and battery. Defendant Jewett moved for summary judgment on the theory that assumption of risk was a complete defense for his actions. "Defendant asserted that by participating in the touch football game that resulted in her injury plaintiff impliedly agreed to reduce the duty of care owed to her by defendant ... to only a duty to avoid reckless or intentionally harmful conduct and that the undisputed facts established both that he did not intend to injure plaintiff and that the acts of defendant that resulted in plaintiffs injuries were not reckless" (*Knight v. Jewett*, 1992, 698). Also, defendant claimed that plaintiff watched professional football on television and was familiar with the risks associated with playing football. Plaintiff, however, stated that she assumed that the game they were playing was "mock football" and not a serious, competitive sport.

The California Court concluded "that a participant in an active sport breaches a legal duty of care to other participants (i.e., engages in conduct that properly may subject him/her to financial liability) only if the participant intentionally injures another player or engages in conduct that is so reckless as to be totally outside the range of the ordinary activity involved in the sport" (711). Jewett's conduct was found to be negligent or careless but not intentional. The touch football game did not breach a legal duty of care owed by defendant to the plaintiff. The case fell within primary assumption of risk, so comparative fault was not used.

The *Knight v. Jewett* case gave the sport industry a pass on liability in contact sports. The 2007 California golf case *Shin v. Ahn* took the primary assumption of risk from contact sports to noncontact sports, and what can be observed in the following cases is that assumption of risk has been further defined as part of physical activity. Shin and Ahn were part of a threesome playing golf. As they moved to the next tee, "plaintiff took a shortcut which placed him in front of the defendant and to his left. He stopped ... even though he knew (1) that he was in front of the tee box, (2) that defendant was preparing to tee off, and (3) that he should stand behind a player who was teeing off" (583). "Plaintiff's expert stated that golf etiquette requires that a player ensure that no one is in a position to be struck when he or she hits the ball" (583). Shin was hit in the temple by a ball driven by Ahn. Shin sued for negligence as a result of his injury.

The trial court found for the defendant and then reversed itself, saying that issues remained that could be examined by the court at a later date. The California court of appeals affirmed the trial court's decision. The Supreme Court of California affirmed the lower courts' decisions and remanded the case with directions that litigation should continue under primary assumption of risk. An interesting point that sport professionals should consider is the Supreme Court of California's statement that the appeals court "relied too heavily on one of the golf's rules of etiquette involving safety. Golf's first rule of etiquette provides that players should ensure that no one is standing close by or in a position to be hit by the club, the ball or any stones, pebbles, twigs or the like when they make a stroke or practice swing" (590). The court went on to say that "rules of etiquette govern socially acceptable behavior. The sanction for a violation of a rule of etiquette is social disapproval, not legal liability" (590).

Anand et al. v. Kapoor (2010) was a New York case that emphasized the results of the Shin case. Anand was playing on a nine-hole golf course when he suffered a retinal detachment and permanent loss of vision after being hit in the eye by his partner's golf ball. Kapoor's ball went into the rough, and he went to search for it. In the meantime, without waiting for Kapoor, Anand walked along the fairway to his lie. Kapoor found his ball, and without giving a warning, he hit the ball that struck his friend Anand causing the injury. The court ruled for the defendant, finding that being hit by a ball without warning while searching for one's own ball was a risk of playing golf. No mention was made of the rules of etiquette of golf.

Krych v. Bredenberg is a more recent application of the legal doctrine of primary assumption of risk in the context of golf. Walter Krych and Robert Bredenberg were out playing in different groups at a golf course in Erie County, New York. The appeals court examined whether defendant failed to exercise due care by hitting his golf ball from the tee so prematurely as to unreasonably increase the risk of striking plaintiff while plaintiff was in the fairway on the same hole.

Despite testimony indicating that he had an unobstructed view of plaintiff's group ahead on the same fairway, the defendant decided to tee off with his driver, and he hit his golf ball straight down the center where it struck plaintiff in the head as he retreated toward his golf cart following an audible call of "fore." The court noted that defendant Bredenberg's submissions regarding his actions on the golf course raise an issue of fact whether he unreasonably increased the risk of striking plaintiff with his golf ball by teeing off when the plaintiff, who was visible in the fairway on the same hole, was still positioned well within the typical range of defendant's drive. In other words, whether the defendant should have perhaps used more caution in deciding to play his ball while the plaintiff was still clearly in the fairway within the range of his shot was an issue of fact still needing to be resolved and the appellate court, therefore, found summary judgment was properly denied for defendant.

Examples of contemporary assumption of risk decision in skiing (*Fontaine v. Boyd,* 2011), trampoline play (*DeMarco v. DeMarco,* 2017), and use of golf clubs (Rudzinski et al. v. BB, 2010) follow.

Deborah Boyd, an intermediate skier, ran over the back of the skies of Andrea Fontaine, an expert skier, causing her to fall. Fontaine required several surgeries and considerable medical treatment and had permanent injuries to both knees. Fontaine sued Boyd. The first question was the appropriate venue for the case. Fontaine was a Massachusetts resident; Boyd was a Rhode Island resident. The incident occurred in New Hampshire. The case was brought to a Rhode Island court, but it was decided under New Hampshire law, the location of the incident. (Remember, tort law is state law.) The court had to determine "whether a claim of negligence by one skier against another skier for injuries sustained when the two friends collided while skiing recreationally is barred as a matter of law by the doctrine of primary assumption of risk under New Hampshire law" (*Fontaine v. Boyd*, 2011). The court found for the defendant Boyd. The collision, as described, was an inherent risk of skiing.

In a trampoline case applying the legal doctrine of primary assumption of risk, *DeMarco v. DeMarco*, "where plaintiff was injured while jumping on a trampoline at defendants' home, the injury-producing activity did not fit within the narrow group of cases to which the doctrine of primary assumption of risk applied because it was not a sponsored athletic or recreational pursuit that took place at a designated venue" (1226)

Assumption of risk has consistently been upheld in golf for those persons whose golf balls hit others on the course. However, it was also found to be a valid defense when one golfer hit another with his club (*Rudzinski et al. v. BB*, 2010). Two children, ages 9 (BB) and 11 (DB), were playing golf. The 9-year-old had never played before, so the 11-year-old provided some instruction. "As BB was preparing to swing, DB saw an extra ball near the ball BB intended to strike, told BB not to swing, and went to move it" (2). DB was hit in the face, requiring hospitalization, but sustained no permanent injuries. Rudzinski filed suit on behalf of DB against BB for negligence, carelessness, gross negligence, and recklessness (among brothers). The question for the court was whether the risk of being hit by a golf club was an inherent risk of golf. The court ruled for the defendant. Because the plaintiff's conduct was "consistent with the inherent risks presented by golf and because there is no evidence of intentionally injurious or reckless conduct, the court finds that DB has failed to establish that BB's duty of care encompassed the risk involved" (11).

Decisions Finding Open and Obvious

"Open and obvious" tends to appear most often in water incidents and at swimming pools. *Sholer v. ERC Management Group et al.* (2011) is an example of this pattern. Cassidy Sholer, an adult, became severely injured after diving into an apartment swimming pool. The pool was open, lights were on, and there was no signage regarding pool depth, prohibiting diving or unsupervised swimming. She made a shallow dive and hit her head. She sued under negligence. The apartment complex countered that the "no diving" risk was open and obvious. They also stated that the victim had been at least mildly intoxicated in order to break the chain of causation. The person who rescued her claimed that the shadows in the pool were such that the depth was difficult to recognize. The trial court and the court of appeals ruled for the defendants on the basis of open and obvious danger. The Supreme Court of Oklahoma reversed the trial court's decision and returned the case to the lower court for further analysis of whether the pool may have had a hazard.

A case involving failure to pad a softball field fence post was considered open and obvious (*Kaitbenski v. Tantasqua Regional School District,* 2009). Taryn Kaitbenski, playing catcher in a varsity interscholastic softball game, ran into an uncovered and unpadded fence post as she tried to catch a pop fly and sustained injuries as a result. She sued the construction companies that built the stadium. They argued that she needed expert testimony to prove her claim and that her injury was open and obvious. This case highlights the need for risk management in the areas of construction and for knowledge of safety standards by those engaged in the building of facilities used primarily for sport and physical activity purposes.

Decisions Involving Spectators

Spectators have been injured from a flying ball or puck during the game (*Sciarrotta v. Global Spectrum et al.,* 2008) and by a player who entered the spectator seating area (*Pickel v. Springfield Stallions, Inc. et al.,* 2010). The *Sciarrotta* decision contains a detailed discussion of the "limited duty" rule, typically applied to baseball facility injuries to spectators. This rule and line of court decisions now heavily influences safety planning for facilities housing sports where objects may fly into the seating areas, notably baseball and hockey facilities. Mrs. Sciarrotta attended an ice hockey game at the Sovereign Bank Arena in Trenton, New Jersey, to see her daughter sing the national anthem. She was injured when hit by a hockey puck driven from the rink during the team warm-up. Her seat was six or seven rows from the ice and above the Plexiglass safety barrier. She sued, alleging negligence by Global Spectrum, the arena, and by Comcast Spectacor Co., owners and operators, and others responsible for managing the sport facility.

The limited duty rule originated in *Schneider v. Am. Hockey & Ice Skating Center, Inc.* (2001) and was further developed in *Maisonave v. Newark Bears Professional Baseball Club, Inc.* (2005) and in the New Jersey Baseball Spectator Safety Act of 2006. The limited duty rule

> applies to sports venues in respect of a specific peril, that of objects leaving the field of play that may injure spectators in the stands. Under the rule, a sports venue owner or operator that provides screened seating (1) sufficient for those spectators who may be reasonably anticipated to desire protected seats on an ordinary occasion, and (2) in the most dangerous section of the stands, has satisfied its duty of care. The rule applies not only while the game itself is in progress, but whenever spectators are located in the stands. (*Sciarrotta v. Global Spectrum et al.,* 2008, 701)

In *Sciarrotta,* the court debated as to whether the application of the limited duty rule was adequate for the hockey warm-up session when many pucks were in play (which increases the risk to patrons) or only for game play involving one puck. The trial court found for the facility; they had fulfilled the limited duty rule. The intermediate appellate court found a question as to whether the protection was adequate for the practice play when so many pucks were in the air and reversed the decision, holding for Sciarrotta. The appellate court reversed and found for the facility; the limited duty rule was satisfied.

Wendy Pickel, a spectator at an indoor football game, was injured when one of the players fell over the wall separating the players from the playing court and ran into her. She sued the owners of the facility and the team for negligence. The defendants argued "that because football was a contact sport in which violent collisions were inherent in the game ... [this] required plaintiff to plead a greater culpability on behalf of the team than mere negligence" (879, 880). The trial court agreed and held for the defendants. Pickel appealed, arguing that the contact sport exception did not apply to spectators, only to participants. The court of appeals reversed and found for Pickel.

Decisions under Statutes

One case example decided under state statute involved the New Jersey Equine Activities Liability Act (*Hubner et al. v. Spring Valley Equestrian Center*, 2010). Gloria Hubner was injured when she fell from her frightened horse as the horse backed into training poles. She sued claiming negligence. The trial court found for the defendant as the claim was barred by the New Jersey Equine Act. Hubner appealed. The Supreme Court of New Jersey ultimately found her claim was barred by the Equine Act. The Equine Act can operate as a complete bar to plaintiff if her injuries were caused by one of the inherent risks of the activity. The court analyzed the state statute in the following manner:

1) Does the situation mirror the words of the statute?
2) Purpose of the statute is to protect equine activities due to their economy and open space preservation. Participant assumes defined risks.
3) Those assuming the defined risks are barred from recovery. It is one of a number of statutes "using assumption of risk principles to allocate responsibility for injuries sustained in inherently dangerous recreational activities."
4) In a previous case, the court discussed the allocation of losses for inherently dangerous recreational injuries. The "primary" assumption of the risk refers to an obvious inherent risk, as to which the facility operator owes participants no duty and a claim based on the risk is barred. The "secondary" sense of assumption of risks arises where the operator has a duty and breaches it but asserts as an affirmative defense that the participant "voluntarily exposed himself to a risk negligently created" by the operator.
5) Risks are to the listed.
6) The difference between the inherent risks and conditions within a facility's control are identified.

7) An exception to the statute is made where the operator acted with "negligent disregard for the participant's safety." (*Huber, et al. v. Spring Valley Equestrian Center*, 2010, 618, 619)

Decisions Involving Waiver of Liability

Stelluti v. Casapenn Enterprises, LLC et al. (2010) featured a situation where the waiver of liability was upheld for the defendant fitness center despite the fact that the fitness equipment fell apart. Gina Stelluti, a member of spinning class, fell forward while her feet remained strapped to the peddles of the bike when the handlebars were dislodged. She sued under negligence, alleging failure to maintain the equipment, set up the equipment, and properly instruct her on the use of the equipment in such situations. The fitness center countered with the liability waiver she had signed. All courts considering this case found for the defendant on the basis of the liability waiver.

Jakubovsky was skiing down a slope at Blackjack Mountain in Michigan when a snowboarder, coming at a high rate of speed, hit her, causing significant injuries as she was pushed into a fence (*Jakubovsky v. Blackjack Ski Corporation et al.*, 2009). The snowboarder was never identified. She sued the resort. The resort claimed immunity under Michigan's Ski Area Safety Act which "provides that skiers are deemed to accept the dangers inherent in the sport of skiing, including injury from skier-to-skier collisions" (3). Jakubovsky claimed that the resort was not immune under the statute because it had violated the Act "by failing to warn skiers of the unmarked trail which the snowboarder took prior to the accident" (3). The Michigan Ski Area Safety Act states the following:

> Each person who participates in the sport of skiing accepts the dangers that inhere in that sport insofar as the dangers are obvious and necessary. Those dangers include, but are not limited to, injuries which can result from variations in terrain; surface or subsurface snow or ice conditions, bare spots, rocks, trees, and other forms of natural growth or debris, collisions with ski lift towers and their components, with other skiers, or with properly marked or plainly visible snow-making or snowgrooming equipment. (*Jakubovsky v. Blackjack Ski Corporation et al.*, 2009, 4)

The defendant succeeded based on the Michigan Ski Area Safety Act. Similar acts exist in many states where ski resorts are located, and in most cases, the act enables the resort to succeed in a court of law.

Summary

Negligence occurs when a person does not exercise reasonable care under all circumstances. It must be foreseeable that a person's conduct will result in harm. The five elements of negligence are duty, breach of the duty, factual cause, scope of liability including foreseeability, and damage. Violation of statutes, ordinances, or regulations are, on occasion, the basis for a negligence action.

The standards of care in sport and physical activity are reasonable person, special relationship, and professional. The reasonable person is a hypothetical person that represents what an ordinary person would do in the situation. Parents and schools have special relationships with children that make them responsible for certain standards of care. A professional standard is established when a body of knowledge exists and a clearly recognized level of performance is universally adhered to by members of that profession. Defenses to negligence are contributory negligence, assumption of risk, and comparative negligence. Contributory negligence means that the victim contributed to his/her own injuries. Assumption of risk is that the participant knew and agreed to the risk when he/she chose to participate in the activity. Comparative negligence is a system of fault used to identify the extent of fault of the victim and the extent of fault of the persons responsible for the victim's injuries.

Premises liability is classified by status of person on the land as either an invitee, licensee, or trespasser. An invitee has been invited onto the land, typically for a business purpose. The owner must keep the premises in a reasonably safe condition, inspect for problems, repair as needed, and warn only of dangers they know about. A licensee is on the land with the owner's consent but does not have a business interest; he/she is a guest. The owner must keep the land in reasonable condition and warn of any known problems; he/she is not required to inspect the land. A trespasser is on the land without the owner's permission and therefore is owed "zero duty" to be protected from harm occurring on the premises.

Immunity is freedom from liability. The types of immunity include governmental immunity, Good Samaritan laws, and volunteer immunity. Damages in tort can be both compensatory and punitive but most often have the goal of making the injured plaintiff "whole" again.

Discussion Questions

1. Identify the elements of negligence and describe the elements in the context of a sport environment.
2. Explain Good Samaritan laws. Find an example of your state's version of this type of law and identify when and why they are used using a public policy rationale.
3. What is contributory negligence and when does it occur?
4. Do recreational use statutes cover high school and collegiate athletics?

Activities

1. Read two assumption of risk cases in a sport in which you are familiar. Given your knowledge of rules and safety within the specific activity, including age-appropriate understandings, assess the court's consideration of the inherent risks of that sport.
2. Read the dissent and the statements on the etiquette of golf in the Shin vs. Ahn case. Did the California court choose to overrule the laws and etiquette of golf in their decision?
3. Select a sport. Identify five foreseeable risks of harm in the sport. Outline an assumption of risk statement for the sport (such as would be included in a typical waiver of liability).

References

Anand et al. v. Kapoor, 942 N. E. 295 (2010).

Coan et al. v. New Hampshire Department of Environmental Services et al., 8 A. 3d 109 (2010).

Davis et al. v. Accor North America, 2010 U.S. Dist. LEXIS 40057.

DeMarco v. DeMarco, 154 A.D.3d 1226 (2017).

Federal Tort Claims Act (1946). 28 USC 1346(b), 2671–2680.

Fontaine v. Boyd, C.A. No. WC-2007-0794, 2011 R.I. Super. LEXIS 27.

Hubner et al. v. Spring Valley Equestrian Center, 1 A. 3d 618 (2010).

Jakubovsky v. Blackjack Ski Corporation et al., 2009 LEXIS 120889.

Kaitbenski v. Tantasqua Regional School District, 26 Mass. L. Rep. 128 (2009).

Kleinknecht v. Gettysburg College, 989 F. 2d 1360 (1991).

Knight v. Jewett, 3 Cal. 4th 296; 834 P. 2d 696 (1992).

Krych v Bredenberg, 172 A.D.3d 1884 (2019).

Maisonave et al. v. the Newark Bears Professional Baseball Club, 881 A. 2d 700 (2005).

Pickel v. Springfield Stallions, 926 N. E. 2d 877 (2010).

Restatement of the Law of Torts (Second). (1976). American Law Institute.

Restatement Third, Torts: Liability for Physical and Emotional Harm. (2011). American Law Institute.

Rudzinski et al. v. BB, 2010 U.S. Dist. LEXIS 68471.

Schneider et al. v. American Hockey and Ice Skating Center, 342 N. J. Super 529 (2001).

Sciarrotta et al. v. Global Spectrum et al., 944 A. 2d 630 (2008).

Shin v. Ahn, 165 P. 3d 581 (2007).

Sholer v. ERC Management Group et al., 2011 OK 24.

Stelluti v. Casapenn Enterprises, 1 A. 3d 678 (2010).

The Volunteer Protection Act of 1997, 42 USCS Sec. 14503.

Recommended Reading

Cole, M. G. (2007). No blood no foul: The standard of care in Texas owed by participants to one another in athletic contests. *Baylor Law Review, 59*, 435.

Davis, T. (2008). Emerging legal issues affecting amateur & professional sports: Tort liability of coaches for injuries to professional athletes: Overcoming policy and doctrinal barriers. *UMKC Law Review, 76*, 571.

Diekmann, S., Egan, C., Rasmussen, C., & Shen, F. X. (2019, Fall). The failure of youth sports concussion laws and the limits of legislating health education. *Yale Journal of Health Policy, Law & Ethics, 19*, 1.

Hamilton, V. E. (2019, December). Play now, pay later? Youth and adolescent collision sports. *Hastings Law Journal, 71*, 151.

Varriale, C. (2005, Nov. 18). New Jersey Supreme Court crafts hybrid rule for injured patrons at baseball stadiums. *Sports Litigation Alert.* https://sportslitigationalert.com/new-jersey-supreme-court-crafts-hybrid-rule-for-injured-patrons-at-baseball-stadiums/

2

Intentional Torts and Criminal Law

OBJECTIVES

Upon completing this chapter, you will,

- differentiate between civil and criminal law: courts, decisions, and punishments;
- recognize differences between negligence and intentional tort in sport;
- understand and be able to describe the role of immunity as a defense to torts;
- recognize the differences between battery and assault; and

Introduction

Intentional torts are injuries caused by a deliberate act. Under the law, intent means that "the person acts with the purpose of producing a consequence (act) or the person acts knowing that the consequence is substantially certain to result" (*Restatement Third, Torts: Liability for Physical and Emotional Harm,* Section 1). The actor may not intend to injure someone. The intentional torts most often encountered in sport and physical activity are torts to persons and property. Sport managers will also encounter intentional torts in economic relations. The accepted contact between players in many sports and the aggressive nature of some sport competitions have caused courts to find most incidents of play or practice involving injury among sport teammates or opposing players (i.e. co-participants) to be intentional torts. They are not considered to be negligent, something one did not know would happen. The intentional tort categories in which violent actions are intended are the vehicle for many sport decisions. The court will ask if the athlete intended to injure the fellow athlete or if the defendant's actions were so far beyond the expectations and rules of the particular sport that recklessness bordered on intent.

An example of an intentional tort is a person hitting another in the heat of competition, such as occurs in the sport of hockey. The actor expects the act to be carried out. However, the actor does not intend that an injury will be sustained to the opposing player because of their actions. Thus, there is no clear intent to harm the person. In an intentional tort in sport, the court will attempt to discern if there was intent merely to do the act or there was intent to do the act and to harm the plaintiff. An act executed with intent to harm another is not only an intentional tort but could also be a criminal offense. If a substantial injury or death should occur, the person who carried out the act could be liable for a criminal act.

Intentional Tort Law versus Criminal Law

There are major differences between intentional tort law and criminal law. The purpose of intentional tort law is to vindicate and honor the victim while enforcing appropriate standards of care. The role of criminal law, by contrast, is to support the state's interest in deterring crime. Litigation in tort law is between individuals or individuals and agencies. In criminal law, the state or federal government brings a cause of action against an individual person or agency/organization. For example, the State of New York brings an action against a person. On occasion, the same act can result in both tort and criminal law. An example of this is a state bringing a cause of action to prosecute a person for a crime, while the person harmed brings an action to recover compensation.

Intentional Torts to Persons

Intentional torts to persons include battery, assault, false imprisonment, and recklessness. They occur between persons engaging in an activity, or between a coach, teacher, or supervisor and a player or client. The civil rights statute 42 USC Section 1983, as it relates to intentional torts, is also reviewed in this section.

Battery

Battery is intentional, harmful, or offensive contact with another person without that person's consent. To be a battery, the physical contact must be intentional. However, there does not have to be intent to injure, and injury or damage does not have to occur. Continuous intentional tagging and pushing in game play or engaging in locker room pranks could become batteries in certain extreme cases. Horseplay is often found to include battery.

Numerous batteries, seldom recognized as such, exist in the traditional rituals of recreational and competitive sports. Hazing is considered to be among these batteries and is more often prosecuted too under state laws that bar hazing activities, especially as it relates to sports or fraternity initiation rituals. In addition to batteries within the competitive arena, there are also batteries that occur as a result of athletes injuring spectators. For years, aquatic competitions ended with winners, losers, coaches, officials, and spectators being thrown into the water. When aquatic officials complained of these unsafe practices, administrators responded by stating that restricting such behavior would take the fun out of the event. Finally, serious life-threatening and debilitating injuries resulting from horseplay caused administrators to view this behavior in a different light. Today, most national swimming meets no longer finish with everyone in the water.

Pushing, shoving, chasing, and tagging are to be avoided in physical activity environments unless such activity is an element of regular game play, and officials are present to control the level of physical contact and safety. The majority of serious injuries attributed to horseplay occur in the home or in unsupervised recreational areas.

Battery does not take place if the other party consented to the act. Thus, consent is a complete defense to battery. Consent, however, is difficult to assess and even more difficult to prove! For example, does a person competing in and winning a swimming event give consent to a fellow team member to toss that person into the water in celebration of the victory? No matter the context, sexual contact among adults without consent is battery. Sexual contact between an adult and a minor with or without consent is likely a criminal act under state law.

Assault

Assault is the apprehension or belief that one will experience imminent contact. Assault does not require physical contact since the person harmed has not consented or agreed to the alleged harmful act. When a person is threatened by an action where they believe another is preparing to hit them, an assault has occurred. A critical distinction is that it is not necessary that the assaulting person intends to harm the individual. The person threatened need not be in actual fear of the other person's actions; only apprehension or threat is required. An example of an assault is a 6'4" basketball coach lunging toward a 5'2" seventh-grade athlete, telling him to move toward the basket now! If the two are in fairly close range, the young person may be in fear of being hit, although he is not actually touched. This is potentially the intentional tort of assault. The threat must be physical—words alone will not constitute an assault. If physical contact is made, it is indeed a battery.

False Imprisonment

False imprisonment is the unjustified, unlawful, and intentional confinement, restraint, or detention of a person within specific boundaries against that person's will. Wrongful intent need not exist, nor is there a need for substantial damage. For example, store managers who restrain shoppers suspected of shoplifting could be charged with false imprisonment. While false imprisonment court decisions are uncommon in sport and physical activity, professionals who routinely restrain persons in locker rooms or gyms as punishment could technically be held liable for false imprisonment.

Recklessness

Recklessness describes a significantly high level of risk of which the actor is aware. A person acts recklessly in engaging in conduct if:

a) the person knows of the risk of harm created by the conduct or knows facts that make the risk obvious to another in the person's situation; and

b) the precaution that would eliminate or reduce the risk involves burdens that are so slight relative to the magnitude of the risk as to render the person's failure to adopt the precaution a demonstration of the person's indifference to the risk (*Restatement Third, Torts: Liability for Physical Harm,* Section 2, 2010).

In the past, recklessness was often mainly a tort of professional sport. Today, intentional torts occur in many forms and at all levels of sport competition as the courts have long found it difficult to assess sport injuries only as intentional torts. However, as players have increasingly sustained severe injuries from the violation of game rules, these acts have been judged under either a reckless standard or as intentional torts. How far beyond the rules of the game can a participant—even a professional athlete—be expected to assume a risk of injury? Courts appear to sense a need to declare that a player assumes all risks of injury up to the limits of the rules. However, when the injury is a clear violation of a safety rules, it likely qualifies as an intentional tort.

42 USC Section 1983

42 USC 1983 is a statute often used in civil rights cases that permits tort claims for deprivation of federal rights under the color of state law. Defendants are state or local government officials; victims may also sue under this law as private individuals.

Section 1983 provides a private right of action for damages to individuals who are deprived of "any rights, privileges, or immunities" protected by the U.S. Constitution or federal law by any person acting under the color of state law.... As such state officials may be held liable under Section 1983 if there is, at minimum, an underlying constitutional tort.... however, the defense of qualified immunity generally shields officials in the performance of their discretionary duties from liability of civil damages "insofar as their conduct does not violate clearly established statutory or constitutional rights of which a reasonable person would have known" (U.S. Code, 2011, 111, 112).

Victims of intentional torts may use 42 USC 1983 in place of or in addition to intentional torts to gain personal rights. *J. K. v. Arizona Board of Regents et al.* (2008) and *Fitzgerald v.*

Barnstable School Committee (2009) are cases involving 42 USC 1983.

J. K. is discussed under battery while *Fitzgerald* follows here because the case established the connection between sexual assault and 42 USC 1983.

In 2001, a kindergarten student, Jacqueline Fitzgerald, told her parents that when she wore a dress to school, "an older student on her school bus would bully her to lift her skirt" (*Fitzgerald v. Barnstable School Committee,* 2007, 169). Later, the third grader also asked her to do more. Her mother reported the incidents to the school. The school studied the situation and the local police department conducted an investigation. All involved parties decided that insufficient information existed to find the young man criminally responsible. Their solution was to provide a different bus schedule for Jacqueline or separate the kindergarteners from the third graders on the bus. Mrs. Fitzgerald felt the solution was a punishment for her daughter and recommended that the young man be moved to a different bus. The school refused. There was a second encounter between the students in a gym class and Jacqueline began to miss many school days and all of her gym classes.

In 2002, the Fitzgerald parents sued the Barnstable School Committee and the superintendent. The claim against the school committee was for violation of Title IX, while the claim against both the School Committee and the superintendent was under 42 USC 1983. At the time of the lawsuit, for a Title IX complaint to succeed, the following elements had to be established: the school was covered under Title IX as a recipient of federal funds; the harassment was severe, pervasive, and offensive; the student had to be deprived of educational opportunities as a result of the incidents; and educators had to have had actual knowledge of the situation and had done nothing about it. The case met all elements except the last one: the school had addressed the situation and provided a solution, which the parents deemed unreasonable. Thus, the Title IX statute failed to protect the young girl. The statute 42 USC 1983 was also a part of the pleadings to the court. The appellate court ruled that the plaintiff had to comply with Title IX, not with 42 USC 1983. *Fitzgerald* lost in the Court of Appeals. However, the case was appealed to the United States Supreme Court. The U.S. Supreme Court reversed the appellate decision, stating that 42 USC 1983 and the Equal Protection clause of the Fourteenth Amendment to the Constitution, as well as Title IX, needed to be considered by the trial court. The case was remanded back to the lower court for further proceedings. Often, cases that are remanded are then eventually settled and do not return to subsequent judicial intervention in court.

Intentional Interference with Property

Intentional interference with property includes trespass to land, trespass to chattel, and conversion. Substantial damage is not required in intentional interference with property. Trespass to land (real estate) is an intentional entry—walking onto land or the projection of an object (e.g., shooting an arrow or hitting a golf ball) onto the land in possession of another. The action must have been executed without permission (either implied or expressed) from the owner of the property. The intent need only be to enter; no intent to harm is required. For example, a coach or teacher who advises students to pass through a property owner's yard on their way to a playing field or campgrounds could be found liable for encouraging minors to trespass on land.

Trespass to chattel, instead, is interference with a person's personal possessions. The action must be intentional. Stealing a motorboat is trespass to chattel; intentionally hitting a sailboat in open waters may be trespass to chattel. Actual damage must exist. Trespass to chattel exists when a person who rightly has access to the property of another refuses to return the property. Conversion is trespass to land or chattel that so substantially interferes with the owner's possession of the property that it is only fair to require the defendant to pay for the property (*Restatement of the Law of Torts, Second,* 1965, 222A). Many courts hold that a purchaser of stolen property is a converter whether or not he/she is aware that it is stolen. Other states have ruled that a person who becomes aware that property was stolen and returns the property will not be held for conversion.

Business Torts: Fraud, Deceit, and Misrepresentation

Fraud and deceit are torts often appearing in athletics. Recruiting is an area in which fraud, deceit, and misrepresentation have been alleged. Fraud and deceit may also appear in the purchase of equipment and the construction of buildings. According to the *Restatement of the Law of Torts, Second* (1965), the elements of fraud and deceit:

1) a false representation of a material fact;
2) knowledge that the fact is false;
3) intention to induce the other party to rely on the representation;
4) the other party's reliance on the representation; and
5) substantial damage as a proximate result of the other party's reliance. (525)

A school's description of a league rule and a health spa's explanation of anticipated health improvements are examples of situations that could make agencies vulnerable to litigation under a legal theory of misrepresentation. The opinions of coaches, teachers, trainers, doctors, and lawyers—on issues about which they are expected to possess knowledge—may be considered facts.

A misrepresentation of a law will not be actionable unless it is made by a person in a position of confidence, or by one expected to have knowledge of the law. For example, a college coach, administrator, or recruiter may be actionable for misrepresenting the National Collegiate Athletic Association (NCAA) rules regarding eligibility or recruitment. An athletic recruiter may be liable for misrepresenting a university's requirements to a potential student-athlete.

The difference between fraud and misrepresentation is that fraud involves the intent to deceive. The deception was planned. Instead, misrepresentation:

1) falsely denying knowledge of the facts;

2) actively concealing the facts;

3) discloses only parts of the facts; or

4) provides a false picture.

Persons who claim misrepresentation must differentiate between nondisclosure and misrepresentation. If the question was never asked, the person making the representation may not have been obligated to disclose the facts. Nondisclosure or failure to disclose is usually not actionable unless there is a relationship between the plaintiff and the defendant that required that there be disclosure or the plaintiff relied on the defendant's special skill and knowledge in making the decision.

Unlike other intentional torts, there must be substantial damage before one can make a claim under fraud, deceit, or misrepresentation. Damages usually include losses resulting from the injury. They may include lost work time, customers, time in school, or money. Some courts' awards are only for out-of-pocket expenses or expenses that can be verified by receipts; others may permit more abstract losses to be covered. Only when recklessness is involved are punitive damages awarded.

Defenses to Intentional Torts

Defenses to intentional torts are reasons to justify the actions of the actor. they include consent, self-defense, defense of other people or one's own property, necessity, and discipline.

Consent

Consent occurs when a reasonable person does not object to or attempt to stop the action of another. It may be verbal consent or implied consent as a result of silence. A minor is not able to consent. As the minor moves closer to the age of majority or gains the ability to understand and weigh risks, he/she becomes capable of consenting. If the consent occurs under duress, it will not be considered valid in the eyes of the court. Participation in a game involves a manifestation of consent to those bodily contacts that are permitted by the rules of the game. It should be noted that a person must know the risks involved in an activity and the extent of the damage that could occur before giving informed consent.

Self-Defense

Self-defense and defense of others permits a person who is under attack to take reasonable steps to prevent harm to him/her or to others, when there is not time to obtain professional assistance. Reasonable force may be used to prevent threatened harm, offensive touching, or bodily contact. An individual must sense imminent extreme danger; revenge is not a defense.

A person can use deadly force in self-defense or defense of others only when that degree of force is essential to prevent imminent harm. A person who is attacked should retreat if he/she can do so safely. A person defending him/herself and others in that person's own home may use deadly force and need not retreat. In addition, a person may use reasonable force to defend the rights of family members and others against attack. The property owner may use force that is necessary to protect property. Verbal commands are to be used first. If the verbal commands are not successful, the owner may then use legally appropriate force.

Necessity

Necessity is a privilege, due to unusual circumstances, to harm a person or property even though the person or property has done nothing wrong. A sailing group that is subject to threatening weather can tie its craft to a private dock and make camp on a private shore. In this case, the necessity is seeking shelter in a life-threatening situation. Those who use necessity as a defense are financially responsible for the extent of any damage to property. However, they are not liable in tort for having entered the property of another without permission.

Criminal Law

Tort law, previously studied, was civil law; the injured party or plaintiff brought a cause of action against the defendant, the person(s) who had caused the harm. In criminal law, the wrong is considered harm to society, not a wrong to another individual. Therefore, a prosecutor, an official of the federal or state government, brings a cause of action against the person accused of the harm (defendant) in a criminal court. The prosecutor has the burden of proving "beyond a reasonable doubt" the elements of the crime. In both criminal and civil court, a judge or jury determines the guilt or innocence of the defendant. Criminal law is a combination of federal and state law. Federal law applies when the incident occurs in a military, international, interstate, or navigational environment. Although state laws differ, there is considerable commonality among state laws. In other words, an aggravated assault, a criminal offense in the state of Florida, may likely require the same elements be proven, as the same criminal offense in the state of Georgia.

In criminal law, a guilty defendant is punished by jail or prison, execution, the death penalty, and/or fines paid to the state or federal government. There are two broad classes of crimes, felonies and misdemeanors. In general, felonies carry a maximum incarceration sentence of more than a year. Misdemeanors usually carry a sentence of less than a year. In criminal litigation the burden of proof is always on the state. The state must prove guilt. Also, criminal litigation requires that the state or federal government satisfy each element of the statutory definition of the crime and that the defendant has been found culpable "beyond a reasonable doubt." Usually, a warrant is issued on "probable cause," which is a much lower legal standard.

Litigation in Intentional Torts

Litigation in sport-specific intentional torts differs from general intentional tort cases. An intentional tort requires only the intent to execute an act while court decisions deciding about intentional torts in sport require both the intent to act and the intent to injure.

Battery and Assault

Examples of court decisions of battery in sport include a volunteer coach beaten by opposing team coaches in a little league baseball tournament (*Hill et al. v. Bridgeview Little League Association et al.*, 2000, 2001), a person injured by a drunken spectator at a tailgate party (*Bearman v. Notre Dame*, 1983), a head injury in a high school basketball game (*Brokaw v. Winfield-Mt Union Community School District et al.*, 2008), and a case of student sexual assault (*J. K. v. Arizona Board of Regents et al.*, 2008).

John Hill was attacked and beaten by the Loy brothers while coaching third base in a Little League tournament. The brothers were coaching the opposing team. Hill sustained several injuries, including a gouged eye and a broken nose. He sued the Loys, Bridgeview Little League (Bridgeview), the opponents, and Justice Willow Springs Little League (Justice), who was the tournament sponsor. Negligence claims were filed against Bridgeview and Justice for failing to protect Hill. The trial court "entered an order of default against the Loys for failure to answer or otherwise plead" (1177).

The jury verdict for Hill was $632,710 and $125,000 for his wife. Fault was apportioned equally between Bridgeview and Justice. The defendants appealed, challenging the finding of negligence and the exclusion of the Loys from the apportionment of fault. The Illinois Supreme Court reversed the trial court's decision finding that Bridgeview could not foresee the actions of the Loys, and that Justice did not owe a duty to Hill. Hill could therefore still sue the Loys for intentional tort.

A more recent example was *Oakley v. Dolan* (2020), where a famous fan was removed from Madison Square Garden (MSG). The fan was former Knicks player Charles Oakley who claimed that the defendant (MSG executive Dolan) constantly singled him out and sent security to harass him when he attended games. Security shoved him to the ground and then physically removed him. Oakley pushed their hands away and was then thrown to the ground by six security guards. Oakley sued the MSG employee for battery after his forceful removal.

Spectator Misconduct and Violence

One of the most publicized cases of spectator misconduct in sport is *Bearman v. Notre Dame* (1983). Christenna Bearman suffered a leg fracture when she was knocked down by a drunken spectator as she returned to her car following a Notre Dame football game. The circuit court initially granted Notre Dame a motion for judgment on the evidence. Bearman appealed, arguing

> she was a business invitee of the University of Notre Dame; therefore, Notre Dame owed to her a duty to protect her from injury caused by the acts of other persons on the premises. On the other hand, Notre Dame argued that absent notice or knowledge of any particular danger to a patron, the University cannot be held liable for the acts of third persons. (1197)

The Indiana appeals court reversed the trial court, and remanded, based on this statement:

> The University is aware that alcoholic beverages are consumed on the premises before and during football games. The University is also aware that "tailgate" parties are held in the parking areas around the stadium. Thus, even though there was no showing that the University had reason to know of the particular danger posed by the drunk who injured Mrs. Bearman, it had reason to know that some people will become intoxicated and pose a general threat to the safety of other patrons. Therefore, Notre Dame is under a duty to take reasonable precautions to protect those who attend its football games from injury caused by the act of third persons. (1198)

Although *Bearman* involved a battery and is often thought of as a battery case, the final legal analysis was under premise liability, the liability of property ownership focused on a landowner's overall responsibility to protect their invitees from foreseeable dangers and harm from third parties.

In *Brokaw et al. v. Winfield-Mt Union Community School District and McSorley*, 2008, Jeremy Brokaw, a high school junior and starting guard for the basketball team, was struck in the head by the elbow or fist of an opposing team guard, McSorley. Brokaw fell to the floor, sustaining head injuries including headaches, hallucinations, post-concussion syndrome, and epilepsy symptoms. McSorley was ejected from the game on a technical foul. He received a one game suspension from the league and a five-game suspension from his high school. Brokaw's parents sued McSorley for assault and battery including punitive damages and sued McSorley's school district for negligent supervision. The district knew that McSorley behaved aggressively and did nothing about it. The trial court ruled McSorley committed a battery and awarded Brokaw's parents $13,000 for medical expenses and $10,000 in damages to Brokaw. Punitive damages were denied as the incident did not rise to the level of recklessness. The claim for negligent supervision was also denied.

An example of the many notorious sexual assault cases in sport that were deemed to be criminal batteries by the courts includes an assault of a woman by a football player (*J. K. v. Arizona Board of Regents et al.*, 2008). J. K. was allegedly sexually assaulted by a football player in a University of Arizona dorm where they both resided. J. K. had never met Henderson (the football player) before the attack. Henderson had a history of misconduct and sexual harassment. A university investigation concluded "that the 'football player' had more likely than not sexually assaulted J. K. in violation of the Student Code of Conduct" (9). In addition, the university public safety department's "formal investigation concluded that Henderson had non-consensual sexual intercourse with J. K. and that there was probable cause for criminal prosecution" (9). The local prosecutor refused to prosecute the case. J. K. filed a complaint against the football player and the Arizona Board of Regents et al. in the Maricopa County Superior Court; the defendants removed the case to the federal district court in Arizona. The complaint included a violation of Title IX in the conduct of the investigation proceedings and follow-up on campus and a violation of her due process rights under 42 USC 1983 against Koetter, the football coach. The plaintiff contended that but for:

> a) Koetter's knowledge of Henderson's predatory sexual harassment and threatening behavior,
>
> b) his affirmative actions in facilitating and permitting Henderson to return to ASU in August 2003 after already being expelled from the Summer Bridge for sexual harassment,
>
> c) his affirmative action in concealing relevant information from Clubb and Sullivan at Student Affairs ... in addition to alleging that Koetter failed to act, Plaintiff alleged that Koetter affirmatively ensured that Henderson returned to school, where he was assigned to the very dormitory where his acts of sexual harassment against females had occurred just one month earlier. (22)

As a result of these findings, Coach Koetter's motion for summary judgment was denied. Many of the individual defendants for the Arizona Board of Regents were dismissed and the issue of ASU's willful destruction of documentation regarding the football player's earlier misconduct was settled. As to the Title IX claim, it was stated "the court cannot hold as a matter of law that ASU's response to Henderson's known misconduct during the Summer Bridge program, as well as J.K.'s allegation that Henderson raped her, were not 'clearly unreasonable'" (53, 54).

Recklessness

Recklessness is a concept that often relates to sport cases in that an athlete assumes certain risks when engaging in sport, risks beyond those assumed in regular life activities. The rules of each game or activity and the duties of the referees and persons in charge, when appropriate, are to control the situation. Unfortunately, games and sport activities often get out of control, and those injured in these out of control situations need a legal cause of action. Recklessness is one of those necessary legal causes of action. Early seminal cases in sport that paved the way for the standard recklessness are discussed first, as well as a discussion of contemporary decisions from a range of sports and activities.

Hackbart v. Cincinnati Bengals, Inc. (1979) has played an important role in establishing the concept of recklessness and helped establish clarity on the traditional tort defenses of privilege and concept in the sport context. On September 16, 1973, Hackbart, a veteran free safety for the Denver Broncos, was involved in a play that resulted in a pass interception by the Broncos. Acting as an offensive player, Hackbart attempted to block Clark, an offensive back for Cincinnati, by throwing his body in front of him. Clark struck Hackbart, who was still on his knees, with a blow to the back of his head. No penalty was called, and Hackbart continued to play. Later, Hackbart had pain; it was eventually discovered he had a neck fracture. The trial court judge resolved the liability issue in favor of the Cincinnati Bengals and Clark, reasoning,

> professional football is a species of warfare and that so much physical force is tolerated and the magnitude of the force exerted is so great that it renders injuries not actionable in court, that even intentional batteries are beyond the scope of the judicial process.... Despite the fact that the defendant Charles Clark, admitted that the blow which had been struck was not accidental, that it was intentionally administered, the trial court ruled as a matter of law that the game of professional football is basically a business that is violent in nature, and that the available sanctions are imposition of penalties and expulsion from the game. (518–519)

This case weighs the notions of violence, consent, and assumption of risk. The court of appeals reversed and remanded the case for a new trial, holding that the tort law was applicable to an athletic event and that recklessness—not assault and battery—was a standard for measuring liability.

Reckless misconduct, later referred to as recklessness, was applied in an amateur sport league for high school age boys in the seminal sport case of *Nabozny v. Barnhill* (1975). Nabozny was the goalkeeper for the hansa team; Barnhill was a forward for the Winnetka team. The goalkeeper was kicked in the head by a midfielder while the goalkeeper was on his left knee in the penalty zone. Experts agreed that the contact in question should not have occurred. The court stated,

> when athletes are engaged in an athletic competition; all teams involved are trained and coached by knowledgeable personnel; a recognized set of rules governs the conduct of the competition; and a safety rule is contained therein which is primarily designed to protect players from serious injury, a player is then charged with a legal duty to every other player on the field to refrain from conduct proscribed by a safety rule. A reckless disregard for the safety of other players cannot be excused. To engage in such conduct is to create an intolerable and unreasonable risk of serious injury to other participants. We have carefully drawn the rule announced herein in order to control a new field of personal injury litigation. Under the facts presented in the case at bar, we find such a duty clearly arose. Plaintiff was entitled to legal protection at

> the hands of the defendants.... it is our opinion that a player is liable for injury in a tort action if his conduct is such that it is either deliberate, willful, or wanton or with a reckless disregard for the safety of the other players so as to cause injury to that player, the same being a question of fact to be decided by a jury. (260–261)

The case was reversed and remanded to the circuit court for a new trial.

Examples of contemporary cases are taken from a recreation league, colleges, theme park, golf course, and ski resorts. *Feld et al. v. Borkowski et al.* (2010) involved teammates on an intramural slow-pitch softball team composed of high school students. Feld was playing first base, while Borkowski was practicing batting when he hit a high-flying ball and let go of the aluminum bat hitting Feld. Borkowski yelled a warning, but it was too late. Feld's left eye was severely injured. Feld, through his parents, filed suit in negligence. Borkowski responded that softball was a contact sport and was an exception to the rule of negligence. Feld then changed the charge to reckless conduct. To support the reckless conduct action, an expert witness stated that the "only way a right-handed batter could hit a first baseman with a bat in such a manner is if the batter followed though and rotated around after striking the foul ball and deliberately threw the bat or let go of the bat in such a way that it was flung with considerable force through the air toward the first base position" (74). The district court found for Borkowski, noting that softball was a contact sport. The Feld family appealed. The appeals court ultimately affirmed the decision for the defendant Borkowski.

In *Borella v. Renfro* (2019), a 17-year-old junior hockey player was injured in a hockey game, resulting in partial loss of use of a hand. The case involved what was described as a "freak accident" during a hockey game where the plaintiff fell as a result of a check by another 17-year-old player, and the other skater's skate blade slashed the plaintiff's wrist. Borella sued the referees, the opponent coach, his coach, and the rink owners for recklessness and negligence. The court found for defendant on all counts, holding that "the record is devoid of evidence from which a jury rationally could conclude that the player's conduct is extreme misconduct outside the range of the ordinary activity inherent in the sport, [so] there is no legal liability under the recklessness standard" (618).

Another ice hockey case, this time involving adult recreational sports participants, was *Archibald v. Kemble* (2009). Both men were playing in an adult "no check" league. No check means no body contact. Kemble, an 18-year-old, jammed his right skate into Archibald's left skate, sending Archibald into the boards and shattering his femur. Archibald was transported to the hospital and required multiple surgeries. He ultimately had a permanent injury. The trial court found it to be a case of recklessness. A debate existed as to whether recklessness in sport should be analyzed under negligence or intentional tort.

The United States Coast Guard Academy was playing a soccer match with Trinity College when cadet Trujillo was struck in the head by Yeager, a Trinity player. Trujillo sued Yeager for careless neglect and reckless use of force in creating the injury (*Trujillo v. Yeager et al.*,

2009). He also sued Yeager's coach, Pilger, for negligence in failing to properly educate his athlete. Yeager, the defendant, moved to dismiss the complaint stating that one cannot be held liable for negligence for injuries occurring in the course of a competitive contact sport. Trujillo's negligence count was dismissed. Most states have adopted an intentional or reckless standard of care for injuries occurring in competitive sport. Trujillo's complaint against the opponents' coach also failed, with the Court "holding that coaches liable in negligence, particularly to players on a different college's team, would unreasonably threaten to chill competitive play" (91).

Recklessness incidents occur more often in golf and skiing than in other sports. In golf, an Ohio court (*Alexander v. Tullis*, 2006) and one in Hawaii (*Yoneda v. Tom et al.*, 2006) involved golfers struck by fellow golfers' balls, including one hit by a ball in their eye. This legally qualifies as a bad day at the golf course in almost all states! Both courts found for the defendants. In *Yoneda*, the court stated, "There was an inherent risk that golf participants would be hit by errant shots and because plaintiff adduced no evidence that defendant golfer intentionally injured him or acted recklessly beyond the ordinary activities of golf, the doctrine of primary assumption of risk applied, barred plaintiff's actions against defendant golfer" (*Yoneda v. Tom et al.*, 2006). The same reasoning was used by the court in the *Alexander* decision.

In skiing, the incidents causing serious injury often involve equipment problems (*Jozewicz v. GGT Enterprises, LLC; K2 Corporation et al.*, 2010) and insufficiently marked resort boundaries (*Ciocian v. Vail Corporation*, 2010). Laura Jozewicz's ski binding released for no reason on her rental ski, causing her to fall and injure her neck. Through discovery during litigation, it was discovered that the company had failed to remove a binding from her rental ski that was on recall by the Consumer Product Safety Commission. The defendants countered that she had signed an equipment rental and release agreement:

> I understand that the binding system cannot guarantee the user's safety. In downhill skiing, the binding systems will not release at all times or under all circumstances where release may prevent injury or death, nor is it possible to predict every situation in which it will release.... I understand that the sport of skiing, snowboarding, skiboarding, snowshoeing, and other sports (collectively "RECREATIONAL SNOW SPORTS") involve inherent risks of INJURY and DEATH. I voluntarily agree to expressly assume all risks of injury or death that may result from these RECREATIONAL SNOW SPORTS, or which relate in any way to the use of this equipment. (Alta Ski Resort, 3)

The federal district court held that the pre-injury release was unenforceable and invalid as a matter of public policy. They noted that the "implication of allowing distributors and retailers to contract away liability for noncompliance with established safety standards would increase the risk of injury and would be contrary to Congress's express public policy concerns.... Public policy should encourage compliance with safety laws, not disregard for such laws" (11). A Colorado case in which the court found that ski area boundaries were not adequately marked is *Ciocian v. Vail Corporation* (2010). Ciocian was on a snowboard and skied off a 19-foot retaining wall onto a paved access road, sustaining serious injuries. The trial court found for the resort. There was no issue of material fact, and the resort's exculpatory agreement was clear and unambiguous and did not violate public policy. On appeal, the court focused on the following question: Was the area of the injury properly marked according to Colorado Revised State Statute 33-44-107 (2010)? Evidence provided by the skiers and ski patrols present was that the boundary signs were not readily visible to a skier, and "there was no way she could have known" (*Ciocian et al. v. Vail Corporation et al.*, 2010, 1132). The appellate court reversed and remanded the case.

In Minnesota (*Meyers v. Lutsen Mountains Corporation*, 2009), the release utilized by the ski resort was upheld by the courts. Meyers, a self-described expert skier, "lofted" into an area of rocks and trees on the edge of an intermediate hill, sustaining severe injuries. The release upheld by the court was detailed. Clear and unambiguous waivers are usually favorably viewed by courts and found to sufficiently transfer risk to the participant skier given the inherent and well-recognized risks of skiing in a natural environment. In *Kibler v. Blue Knob Recreation, Inc.*, 184 A.3d 974 (Pa. 2018), it was ruled that there is no liability where the skier signed an agreement. Pennsylvania law recognizes skiing as a sport with inherent risk (979) with no recklessness on the part of the defendant; even when an employee drove an ATV "up the middle" of the slope, creating a rut (980-81), it was not reckless (986). Further, a waiver found to be enforceable and okay almost no matter what because of the nature of skiing. "The signer is a free agent who can simply walk away without signing the release and participating in the activity, and thus the contract signed under such circumstances is not unconscionable" (982), even when they didn't read it.

Hazing

Hazing may be treated as a civil or criminal incident. An example of one of the many extreme cases of hazing follows. "Brian Seamons was tied unclothed to a horizontal towel bar with athletic tape by his Sky View High School football teammates in the boys' locker room" (*Seamons et al. v. Snow et al.*, 1996, 1229). He had been grabbed while showering, his genital area taped, and he was hung on the towel bar. A girl he had dated was brought into the locker room to see him. According to the facts, members of the team looked on.

Brian reported this incident to school administrators and other authorities, including the football coach ... and the school principal.... The coach brought Brian before the football team, accused Brian of betraying the team by bringing the incident to the attention of the administration and others and told Brian to apologize to the team. When Brian refused to apologize, the coach dismissed Brian from the team. The five individuals who assaulted Brian were permitted to play in the next football game. The school district responded to the whole incident by canceling the final game of the season, a state playoff game.... Eventually the principal suggested to Brian and his parents that Brian should leave the high school. Brian did so and enrolled in a distant county (1230).

Seamons's complaints were under constitutional and tort law. The trial court found for the school. The plaintiff appealed. The appellate court affirmed all decisions, except the First Amendment claim. In 1998, the district court failed to find for Seamons on the First Amendment issue. The federal appeals court, however, reversed and remanded the case for further action.

Criminal Litigation

In criminal law, the state or federal government charges the person with a crime and prosecutes the case. *State of Ohio v. Guidugli* (2004) occurred in an intramural basketball game at the University of Cincinnati. Campus police were called to the situation where there were few eyewitnesses and a great deal of pushing and shoving going on. The intramural supervisor, Steinman, saw the student "Guidugli" punch one of the opposing players with a full swing toward the player's eyes. The defendant was convicted of misdemeanor assault for his role in the fight. He pleaded self-defense, which was unsuccessful. He was charged with criminal assault and given a 180-day suspended jail sentence.

A case that stunned the sport nation was the state of Kentucky's action against Stinson, a football coach at Pleasure Ridge Park High School, in Louisville. A 15-year-old player under his direction collapsed and died from a heat stroke, sepsis, and multiple organ failure. The athlete's body temperature was found to be 107 degrees at the time of death. Prior to the day of the incident the same athlete had collapsed during a practice in 94-degree heat. The local prosecutor charged Stinson with reckless homicide. Although Stinson was found not guilty, the incident serves as a warning to coaches practicing in severe weather and other hazardous conditions (Marck, 2011).

The more recent University of Maryland heatstroke case involving football student athlete Jordan McNair ended in a settlement by the McNair family with the university for $3.5 million (Acevedo, 2021). Negligence claims based on actions that occurred during an off-season workout were leveled against the university, athletic department, and medical staff present on the day this tragic incident happened. This case should be studied to learn how best practices in emergency preparedness should be implemented for both in-season and off-season workouts, as well as voluntary practices that athletes are often expected to attend despite being designated as voluntary by coaching staff.

Summary

Intentional torts are injuries that are caused by deliberate acts or deliberate failure to act. Intentional torts to persons include battery, assault, false imprisonment, and recklessness. Intentional torts to property include trespass to chattel, trespass to personal property, and conversion. Business torts are fraud, deceit, and misrepresentation. Defenses to intentional torts include consent, self-defense, defense of others, necessity, and discipline.

Criminal law involves harms to society. A prosecutor brings the cause of action against the person who caused the harm. The burden of proof must be "beyond a reasonable doubt." Crimes are listed as felonies or misdemeanors, with punishments including jail and prison sentences, fines, community service, and even death in some states. Historically, society and the courts held that the person engaged in physical activity assumed all the risks inherent in the sport. In some cases, the triers of fact have even ruled that participants assume the risk of intentional torts that might occur in the heat of battle during competitive or recreational sport.

Discussion Questions

1. Contrast negligence with intentional tort. When does each occur?
2. How does the application of criminal law differ from the application of civil law?
3. What is the difference between battery and assault?

Activities

1. Students aspiring to employment in collegiate athletic departments should read the case *J. K. v. Arizona Board of Regents, et al.* (2008) to create a risk management outline to be used in such a situation. Legal, ethical, and public relations decisions should be considered.
2. Locate two recent cases involving hazing in either college or interscholastic athletics. Did the state in which the case was decided have a hazing statute in place when the incident occurred? If such a statute existed, what role did it play in the decision? Who won the case?
3. Using the Jordan McNair case facts brought against the University of Maryland and its athletic department, identify what practices or procedures failed to protect the athlete from the heat-related death he suffered.

References

Acevedo, M. (2021, January 16). University of Maryland settles with family of student who died of heatstroke. *NBC News*. https://www.nbcnews.com/news/us-news/.

Alexander v. Tullis, 2006 Ohio 1454 (Ohio Ct. App. 2006).

Archibald et al. v. Kemble, 971 A. 2d 513 (2009).

Bearman v. University of Notre Dame, 453 N. E. 2d 1196 (1983).

Borella v. Renfro, 96 Mass. App. Ct. 617 (2019).

Brokaw, v. Winfield-Mt Union Comm. School Dist. & McSorley, 2008 Iowa App. LEXIS 1138.

Ciocian v. Vail Corporation, 251 P. 3d 1130 (2010).

Feld v. Borkowski, 790 N. W. 2d 72 (2010).

Fitzgerald v. Barnstable School Committee, 504 F. 3d 165 (2007); 129 S. Ct. 788 (2009).

Gregorie v. Alpine Meadows Ski Corporation, 2011 U.S. Dist. LEXIS 20275; 405 Fed. Appx. 187 (2010).

Hackbart v. Cincinnati Bengals, 601 F. 2d 516 (1979).

Hill v. Bridgeview Little League Association, 745 N. E. 2d 1166 (2000).

J. K. v. Arizona Board of Regents, 2008 U.S. Dist. LEXIS 83855.

Jozewicz v. GGT Enterprises, 2010 U.S. Dist. LEXIS 53937.

Kibler v. Blue Knob Recreation, Inc., 184 A.3d 974 (2018).

Marck, D. (2011). Necessary roughness?: An argument for the assignment of criminal liability in cases of student-athlete sustained heat-related deaths. *Seton Hall Journal of Sports & Entertainment Law, 21*, 177.

Meyers v. Lutsen Mountains Corporation, 587 F. 3d 891 (2009).

Nabozny v. Barnhill, 334 N. E. 2d 258 (1975).

Oakley v. Dolan, 980 F.3d 279 (2020).

Restatement of the Law of Torts, (Second). (1965). American Law Institute.

Restatement Third, Torts: Liability for physical and emotional harm. (2010). American Law Institute.

Seamons v. Snow, 206 F. 3d 1021 (2000).

State of Ohio v. Guidugli, 811 N. E. 2d 567 (2004).

Trujillo v. Yeager, 642 F. Supp. 2d 86 (2009).

Yoneda v. Tom, 133 P. 3d 796 (2006).

Recommended Reading

Feingold, D. (2011). Who takes the heat? Criminal liability for heat-related deaths in high school athletics. *Cardozo Journal of Law & Gender, 17*, 359.

Lee, J. W., & Lee, J. C. (2009). Sport and criminal behavior. Carolina Academic Press.

Otto, K. A. (2009). Criminal athletes: An analysis of charges, reduced charges, and sentences. *Journal of Legal Aspects of Sport, 19*, 67.

Rapp, G. C. (2008). The wreckage of recklessness. *Washington University Law Review, 86*, 111 (including expanded discussion of recklessness in sport, pp. 113–120).

Scales, A. (2009). Student gladiators and sexual assault: A new analysis of liability for injuries inflicted by college athletes. *Michigan Journal of Gender and Law, 15*, 205.

Solomon, A. (2018). Preventing recurrences of the cover-ups at Penn State and Baylor (and now Michigan State): Where does it end? *Marquette Sports Law Review, 28*, 379.

3

Product Liability

OBJECTIVES

Upon completing this chapter, you will,

- understand the policy rationale for imposing liability on the manufacturers and sellers of defective sports and physical activity equipment;
- be able to differentiate between manufacturing and design defects;
- understand the importance of warnings to protect users from harm;
- be able to distinguish express and implied warranties; and
- be able to explain the defenses available to manufacturers in product liability cases.

Introduction

Product liability is of concern to manufacturers, retailers, and sellers of sport and physical activity equipment. Owners and agencies leasing sport and physical activity equipment may also be sued under product liability. Historically, product liability has been considered strict liability, where the manufacturer, wholesaler, and retailer of a faulty product are automatically liable for putting an unreasonably dangerous product in the marketplace, and with the exception of the very few courts that have decided to include a product liability category of negligence in a decision, it remains strict liability today. While "services" are not covered under product liability, occasionally a service provider may be included as a defendant in a product liability lawsuit.

Participants in sports and physical activity generally assume that the products they purchase or lease are safe and will enable them to perform to their maximum capacity in the sport or activity. Often, however, the product is so technically complex that users are not able to examine the equipment for any faults or flaws. This complexity increases with advances in technology and in many cases, makes it impossible for even skilled performers to assess the condition of their equipment. Because sport and physical activity equipment is expensive, users expect the equipment to be safe and appropriate to the activity. Furthermore, since the user is typically not in the best position to assess the safety of the equipment he/she is using, the responsibility for discovering product defects and correcting them is appropriately borne by those who design and manufacture the product, rather than the consumers of such products.

Sport professionals, sport personnel, team or sport club managers, and others responsible for the selection and purchase of sport and fitness equipment need to be aware of product liability. They must be able to protect their organizations against the purchase and installation of faulty products, know the organizations' rights when products fail, and effectively relay manufacturers' warnings to appropriate audiences.

Under product liability, the manufacturer, wholesaler, retailer, supplier, and vendor are liable for placing a defective product—one that might cause injury—on the market. Product liability theory presumes that the manufacturer and seller are in the best position to become aware of problems, to eliminate defects, and to absorb losses from product changes and/or litigation. A product is considered defective under product liability when the defect existed at the time the product left the manufacturer or retailer (defendant) and the defect caused the injury. Components of the product liability statute also include noncompliance with safety standards, misrepresentation, and failure to recall. The Consumer Product Safety Commission also allows for an action in federal court against a manufacturer in violation of a consumer product safety rule.

Defenses to product liability include contributory negligence, assumption of risk, misuse, and the Uniform Commercial Code (UCC) disclaimers. Product liability is governed by state and federal laws. States may differ in their laws and in the interpretation of similar laws. *Restatement (Third) of Torts: Product Liability* (1998) is the guide for the discussion that follows. It defines a product as a "tangible personal property distributed commercially for use or consumption. Other items, such as real property and electricity, are products when the context of their distribution and use is sufficiently analogous to the distribution and use of tangible personal property" (267). A person, according to Section 20, who sells or distributes a product is defined in the explanation below:

a) One sells a product when, in a commercial context, one transfers ownership thereto either for use or consumption or for resale leading to ultimate use or consumption. Commercial product sellers include, but are not limited to, manufacturers, wholesalers, and retailers.

b) One otherwise distributes a product when, in a commercial transaction other than a sale, one provides the product to another either for use or consumption or as a preliminary step leading to ultimate use or consumption. Commercial non-sale product distributors include, but are not limited to, lessors, bailors, and those who provide products to others as a means of promoting either the use or consumption of such products or some other commercial activity.

c) One also sells or otherwise distributes a product when, in a commercial transaction, one provides a combination of products and services and either the transaction taken as a whole, or the product component thereof, satisfies the criteria in ... (a) or (b). (284)

Categories of Product Defect

Product liability exists when a manufacturer, retailer, or seller sells or distributes a defective product. The categories of product defect include a manufacturing defect, a design defect, or defect as a result of providing inadequate instructions or warnings. *According to the Restatement (Third) of Torts: Product Liability* (1998), Section 2, a product

a) contains a manufacturing defect when the product departs from its intended design even though all possible care was exercised in the preparation and marketing of the product;

b) is defective in design when the foreseeable risks of harm posed by the product could have been reduced or avoided by the adoption of a reasonable alternative design by the seller or other distributor or a predecessor in the commercial chain of distribution, and the omission of the alternative design renders the product not reasonably safe;

c) is defective because of inadequate instructions or warnings when the foreseeable risks of harm posed by the product could have been reduced or avoided by the provision of reasonable instructions or warnings by the seller or other distributor, or a predecessor in the commercial chain of distribution, and the omission of the instructions or warnings renders the product not reasonably safe. (14)

Manufacturing Defect

A manufacturing defect is an unreasonably unsafe product created in the construction process; it may include the improper construction of a part (or parts) or the improper assembly of the parts. A manufacturing defect means that the product does not perform or was not built as the manufacturer planned or according to the design. As a result of the change, an unsafe product has been created. With a manufacturing defect, the defect may occur in all of the products or may occur in in only a few random products.

For example, in 2009, the U.S. Consumer Product Safety Commission (CPSC) in association with the manufacturer issued a nationwide recall of a specific brand and model of basketball hoops. Approximately 1,700 in-ground basketball hoops were recalled because the bolts at the base could fail, causing the unit to fall. This would be considered a manufacturing defect because the defect occurred during the manufacturing stage rather than during the design process and some, not all, of the hoops manufactured were defective. To determine liability for manufacturing defects, strict liability is used.

Design Defect

A design defect means that the product, when built according to the manufacturer's plan, contains a design flaw or fault that will subject the user of the product to unreasonable harm; the original plans or specifications are flawed. A design defect makes all of the products unreasonably dangerous, not just a few of them. This unreasonable danger is one that has not been contemplated by the user or consumer. The manufacturer is held to the status of an expert in the design area. An examination of the manufacturer's schematics or design plans must reveal a flaw in the design and analysis of the manufacturing protocol that demonstrates that the product was created according to the faulty design. Those persons who created the design and specifications will ultimately be held responsible.

The role of the manufacturer and the seller or distributor for failure to note the design flaw will be based upon whether the defendant had expertise or reason to know (through complaints or otherwise) that the design flaw might exist. However, a recent trend being used by some courts is considering the obviousness of the danger as one factor in determining if the product is unreasonably dangerous, rather than as a complete defense to product liability.

The Restatement (Third) of Torts: Product Liability (1998) exclusively adopts a risk/utility analysis in determining whether a design defect exists. Under this approach, a product will be found defective as designed only if the magnitude of the risk created by the design is greater than the utility of the product (*Restatement [Third]*, Sec. 2[b]). Specifically, the *Restatement (Third) Torts* Section 2(b) provides that a product is defective when "the foreseeable risks of harm posed by the product could have been reduced or avoided by the adoption of a reasonable alternative design by the seller or other distributor, or a predecessor in the commercial chain of distribution, and the omission of the alternative design renders the product not reasonably safe" (14).

Instructions

Adequate instructions on how the product is to be used and information about potential hazards in the use of the product are to be provided. These instructions are to include assembly, cleaning, periodic inspection, routine care, and method of repair. If the equipment is to be installed under supervision, it should be noted.

The nature of some products causes them to be considered dangerous. At times, the purchaser may not understand the obvious danger of a product he/she is using. For example, all boats and personal watercraft present a hazard to any person who is unable to right his/her body and come to the surface after being thrown into the water. For anyone unable to execute this minimal personal rescue skill, the use of all watercraft is hazardous.

Warnings

When manufacturers or sellers become aware of a dangerous product, they have an obligation to warn the user about the specific danger(s) involved. Merely placing a warning label on a product is not enough. The product must be manufactured to be as safe as is reasonable. What cannot be incorporated into the safe manufacture of the product must be explained in the warning. Warnings must be adequate to perform their intended function of risk reduction (*Pell v. Victor J. Andrew High School and AMF,* 1984). Warnings may be inadequate, however, if they:

- do not specify the risk presented by the product;
- are inconsistent with how a product should be used;
- do not provide the reason for the warnings; or
- do not reach foreseeable users.

When the danger is not apparent, there is a duty to warn the user of the product. When the danger is obvious, some courts have ruled that there is no duty to warn. Other courts have ruled that even though the danger might be considered obvious to some people, the duty to warn remains with all involved in manufacture, retail, and leasing. When the user has knowledge of the danger of a product as a result of his/her experience and expertise, there is no duty to warn. For example, a competitive surfer has knowledge of the dangers of surfing and understands the precautions taken to use surfing equipment safely. No duty to warn exists when the dangers of a product are known within a profession. The duty to warn cannot be delegated.

In understanding the nuances of product liability law, it is necessary to differentiate between defective and dangerous products. Defective products are to be removed, while dangerous products should contain warnings. Products may be dangerous only when used or misused in certain ways. If manufacturers or sellers can foresee any of these uses or misuses, or alternatively if a court of law could decide that they should have foreseen a use or misuse, the manufacturer or seller must warn users about foreseeable dangers. Manufacturers must simulate how products will be used by consumers and whether the product could be dangerous in its present or future use. They should reasonably anticipate the environment in which it could be used and warn against dangers they can foresee. For example, children using a portable basketball hoop in a driveway or on a neighborhood street may not appreciate that dunking on the hoop may cause the entire structure to tip over, potentially injuring the participants or others nearby, because the hoop is not permanently fixed in the ground.

The objective of a warning in product liability—but also in tort law, generally speaking—is to alert the user to a danger of which the user is not aware. Determining whether a danger is obvious to the user must take into account the user's expertise, skill, and knowledge. Therefore, products that may typically be expected to be used by children, where the user may not have the expertise or maturity to appreciate the danger, are particularly prone to requiring warnings.

Manufacturers, sellers, and owners (including sport and physical activity professionals) may have a duty to warn. They need to be aware of when to warn and have a systematic process of informing clients about the warnings. A person held to a duty to warn, according to Wittenberg (1985), is to provide a warning that is

> 1) Conspicuous—it will attract the user's eye
>
> 2) Specific—it will be understood by the user
>
> 3) Forceful—it will convince the user of the range and magnitude of the potential harm that could occur. (pp. 1–33)

Manufacturers, wholesalers, retailers, sellers, and persons supervising the use of a product can be held for failure to adequately warn users of foreseeable dangers or failure to pass on the warnings to others. These dangers include foreseeable use and misuse of the product. A warning of danger must: a) identify the risk, b) provide the reason for the warning, and c) reach the user. The user is to be warned and to understand the importance of the warning. Warnings are to be written in such a manner that users recognize the significance of the warning. When the significance of the warning is obvious, there is a far greater chance the warning will be taken seriously. Manufacturers, retailers, and wholesalers must place the warning on the product in such a way that it cannot be missed.

The manufacturer is to provide the product user with information and directions regarding the qualities, characteristics, and uses of the product. The information is to be written in such a way that if caution were essential, a reasonable person would recognize the need to exercise caution. The objective is to avoid injuries that could occur from ignorant misuse of the product. Instructions are to be provided to enable the purchaser to pass on the instructions and warnings to all potential users of the product.

When a warning is justified, the courts will determine the adequacy of the warning on a case-by-case basis, considering whether it was noticeable, accurate, clear, and strong. It must capture the attention of those who will use the product and inform them of the dangers in the use of the product. Even in situations where the user is sophisticated, a warning to remind the user of the potential danger associated with the product may be in order.

Manufacturers, retailers, and supervisors of activity have a duty to instruct the participant on the safe use of the equipment and to warn against dangers. The warning must be sufficient to enable the average person to understand the probability, frequency, and magnitude of the occurrence of the risk and the extent of the potential injury. It is this duty to warn and to instruct about the dangers of the use of certain equipment that is the responsibility of those who supervise, manage, or teach physical activity.

When a manufacturer provides a warning to a sport professional, such as the manager of a fitness center, the manufacturer also gives responsibility to that person to properly inform or pass on the warning to those who will use the equipment. Warnings are to be placed on the face of the equipment or on the wall above the equipment; they are not to be thrown out in the empty cartons used to ship or deliver the product. Professionals have an additional duty to inform and to warn participants about the skill and physical capacity essential to safely use certain pieces of equipment. This includes the duty to warn and to provide instruction sufficient to enable the average person to ascertain the need for experience before using various pieces of equipment.

Participants need to know and understand when the equipment is beyond their skill level. Warnings need to be tailored to the specific skill level of the performer.

Misrepresentation

Misrepresentation is an inaccurate statement that leads another to believe a "fact" that is not actually true. The statement may be an unintentional error or an intentional falsehood. In *Restatement of Torts (Third): Product Liability* (1998) Section 9, it is stated that "One engaged in the business of selling or otherwise, distributing products, who, in connection with the sale of a product makes a fraudulent, negligent, or innocent misrepresentation concerning the product is subject to liability for harm to persons or property caused by the misrepresentation" (187).

When a product's facts and use statements are misrepresented by the seller, an injured plaintiff may have a cause of action for misrepresentation. The product does not have to be defective or unreasonably dangerous; however, a claim may only be brought for physical injury. Care should be taken to ensure that advertisements, brochures, and salespersons' comments given face-to-face or over the phone or internet do not directly or inadvertently cause product misrepresentations. Salespersons are to be monitored by management to ensure that purchasers are informed of the potential hazards and risks in the use of equipment.

Breach of Warranty

A warranty is a guarantee by a manufacturer, wholesaler, or retailer to a buyer that the product will perform according to identified standards for a specified period of time. Requirements for maintenance, intended use, and other specifications must be given to the buyer. The warranty is a part of the contract between the buyer and seller. If the seller violates the warranty, the seller breaches the contract; if the buyer violates the warranty, the buyer breaches the contract. In warranty, the liability of the industry exists without regard to fault. For example, if the product does not meet the specifications of the fitness industry, the liability of the manufacturer, retailer, or wholesaler is automatic; there is no need to investigate the intent of the parties. Breach of warranty, also covered by the Uniform Commercial Code (UCC), may occur through breach of express or implied warranty.

Many laws relating to business are similar from state to state. "The states, not the federal government, are the primary source of law on commercial transactions in the U.S. in all 50 states and the District of Columbia, at least some of that commercial law is based on the UCC" (Cornell legal information institute, n.d.).

Express Warranties

Express warranties are written statements about the product; implied warranties are warranties that the purchaser assumes. An express warranty is a statement or document containing promises or descriptions of the product. Sections 2-313, 2-314, and 2-315 of the Uniform Commercial Code (UCC) cover express or verbal warranty, implied warranty of merchantability, and implied warranty of fitness for a particular purpose. UCC 2-313 explains the express warranties that a manufacturer, wholesaler, retailer, or supplier may make.

UCC 2-313 Express Warranties by Affirmation, Promise, Description, Sample

1) Express warranties by the seller are created as follows:
    a) Any affirmation of fact or promise made by the seller to the buyer that relates to the goods and becomes part of the basis of the bargain creates an express warranty that the goods shall conform to the affirmation or promise.
    b) Any description of the goods that is made part of the basis of the bargain creates an express warranty that the goods shall conform to the description.
    c) Any sample or model that is made part of the basis of the bargain creates an express warranty that the whole of the goods shall conform to the sample or model.
2) It is not necessary to the creation of an express warranty that the seller use formal words such as "warrant" or "guarantee" or that he have specific intention to make a warranty, but an affirmation merely of the value of the goods or a statement purporting to be merely the seller's opinion or commendation of the goods does not create a warranty. (UCC 2-313)

In breach of an express warranty, the plaintiff must establish that:

- The warranty was made. The seller made the statement.
- The seller's statement was part of the bargain. The purchaser relied upon the seller's statement in making his/her decision to purchase.
- The product did not conform to the warranty. The product's behavior is not in line with the warranty.

- A causal connection exists between the breach of the warranty and the plaintiff's economic or physical injury.

A breach of an express warranty occurs when the plaintiff is injured and the seller or manufacturer made statements of fact about the product that were false. These statements may be express; for example, the plaintiff was told, or it was implied, that the lifejacket would support a person of ordinary size in deep water. The statement must be made to the plaintiff or made generally to the public. The plaintiff must have relied on the statement, and the reliance on the statement or "facts" must be the cause of the injury.

When the goods are described—and that description is made a basis of the bargain or relied upon by the purchaser—there is an express warranty that the goods shall conform to the description (UCC 2-313 [1, b]). The description can be contained in a brochure, blueprint, written specification, or sample model.

Implied Warranties

Implied warranties exist at the time the person contracts for an article of goods. The purchaser assumes that the product will be what it purports to be and that it will be fit for its intended use. These warranties do not have to appear in writing, nor be mentioned. It is assumed that a boat will float and that a bathing suit will not shrink in water. The goods are expected to pass without objection in the trade and are to be fit for the ordinary purposes for which such goods are used.

Implied warranties include merchantability and fitness for a particular purpose. Merchantability means that the product is suitable for the purposes for which it was created. The level of suitability is to be average or reasonable; it need not be perfect. According to UCC 2-314, this section's ultimate objective "is to require the seller to assume responsibility for a substandard product."

UCC 2-314 Implied Warranty: Merchantability: Usage of Trade

1) Unless excluded or modified ... a warranty that the goods shall be merchantable is implied in a contract for their sale if the seller is a merchant with respect to goods of that kind. Under this section, the serving for value of food or drink to be consumed either on the premise or elsewhere is a sale.

2) Goods to be merchantable must be at least such as

    a) pass without objection in the trade under the contract description; and

    b) in the case of fungible goods, are of fair average quality within the description; and

    c) are fit for the ordinary purposes for which goods are used; and

    d) run, within the variations permitted by the agreement, of even kind, quality, and quantity within each unit and among all units involved; and

e) are adequately contained, packaged, and labeled as the agreement may require; and

f) conform to the promises or affirmations of fact made on the container or label if any.

3) Unless excluded or modified ... other implied warranties may arise from course of dealing or usage of trade. (UCC 2-314)

Fitness means that the product has been made for a particular purpose. UCC 2-315 describes fitness in the following way:

> Where the seller at the time of contracting has reason to know any particular purpose for which the goods are required and that the buyer is relying on the seller's skill or judgment to select or furnish suitable goods, there is unless excluded or modified under the next section an implied warranty that the goods shall be fit for such purpose. (UCC 2-315)

When the buyer identifies a particular purpose for the product, the seller must address that purpose when making the sale. A clear statement of the product's fitness for that purpose should be presented. Often, sports and physical activity products have written labels or hangtags identifying the fitness of the product for certain purposes. For example, a bicycle used for racing may be differentiated at the point of sale, in terms of labeling or advertising, from a bike primarily intended for leisure purposes. A prospective buyer should be able to ascertain the fitness of a particular piece of equipment to achieve the desired purpose at the point of sale, through product descriptions or talking with a salesperson. For example, if a runner is purchasing a new pair of shoes to be used in a marathon and discloses the particular purpose for which the shoes are being purchased to the seller, the seller must sell the runner a pair of running shoes that are fit or suitable for this particular purpose. When a product is not fit for that purpose, the buyer has a cause of action under implied warranty of fitness for a particular purpose.

Federal Consumer Product Safety Act

The National Commission on Product Safety was created by Congress in 1968. Its purpose was to explore the need for federal regulation of consumer products. Congress found a high level of unacceptable products—ones from which people were not able to protect themselves (15 USCA 2051 [1]). The Commission recommended the establishment of the Consumer Product Safety Act (CPSA). This act was established

> to protect the public against unreasonable risks of injury associated with consumer products; to assist consumers in evaluating the comparative safety of consumer products; to develop uniform safety standards for consumer

> products and to minimize conflicting state and local regulations; and to promote research and investigation into the causes and prevention of product-related deaths, illnesses, and injuries. (15 USCA 2051 [b])

The CPSA requires manufacturers to inform the Commission of substantial product hazards—ones believed to cause serious harm to users. The term

> "consumer product" means by article, or component part thereof, produced or distributed (i) for sale to a consumer for use in and around a permanent or temporary household or residence, a school, in recreation, or otherwise, or (ii) for the personal use, consumption, or enjoyment of a consumer in or around a permanent or temporary household or resident, a school, in recreation, or otherwise. (15 USCA 2051 [1])

Under safety information and research mandates, the CPSA maintains a National Electronic Injury Surveillance System (NEISS) that gathers information from representative hospital emergency rooms in the United States and its territories. Statistically valid estimates of frequency and severity of injuries associated with specific consumer products are the reported results.

An individual injured by a product whose manufacturer is in violation of the consumer product safety law may bring an action in federal court. The plaintiff must prove that the manufacturer has distributed a product that presents a hazard, and that the manufacturer failed to give notice to the CPSA despite knowledge of the hazard. The failure to give notice must be the proximate cause of the plaintiff's injury. In addition to being made whole or receiving compensatory damages, a successful victim may recover the costs of the lawsuit and attorney fees.

Professionals may not "manufacture for sale, offer for sale, distribute in commerce, or import into the United States any consumer product that is not in conformity with an applicable consumer product safety standard" (15 USCA 2068). Any person who knowingly violates Section 2068 is subject to a civil penalty of $5,000 or less for each violation. The maximum penalty is not to exceed $1,250,000 (15 USCA 2069). These figures are to be adjusted yearly for increases. The Commission recalls over 200 products each year; most of the recalls are voluntary.

Compliance with Product Safety Statutes

Within the *Restatement (Third) of Tort: Product Liability* (1998), there is a section titled "Noncompliance and Compliance with Product Safety." The statutes or regulations contained therein state, in connection with liability for defective design or inadequate instructions or warnings:

a) a product's noncompliance with an applicable product safety statute or administrative regulation renders the product defective with respect to the risks sought to be reduced by the statute or regulation; and

b) a product's compliance with an applicable product safety statute or administrative regulation is properly considered in determining whether the product is defective with respect to the risks sought to be reduced by the statute or regulation, but such compliance does not preclude as a matter of law a finding of product defect. (120)

State Product Liability Law

Buckley (1993) noted that there are five elements of product liability that are found in most state statutes or case law. These five elements are listed below:

1) The defect must render the product unreasonably dangerous to use.
2) The seller or manufacturer must be in the business of selling products such as the flawed one(s).
3) The product cannot have been substantially changed between the time it left the seller's or manufacturer's hands and the time it reached the ultimate user.
4) The defect must have proximately caused the ultimate user's injuries.
5) The ultimate user must have used the product properly (i.e., in a way that the product was designed to be used).

Defenses

Defenses to product liability are contributory negligence, assumption of risk, misuse, and disclaimers. Apportionment of responsibility between and among plaintiffs, sellers, and distributors of defective products considers the contributory negligence of the plaintiff as well as the liability of the defendant.

Contributory Negligence

Contributory negligence means that the user was negligent in his/her use of the equipment. A user who ignores the manual and warranty, assembles the equipment in a faulty manner, or uses a product in a new and unusual way not anticipated by the manufacturer or the retailer is contributorily negligent. Users who fail to discover a defect that a reasonable person should have discovered are contributorily negligent. In states that have comparative negligence, contributory negligence will be used in arriving at the percentage of fault.

Assumption of Risk

Assumption of risk is recognized in most product liability situations. Assumption of risk requires that the plaintiff knew of the risk of danger or should have known of the risk of danger. The user must:

1) Be aware of the danger.
2) Recognize and appreciate the
   a) significance, and
   b) magnitude of the risk associated with the use of the product.
3) voluntarily take the risk.

Knowledge and appreciation of the danger means that the user must *actually* have known of the danger rather than *should* have known of the danger. This means that the injured person was properly informed of the danger. It also means that when an elite athlete is injured, his/her previous experience and observation of others sustaining injury as a result of using a product will serve to inform him/her of potential hazards in the activity.

A person assumes a risk when he/she discovers a product defect, ignores the risk, and uses the product. The courts will examine the owner's liability in ignoring a discovered product defect.

Misuse

Mishandling, abuse, or the use of a product for abnormal purposes is called misuse. The manufacturer, wholesaler, and retailer are liable for warning the user about foreseeable misuse. A product must be used for its intended purpose—the function for which it was designed. Use of a product for a purpose other than that envisioned by the manufacturer is considered misuse and could bar recovery to the injured party. When the manufacturer, wholesaler, and retailer become aware that their products are being used in ways other than the intended purpose, they are to provide warnings to the public and to all new product purchasers. To avoid liability, sport and physical activity professionals, such as fitness center managers, are to demand that participants use equipment only for the manufacturer's intended use. When professionals wish to use equipment in ways other than its intended use, they should seek written permission from the manufacturer and request that reasons be provided for denial of requested use.

Disclaimers

A disclaimer is a defense in breach of warranty lawsuits. A manufacturer and a seller may place disclaimers or statements declaring they are not responsible or liable for the product if the product is used for a purpose or in a manner beyond the limits of those uses recommended by the manufacturer, retailer, etc. These statements explain product use and disclaim responsibility for products used in ways other than those recommended. "As is" and "with all faults" are disclaimers about the quality of the product.

Disclaimers must be conspicuous and unambiguous and clearly convey their message. An injured party needs to give notice to the defendant of the breach of warranty within a reasonable time after the injury. This enables the defendant to investigate and when warranted, take action on the product for the benefit of other consumers.

Damages

Product liability damages are usually compensatory. On occasion, punitive damages are awarded. Compensatory damages provide for the expenses directly involved in the injury and rehabilitation. Punitive damages are awards assessed against the party responsible for the harm in an effort to stop the party from continuing to create the harm. Usually, the defendant's level of liability must be reckless before punitive damages are awarded. Prior knowledge of the defective condition and failure to do anything about it may result in punitive damage awards. Failure to inspect or to test may also be reasons for the award of punitive damages.

Litigation

In *Ontiveros v. 24 Hour Fitness USA, Inc.* (2008), Susana Ontiveros was a member at a 24-hour fitness center in Los Angeles. This fitness center contained numerous exercise machines and also offered aerobic exercise classes. For an additional fee, Ontiveros received an upgraded membership that gave her access to additional equipment, services, and amenities, such as equipment to test her blood pressure. To obtain this membership, Ontiveros was required to sign a membership agreement containing a release from liability, which included the following stipulation:

> You understand and acknowledge that [defendant] is providing recreational services and may not be held liable for defective products. By signing below, you acknowledge and agree that you have read the foregoing and know of the nature of the activities at [defendant's facilities] and you agree to all the terms of the front and back pages of this agreement and acknowledge you have received a copy of it and the membership policies. (*Ontiveros v. 24 Hour Fitness USA, Inc.*, 2008, 427)

Ontiveros declared that she was familiar with exercise machines and therefore did not need or receive assistance concerning proper use of equipment. Ontiveros was injured while using a stairstep machine, alleging that she fell backwards onto the floor because of the failure of a component of the machine. She brought suit against the fitness center, asserting a product liability claim using strict liability. Ontiveros asserted that the fitness center provided her no services, making them part of the product distribution chain and liable for defective equipment under the strict liability doctrine.

The court ruled in favor of the fitness club, finding that the dominant purpose of the membership agreement she signed was for fitness services. Thus, she had no valid claim under the strict liability doctrine. Had the gym simply made exercise equipment available for her use, the gym could have been held strictly liable for defective equipment. However, the membership agreement between the plaintiff and defendant included aerobics classes, dance classes, yoga, and additional health testing centers that the court concluded was indicative of fitness services. Since it was primarily a fitness service that the plaintiff was provided, the defendant could not be found liable for her injuries using product liability.

In another fitness gym case, this time involving a treadmill, *Ingram v. Life Fitness* (2016) ruled in favor of the gym on the basis of assumption of "obvious and inherent risks" and found no basis for a strict product liability claim against the manufacturer. In this case Ingram, the fitness gym client, suffered injuries when she jumped off a treadmill that was still running while at the Life Fitness gym. Through testimony, the court found Ingram was a longtime user of treadmills, that she regularly used the sports club, that she had several times seen other club members jump off treadmills that were still running, and that she had used treadmills at the club at least 10 times. Given plaintiff's familiarity with the use and operation of treadmills, she assumed the obvious and inherent risks attendant to their use. As related to the product liability claims, the court dismissed the strict product liability claim in this case because there was no evidence that the treadmill malfunctioned in causing Ingram's injury. This case serves as a reminder to never jump off a moving treadmill or instead to walk safely on the sidewalk, which isn't likely to move!

Football Helmet Litigation

When one thinks of product liability in sport, one usually thinks of football. Among the more notable football product liability cases are *Bryns v. Riddell, Inc.* (1976), *Rawlings v. Daniels* (1981), *Hemphell v. Sayers* (1982), *Galindo v. Riddell, Inc.* (1982), *Carrier et al. v. Riddell, Inc. et al.* (1983), *Fiske v. MacGregor, Division of Brunswick* (1983), *Gentile v. MacGregor Mfg. Co.* (1985), *Lister v. Bill Kelly Athletic, Inc.* (1985), *Austria v. Bike Athletic Co.* (1991), *Rodriguez v. Riddell Sport Inc.* (2001), and *Green v. Schutt Sports Manufacturing et al.* (2010). Cases involving Riddell include *Byrns, Galindo, Carrier,* and *Rodriguez.*

The football helmet cases litigated that were reviewed spanned a period of time from the Byrns case of 1976 to the 2010 decision in *Green*. The majority of the cases were litigated by high school athletes over claims of defective design or defective manufacture. A few cases claimed a failure to warn. Litigation examples include the lawsuits filed by Byrns (1976), Daniels (1981), and Green (2010). Football player Kevin Byrns received an on-side kick, fell to the ground, and was hit by one or more players. The impact resulted in serious head injuries.

His suit against Riddell was that the helmet "was defective by design and manufacture and by reason of such defects was inherently dangerous to the user" (1066). The legal argument was over the helmet's ability to absorb force during impact. The trial court found for the manufacturer. After hearing the views of experts and watching films, the trial court concluded "that the film, as a matter of law, left no reasonable doubt as to the place of impact, thus ruling that the appellant failed to show causation between the impact and the injury" (1069). Byrns appealed the decision. The Supreme Court of Arizona reversed and remanded the case for further proceedings.

Mike Daniels experienced severe brain injuries that reduced his abilities when his football helmet collapsed as he collided with another player during practice. He sued Rawlings for a defective helmet and for failure "to warn of the protective limitations of the helmet" (437). The district court awarded him $1.5 million and was affirmed on appeal.

Green (2010), a high school football player, sued Schutt Sports when he suffered a severe burst, a fracture of a neck vertebra resulting in quadriplegia, during a tackle. His lawsuit was for defective helmet design. The court found that it was the way he executed the tackle rather than the helmet design that caused his injury. On appeal, the Fifth Circuit agreed and found for the manufacturer.

More recently litigated football injury cases include *Narkamura v. BRG Sports* (2019) and *Butler v. BRG Sports* (2019). In both of these Illinois cases, the statute of limitations became the dispositive issue to deny recovery for injuries suffered by athletes related to their helmets. This was the case even when the football players did not know the extent or severity of their injuries until much time had passed since the time of their collisions on the field. Additional cases to analyze involving products liability claims in sport include *DuRocher v. Riddell, Inc.* (2015), a design defect case that involved two former Washington University football players who asserted they suffered concussions and repeated head impacts while playing football and wearing helmets manufactured by the defendant manufacturer Riddle. The court found the plaintiffs met most of the necessary components to state a claim for product liability, including pleading enough with regard to the defective design of their helmets and that the helmet was not reasonably safe as designed.

Recent football helmet litigation has raised traditional product liability claims and defenses but also has begun to make the connection between the failure of the helmets used to protect players and eventual brain damage they incur, specifically chronic traumatic encephalopathy, also commonly known as CTE. This is an area to watch as a sports litigation trend and will likely rely upon product liability theories if the helmets' failure to protect athletes during collisions is found to proximately cause the injuries. Again, proving the causal link may be difficult to establish in these cases, but the potential for future class action litigation against football helmet manufacturers is not too far out of field once one athlete plaintiff's lawsuit is successful in court.

Summary

Product liability is the liability of the manufacturer, retailer, and seller for placing a defective product on the market. A product is defective under product liability when the defect existed at the time the product left the manufacturer or retailer and the defect caused the injury. Product liability may be negligence, misrepresentation, breach of warranty, violation of a Consumer Product Safety Commission rule, or strict liability in tort. Defenses to product liability include contributory negligence, assumption of risk, misuse, and the Uniform Commercial Code (UCC) disclaimers. In product liability cases, the damages can be both compensatory and punitive.

Discussion Questions

1) How should a sport professional implement product warnings?
2) Describe the various kinds of product warranties and give an example of each.

Activities

1) Research a recall involving a sport product on the United States Consumer Product Safety Commission website (http://www.cpsc.gov). Identify the specific risk presented by the product. Why do you think the product recall was necessary to protect the public?
2) Locate two cases in sport, one representing a manufacturing defect and one representing a design defect. Contrast the differences between the two legal claims considered by the courts.

References

Austria v. Bike Athletic Co., 810 P. 2d 1312 (1991).

Buckley, W. R. (1993). *Torts and personal injury law.* Delmar.

Byrns v. Riddell incorporated, 550 P. 2d 1065 (1976).

Butler v. BRG Sports, LLC. 141 N.E. 3d 1104 (Ill. App. Ct. 2019).

Carrier, et al. v. Riddell, inc., et al., 721 F. 2d 867 (1983).

DuRocher v. Riddell, Inc., 97 F. Supp. 3d 1006 (S.D. Ind. 2015).

Ingram v. Life Fitness, 140 A.D.3d 628 (N.Y. App. Div. 2016).

Narkamura v. BRG Sports, 144 N.E.3d 610 (Ill. App. Ct. 2019).

Consumer Product Safety Act, 15 USCA § 2051 (2021).

Fiske v. MacGregor Division of Brunswick, 464 A. 2d 719 (1983).

Galindo v. Riddell, Inc., 437 N. E. 2d 376 (1982).

Gentile v. MacGregor Mfg. Co., 493 A. 2d 647 (1995).

Green v. Schutt Sports Manufacturing Co., 2010 U.S. App. LEXIS 5482.

Lister v. Bill Kelly Athletic, 485 N. E. 2d 483 (1985).

Ontiveros v. 24 hour Fitness USA, 169 Cal. App. 4th 424 (2008).

Rawlings Sporting Goods Company v. Daniels, 619 S. W. 2d 435 (1981).

Restatement (Third) of Torts: Product liability. (1998). American Law Institute.

Rodriguez v. Riddell Sports, 242 F. 3d 567 (2001).

Uniform Commercial Code (UCC) Articles 1 through 9. American Law Institute (2010-2011). https://www.law.cornell.edu/ucc.

Wittenberg, J. D. (1986). Product liability: Recreation and sports equipment (updated). Lawyers Journal Seminars-Press.

Recommended Reading

Deubert, C. R., Cohen, G., & Fernandez Lynch, H. (2016, November). Protecting and promoting the health of NFL players: Legal and ethical analysis and recommendations. *Harvard Journal of Sports and Entertainment Law,* 1.

Polinsky, A. M., & Shavell, S. (2010). The uneasy case for product liability. *Harvard Law Review, 123,* 1437.

Seiberling, M. (2002). "Icing" on the cake: Allowing amateur athletic promoters to escape liability in Mohney v. USA Hockey, Inc. *Villanova Sports & Entertainment Law Journal, 9,* 417.

United States Consumer Product Safety Commission (2021, September 30). Injuries using e-scooters, e-bikes and hoverboards jump 70% during the past four years. https://www.cpsc.gov/Newsroom/News-Releases/2021/Injuries-Using-E-Scooters-E-Bikes-and-Hoverboards-Jump-70-During-the-Past-Four-Years.

Versteeg, R. (2015). Product liability and commercial law theories relating to concussions. *Journal of Business & Technology Law,* 10.

Part II: Constitutional Law

The United States Constitution is the supreme law of the land. Judges in every state are bound by the Constitution of the United States and by the constitutions of their respective states. The First, Fourth, and Fourteenth Amendments to the U.S. Constitution are constitutional laws that most often impact participants and managers in sport and physical activity.

Chapter 4 addresses laws associated with the First, Fourth, and Fourteenth Amendments. The Due Process clause of the Fourteenth Amendment is addressed. Chapter 5 addresses gender equity by discussing the Equal Protection Clause of the Fourteenth Amendment, Title IX, and the Civil Rights Acts of 1987 and 1991. The Americans with Disabilities Act (ADA) of 1990 and related disability laws impacting sport participants and stadiums are discussed in Chapter 6.

All constitutions can be amended. An amendment to the United States Constitution may be proposed by a two-thirds vote of those present in each house of Congress, or by a committee of the legislatures of two-thirds of the states. Amendments may be ratified by the legislature of three-fourths of the states or by conventions in three-fourths of the states. There are times when an amendment may be acceptable within a particular state but will not be acceptable to the entire country. The Equal Rights Amendment's success in numerous states and failure at the federal level is such an example.

The Constitution of the United States guarantees individual rights only with reference to the federal government and to state actions as they are incorporated within the Fourteenth Amendment. When a legal complaint involves a guarantee of an individual right, such as freedom of speech, a court must determine whether the action challenged is a federal or state action. A person challenging a privately owned and operated agency forces the court to determine whether the agency is subject to state protection and regulation.

4

First, Fourth, and Fourteenth Amendments

OBJECTIVES

Upon completing this chapter, you will,

- understand the constitutional protections afforded to sport participants, spectators, and others;
- balance individual rights against the rights of the state;
- identify legal issues associated with regulating speech by students and athletes;
- explain how regulating speech is legally evolving in the social media era; and
- analyze when, and under what circumstances, a sports team can restrict a fan's speech.

First Amendment

The First Amendment of the United States Constitution states that "Congress shall make no law respecting an establishment of religion, or prohibiting the free exercise thereof; or abridging the freedom of speech or of the press; or the right of the people peaceably to assemble, and to petition the government for a redress of grievances." Historically, the First Amendment applied only to actions of the federal government. However, the courts, through the process of incorporation, have made the First Amendment applicable to state actions. First Amendment rights are the freedoms of religion, speech (including symbolic protest), and press. "The First Amendment provides protection for a wide range of expression ... with the goal of preserving an uninhibited marketplace of ideas and fostering self-expression free of government restraint" (Grady et al., 2005, p. 272). In making a decision about the freedoms of religion, speech, and press, the courts balance the needs of the public against the rights of the individual.

When challenging a denial of First Amendment rights, an individual requests that a court of law examine the facts with respect to the particular situation and balance the personal rights in relation to the authority of the state, federal government, or private agency to affect a particular rule, law, or regulation for the benefit of society. Sport and speech have been described as intersecting American icons (Wasserman, 2006). That intersection often creates collisions between fans, the media, and sport organizations (Grady & Moorman, 2008). While "fan expression is a long-standing and expected part" of modern-day sporting events and is "encouraged by the teams, the players, [and] the cheerleaders," how far does the right to engage in this expression go (Wasserman, 2006, 526)? Current application of the First Amendment in sport is seen in cases involving athletes criticizing coaches via social media, fans being ejected from stadiums for wearing t-shirts or holding up signs with offensive messages, and ongoing debate about the proper role of prayer in sport.

Freedom of Religion

Freedom of religion is analyzed under the Establishment and Free Exercise of Religion Clauses. The Establishment Clause separates church and state. For example, the United States Supreme Court decision *Santa Fe v. Doe et al.* (2000) bans prayer at public high school events, including football games. In 1992, the United States Supreme Court found that conducting a religious exercise as part of a high school graduation ceremony was a violation of the First Amendment (*Lee v. Weisman*, 1992). The Supreme Court held that "the Constitution forbids the state to exact religious conformity from a student as the price of attending her own high school graduation" (2660).

In the *Santa Fe* case, current and former students at a Texas public high school complained to school administration about the prayer before varsity football games. In response to the complaint, the school adopted a policy of holding a student election to determine whether an "invocation should be delivered at games" (308). If the results of the election approved the invocation, a second vote was to be held to select the person to give the invocation. The election results favored giving an invocation, and a student was elected to give the invocation. Current and former students then filed another complaint. Eventually, the Fifth Circuit held that "permitting student-led, student-initiated prayer at football games violated the Establishment Clause" (310). The school district petitioned for review by the

U.S. Supreme Court. Their argument was that the facts of the current situation were distinguishable from the prayer policy in the *Lee* case. Graduation was a requirement of all students; a student's attendance at a football game was elective. The court, however, pointed out that football games were mandatory for some students, including band members and cheerleaders. Thus, the high court held the delivery of an invocation prior to home football games violated the establishment of religion clause of the First Amendment.

Good News Club v. Milford (2001) was an example of the Free Exercise of Religion Clause. A New York school district opened its facilities for the public's use—specifically for education, recreation, and the welfare of the community. The policy stated that the schools were not to be used for religious purposes. The Good News Club, a private Christian organization for children between the ages of 6 and 12, requested permission to use the school facilities. Their request was denied under the school district's public use policy. The club brought suit, arguing "that denial of the club's request violated the club's free speech rights under the Federal Constitution's First Amendment" (99).

The district court granted the Good News Club's request for a preliminary injunction, ruling that the school district could not enforce its public use policy. The Good News Club subsequently held meetings in the public school. The district court later decided that exclusion of the club was permissible. The club appealed the decision. The United States Supreme Court ultimately reversed, holding that:

> 1) the district's exclusion of the club constituted viewpoint discrimination in violation of the First Amendment's free speech guarantee, for (a) any group that promoted the moral and character development of children was eligible to use the school building, (b) the club's activities did not constitute mere religious worship that was divorced from any teaching of moral values, (c) there was no reason to treat the club's use of religion as something other than a viewpoint merely because of any evangelical message that the club conveyed, and (d) for purposes of the free speech guarantee, there was no logical difference in kind between the club's invocation of Christianity and the invocation of teamwork, loyalty, or patriotism by other associations to provide a foundation for such associations' lessons; and
>
> 2) the free speech violation was not justified by the district's concern that permitting the club's activities would violate the First Amendment's establishment of religion clause. (99)

Subsequent cases involving freedom of religion have focused on displaying a Ten Commandments monument on the grounds of the Texas state capitol (*Van Orden v. Perry,* 2005) and the required recitation of the Pledge of Allegiance by a school student (*Elk Grove Unified School District and Gordon v. Nedow,* 2004). While not dealing directly with sport, these cases have application to sport contexts and are analogous to the use of religious symbols or pledges in or around sporting events and at other public forums. In *Van Orden,* plaintiffs sued for a declaration finding that displaying the Ten Commandments monument violated the Establishment Clause and sought an injunction to have it removed. In denying the requested relief, the district court concluded that the monument did not contravene the Establishment clause. This was because the state had a valid secular purpose in recognizing and commending the donating organization's efforts to reduce juvenile delinquency, and a reasonable observer would not conclude that the monument conveyed a message that the state was seeking to endorse religion. The Fifth Circuit affirmed the decision on appeal, finding that the monument did not violate the Establishment Clause. Ultimately, the U.S. Supreme Court found that (1) the Establishment of religion clause did not bar any and all governmental preference for religion over irreligion; (2) the *Lemon* test was not useful in dealing with the sort of monument in question; (3) although the Ten Commandments had religious significance, they also had an undeniable historical meaning; and (4) the placement of the Ten Commandments monument on the capitol grounds was a far more passive use of those texts than the posting of the Ten Commandments in public schoolrooms, a practice that the Supreme Court had found to have an improper and plainly religious purpose.

Elk Grove Unified School District and Gordon v. Nedow (2004) involved a public school district in California that required each elementary school class to recite daily the Pledge of Allegiance. The father of one of the students filed suit, alleging that the school district's policy requiring the recitation of the Pledge of Allegiance violated the Establishment and Free Exercise Clauses of the First Amendment. The district court dismissed the complaint. However, the United States Court of Appeals for the Ninth Circuit concluded that the father had standing as a parent to challenge a practice that allegedly interfered with his right to direct his child's religious education, and the district's policy therefore violated the establishment of religion clause.

On appeal before the Supreme Court, it was determined that the father lacked standing to bring the case. However, a concurring opinion by Justices Rehnquist and O'Connor ruled that the school district's policy did not violate the Establishment of religion clause because reciting the Pledge, or listening to others recite it, was a patriotic exercise, not a religious one. Justice Clarence Thomas, in a concurring opinion, found the Establishment of religion clause was a federalism provision intended to prevent Congress from interfering with state establishments. Thus, it made little sense to incorporate the Establishment of religion clause into the Constitution's Fourteenth Amendment so as to be applied against the states. Justice Thomas believed the school district's policy did not infringe upon any religious liberty right that would arise from incorporation of the establishment of religion clause; and the Pledge policy did not infringe the Free Exercise of Religion Clause. It is straight forward to see how cases involving team prayer before sporting events could raise similar constitutional challenges as the legally significant historical cases discussed in this chapter.

Freedom of Speech

Freedom of speech is the freedom to speak, remain silent, discuss with others, advocate, and communicate ideas. Freedom of speech does not protect speech that is libelous, slanderous, lewd, or obscene. The possibility of creating a breach of peace or advocating the commission of a crime is also not protected speech under the First Amendment.

Students, athletes, teachers, government employees, and employees of private industry all possess First Amendment rights available to all citizens. Speech may be verbal or expressive (e.g., protests and demonstrations). In order to determine whether speech merits protection, the courts will examine and balance the following factors:

- the subject of the speech;
- to whom it was directed;
- the forum in which it occurred; and
- the manner of delivery.

Symbolic gestures have been used to influence and alert the public to new and oftentimes controversial ideas. *Tinker v. Des Moines School District* (1969), the case most often cited in symbolic protest, involved three students who wore black armbands in public protest of the government's participation in the Vietnam War. School authorities, knowledgeable on the proposed armband protest, established a school policy on armbands a few days prior to the event.

The students were asked to remove their black armbands, but they refused. They were suspended from school and told not to return until the armbands were removed. The students sought injunctive relief from the courts but were unsuccessful. The federal district Court "upheld the constitutionality of the school authority's action on the grounds that it was reasonable in order to prevent disturbance of school discipline" (505). On appeal, the Eighth Circuit reversed and remanded the lower court's decision, stating that the Constitution did not permit state officials to deny a form of expression that "neither interrupted school activities nor sought to intrude in the school affairs or the lives of others" (514). Here, the court saw the activity as one to stimulate discussion outside of the classroom rather than to disrupt the learning environment.

Another case raising similar student free speech issues is *Morse v. Frederick* (2007). In 2002, Frederick was a high school student who attended a school-supervised and school-sanctioned event to watch the Olympic torch Relay as it passed by their high school in Alaska on its way to the Winter Games in Salt Lake City, Utah. Students were allowed to watch the Torch Relay on both sides of the street as it passed by, under the supervision of teachers and school administrators. Growing impatient waiting for the torch to pass by, some students became rambunctious, throwing plastic soda bottles and snowballs and scuffling with their classmates (397). As the torchbearers and camera crews passed by, Frederick and his friends unfurled a 14-foot banner bearing the phrase "BONG hitS 4 JESUS" (397). Upon seeing the sign from the other side of the street, which was also easily readable to other students, school principal Morse crossed the street and demanded that the banner be taken down (398). Everyone but Frederick complied. Principal Morse confiscated the banner and told Frederick to report to her office, where she suspended him for 10 days, later explaining that she told

Frederick to take the banner down because she thought it encouraged illegal drug use (398). This violated an established school board policy that "specifically prohibits any assembly or public expression that ... advocates the use of substances that are illegal to minors" (398). Frederick appealed his suspension to the school superintendent, who reduced it to eight days, finding that Frederick "was not disciplined because the principal of the school 'disagreed' with his message, but because his speech appeared to advocate the use of illegal drugs" (398).

Frederick then filed suit under 42 USC §1983, alleging that the school board and Morse had violated his First Amendment rights. The district court found for the school board and Morse, ruling they were entitled to qualified immunity and finding that their actions did not violate Frederick's First Amendment right of free speech. "Morse had the authority, if not the obligation, to stop such messages at a school-sanctioned activity," the district court noted (App. to Pet. for Cert., 37a).

On appeal, the Ninth Circuit reversed the lower court decision, finding that even though Frederick "acted during a 'school-authorized activit[y],' and 'proceed[ing] on the basis that the banner expressed a positive sentiment about marijuana use,'" Frederick's First Amendment rights were violated "because the school punished Frederick without demonstrating that his speech gave rise to a 'risk of substantial disruption' (2006, 1118, 1121–1123). Furthermore, the court held "Frederick's right to display his banner was so 'clearly established' that a reasonable principal in Morse's position would have understood that her actions were unconstitutional, and that Morse was therefore not entitled to qualified immunity" (1123–1125). Morse and the school district then petitioned the U.S. Supreme Court to hear the case.

The U.S. Supreme Court agreed to hear the case to resolve two important legal questions: whether Frederick had a First Amendment right to wield his banner, and, if so, whether that right was so clearly established that the principal may be held liable for damages. The Supreme Court found this was a school speech case, agreeing with the superintendent that the school could supervise students' behavior at a school-sanctioned activity. While Frederick himself claimed "that the words were just nonsense meant to attract television cameras," the high court found that the principal thought that the sign would be widely understood by students and others as referring to marijuana use and that it violated the policy against promoting illegal drug use. As phrased by the Court, "the question thus becomes whether a principal may, consistent with the First Amendment, restrict student speech at a school event, when that speech is reasonably viewed as promoting illegal drug use. We hold that she may" (403). As noted by the court in *Morse*, "*Tinker* held that student expression may not be suppressed unless school officials reasonably conclude that it will 'materially and substantially disrupt the work and discipline of the school'" (*Morse*, 403 citing *Tinker*, 513). An often-quoted comment from the *Tinker* opinion explains the proper balance the Supreme Court struck: While students "do not shed their constitutional rights to freedom of speech or expression at the schoolhouse gate," the First Amendment rights of students must be applied in light of the special characteristics of the school environment (*Tinker*,

506). Thus, consistent with First Amendment principles, the Court held "schools may take steps to safeguard those entrusted to their care from speech that can reasonably be regarded as encouraging illegal drug use" (*Morse*, 396). The Supreme Court ultimately concluded that "school officials in this case did not violate the First Amendment by confiscating the pro-drug banner and suspending the student responsible for it" (396).

A recent student speech case that reached the U.S. Supreme Court (since *Morse v. Frederick* was decided in 2007) was *Mahanoy Area Sch. Dist. v. B.L.* (2021). In this First Amendment free speech case, a Pennsylvania high school student Brandi Levy (referred to as B.L. by the courts) tried out for the varsity cheerleading team. Levy challenged her eventual suspension by the school from her junior varsity cheer squad for one year after she posted a picture of herself with the caption using vulgar language to the social media app Snapchat. The post was made during the weekend (so not during school hours) and away from school property at a convenience store nearby the school. Specifically, Levy's post contained her and a friend in a photo with their middle fingers raised and using the "F" word four times in a row, finding apparent fault with "school," "softball," "cheer," and "everything. In other words, it seems she had had just about enough of this varsity cheer team!

Before the district court, it was determined that, while the aspiring cheerleader's punishment was limited to extracurricular activity, specifically her ongoing participation in her junior varsity cheer squad, it was not a legally justified form of punishment or student discipline, especially as it was just vulgar language, which is unequivocally protected speech. On appeal before the Third Circuit, the court also found in the student's favor, holding that because the student's social media post was clearly off-campus speech, it did not occur in a school-sponsored forum, and as it occurred away from campus, over the weekend, and without use of school resources, it was not subject to regulation by the school district. Thus, the fact that the social media post was made "off-campus" became determinative in deciding whether her speech was protected. The Third Circuit, on appeal, also found her speech had not caused any actual or foreseeable substantial disruption of the educational environment, so therefore the student should not have been subject to discipline by the school under the standard outlined in *Tinker.*

The U.S. Supreme Court, in agreeing to hear the student speech case, also held for the student, but provided a slightly different legal roadmap for future courts to use in analyzing student speech cases than the one utilized by the Third Circuit. Justice Breyer, writing for the majority, expressed the legal position that schools have less interest in policing off-campus social media use by students (Hudson, 2021). Thus, as Supreme Court observer Liptak (2021) commented, the Court "did not establish a categorical ban on student speech [occurring] outside of the school" (para 2), but instead "set out factors that courts should assess in weighing the rights of [school] administrators to punish speech [that occurs] in nonschool settings, with one important component being whether parents are better suited to handle the situation" (para. 3). Liptak (2021) noted "it was the first time in more than 50 years that a high school student won a free-speech case in the Supreme Court" (para. 1). Liptak noted the decision updates the *Tinker* standard to the social media era of speech, which is commonly used by school students, but still should give school districts pause before they discipline students over criticizing school decisions. Furthermore, courts reviewing such legal challenges should be cautious in reviewing efforts to sanction student speech, even when it occurs off campus.

Cheering Speech Cases in Stadia and Arenas

More frequently occurring cases involving free speech issues in sport include fans wearing t-shirts or holding signs, flags, or banners that contain or convey messages that may be perceived as offensive to some fans, particularly children. These cases, referred to as forms of "cheering speech" by Wasserman (2006), raise fundamental First Amendment issues. "Cheering speech can be oral, symbolic, or written on signs, banners, clothing, and body parts. It can be in good taste or bad, clean or profane, provocative, clever, or otherwise. And it will be loud and obvious" (Wasserman, 2006, p. 528). These cases often get resolved with the sport facility or athletic department deciding to deny or stop the speech (in the form of a t-shirt, sign, or banner), and typically run afoul of well-established First Amendment case law that often favors the speaker. Calvert and Richards (2004) analyzed one of the more controversial instances of "cheering speech," which occurred in 2004 at the University of Maryland during the men's basketball game between Maryland and Duke. "Maryland fans chanted and wore T-shirts reading 'F--Duke' and directed homophobic epithets at Duke's star player" (Calvert & Richards, 2004, p. 2). In reviewing the incident, Maryland officials considered implementing regulation of student cheering speech, and the NCAA responded that screaming obscenities at players was not acceptable speech (Wasserman, 2006). Furthermore, the University of Maryland sought the counsel of the Maryland Attorney General, who advised that a carefully drafted fan code of conduct would be constitutionally permissible (Wasserman, 2006). Cheering speech is not isolated to collegiate sports involving sports fans' crazy signs or T-shirts. It occurs at all levels of sport, and any determinations that regulate speech must be made carefully based upon the legal considerations detailed in these cases.

Other cheering speech cases raising similar First Amendment concerns of fans sanctioned for cheering or jeering, often more for jeering speech, include *Higgins v. Kentucky Sports Radio* (2020). After UNC beat Kentucky in NCAA March Madness in 2017, Kentucky fans and radio personalities repeatedly blamed a named official for the team's loss, and the radio personalities even discussed the official's personal business and read reviews of that business on the air from so-called "angry fans." The district court found it to be protected speech and the Sixth Circuit affirmed the decision. However, other cases have been decided in favor of the sanctioning organization. In *Donnelly v. Univ. of North Carolina*, 236 N.C. App. 32 (N.C. Ct. App. 2014) the court upheld a lifetime ban of John Donnelly by the University of North Carolina. Donnelly, a UNC alum and supporter of its athletic programs, as well as previous usher at sport events, was banned from its athletic facilities in Chapel Hill after repeated harassment and bizarre incidents involving UNC players and staff members, culminating with Donnelly arriving at the women's soccer team hotel. The court found no First Amendment violation as previous courts have held that harassment is not a form of protected speech.

Cheering speech can also occur on sport merchandise produced for entire fan bases to purchase and can also raise trademark infringement concerns. A T-shirt with the phrase "Muck Fizzou" sold by a Kansas retailer, Joe-College.com, containing the same shade of blue as the school colors of Missouri's rival, the University of Kansas, resulted in a lawsuit by the University of Kansas against the retailer (Nystrom, 2007). Plaintiffs alleged the shirts could cause consumers to believe that the shirts were licensed by the University of Kansas to poke fun at their rivals. The University of Kansas filed suit alleging that Joe-College.com was infringing the university's trademarks (Nystrom, 2007). The school's athletic director also added that the messages on the shirts were in poor taste and cast the school in a bad light. The retailer cited the First Amendment right of free speech as a defense to trademark infringement and claimed signs in his store make clear that the merchandise is not licensed by the University of Kansas, which is a legal disclaimer, in effect. The case resulted in a jury verdict in 2008 for the university and the judge ordered Joe-College.com to pay $667,507 in attorneys' fees, which would put the company out of business (Diepenbrock, 2009). The recurring theme in these cases is that many involved the sport organization or university as defendant responding to the speech with a heavy-handed approach to suppress the speech that, in effect, sanctioned them for speaking (Grady & Moorman, 2008). This suggests that sport organizations may resort to using the mere threat of a lawsuit to stop (or sanction) speech they find offensive or against their professed interests or values, even when the challenged speech is close to the boundaries tolerated by the First Amendment.

Freedom of the Press

Freedom of the press includes freedom to write, draw, and create models. Ideas may be published and conveyed. Absolute freedom of thought and belief is guaranteed under the First Amendment. In *Marcum v. Dahl* (1981), female basketball players at the University of Oklahoma stated to the press that, if the current coach was hired for the following year, they would not play. Shortly after the press released the statement, the athletes' scholarships were not renewed. The athletes filed suit, stating that their First Amendment free speech rights had been violated in the non-renewal of their scholarships. The court concluded "that the plaintiffs' First Amendment rights were not violated by the defendants' refusal to renew the plaintiffs' athletic scholarships" (485). A person's freedom of speech and of press depends upon the circumstances under which the freedoms are used. Certain language is not protected.

Defamation

Defamation is the "holding up of a person to ridicule, scorn, or contempt in a respectable and considerable part of the community.... A communication is defamatory if it tends to do harm to the reputation of another as to lower him in the estimation of the community or to deter third persons from associating or dealing with him" (Black's Law Dictionary). Defamation may be of a living person, a corporation or business, or an association. Defamation does not exist unless the statements are communicated to a third person. If the communication is spoken, it is slander. If the communication is in print, it is libel. To establish liability for defamation, the following elements must be present:

- a defamatory statement concerning another must be made;
- the statement must be published to a third person (publication can be in writing, spoken to the person, or overheard by the third party);
- the person publishing the statement must intend to publish the statement (there is no need of intention to hurt someone); and
- damage must occur.

The status of a person is a factor in defamation. Whether the person is widely known or known only by a few is a factor in what can be said about a person in a public forum, or what can be revealed about the same individual to a third party. People are classified into two categories: public figures/officials and private individuals. Public figures are people known to the community. Athletes, sports professionals, and administrators may be public figures. Private persons are those not widely known in the community. The decision of whether a person is a public figure or a private person will be determined by the judge and/or jury. A key legal determining factor must be recognized: A public figure is defamed only when the defamatory statement is false whereas a private individual is defamed whether the defamatory statement is either true or false.

The "public figure" versus "private individual" comparison is related to the individual's right to maintain his or her reputation and the public's interest in preserving free speech. A need exists for the public to be informed about its leaders. But, at the same time, an individual's personal life should be secure and remain somewhat private. In *New York Times Co. v. Sullivan* (1964), the Supreme Court, under the First Amendment, permitted a true statement to be made against a public official and public figure.

Private individuals continue to have a cause of action under defamation, even though the statement may be true. In *Gertz v. Robert Welch, Inc.*, the court extended the idea of a public figure from one who was known by all, to one who voluntarily injected oneself or was drawn into a particular controversy. As a result of being drawn into the controversy, the Court held that one becomes a public figure for a limited period of time or for a range of issues (345).

Defenses to defamation are truth and privilege. The defendant must establish that what was said was the truth. A defendant may be excused under privilege if his/her conduct was an act in furtherance of some socially useful interest. Privilege is a difficult element to establish. Like truth, it must be established by the defendant.

Damages in defamation may be compensatory and punitive. They may be a result of the damage to one's business or reputation (compensatory) or they may involve punitive damage (awarded to discourage similar actions on the part of the plaintiff or others).

A very public sport-related defamation case was *Curtis Publishing v. Butts* (1967). Curtis Publishing, publisher of the Saturday Evening Post, printed an article that alleged Butts—who at the time was the athletic director at the University of Georgia—was involved in fixing a football game between Georgia and the University of Alabama. Butts, a former football coach at Georgia, was a well-known and respected person, and at the time of the defamation was a candidate for a position with a professional team. George Burnett, an Atlanta insurance salesman, had accidentally overheard, because of electronic error, a telephone conversation between Butts and the head football coach of the University of Alabama, Paul "Bear" Bryant, which took place about one week prior to the game. Burnett was said to have listened while "Butts outlined Georgia's offensive plays... and told ... how Georgia planned to defend.... Butts mentioned both players and plays by name." The readers were told Burnett had made notes of the conversation and specific examples of the divulged secrets were set out. The article went on to discuss the game and the players' reactions to the game, concluding that "the Georgia players, their moves analyzed and forecast like those of rats in a maze, took a frightful physical beating" and said that the players and other sideline observers were aware that Alabama was privy to Georgia's secrets. It set out the series of events commencing with Burnett's later presentation of his notes to the Georgia head coach, Johnny Griffith, and culminating in Butts's resignation from the university.

Butts brought a libel action in federal court for $5 million in compensatory and $5 million in punitive damages. All parties involved conceded that Butts was a public figure under the law. Curtis Publishing Company's only defense was substantial truth. The evidence showed that Butts and the Alabama coach had discussed football but failed to prove that what had been discussed would have been of value to the Alabama coach. Butts' contention was that the magazine's investigative reporting was reckless and wanton misconduct. The jury returned a verdict of $60,000 in general damages and $3 million in punitive damages. The punitive damages award was later reduced.

Of particular importance in the *Curtis* case was the fact that what might have appeared as "kidding" could be taken seriously and completely misconstrued by another. One responsible for reporting information must be diligent in checking the accuracy and reliability of all sources used. In *Sprewell v. NYP Holdings* (2007), plaintiff Latrell Sprewell, a high-profile professional basketball player formerly with the New York Knicks, claimed that he was libeled by statements in articles by sportswriter Berman. The articles regarding the cause of Sprewell's hand injury were published in The *New York Post* and were based, in part, on information provided by confidential sources. It was undisputed that in September 2002, Sprewell sustained a fracture to the fifth metacarpal bone on his right (shooting) hand while on his boat parked in a marina in Milwaukee. He did not inform the Knicks of the injury until he arrived at the team's practice facility on September 30.

Berman wrote an article describing the injury and the fact that the plaintiff had not reported it to the team sooner. Berman, who accompanied the team to its training camp, tried unsuccessfully to contact Sprewell's agent, Gist, to inquire about the cause of the injury.

Marvet Britto, Sprewell's publicist, told Berman that Sprewell himself had "no clue" how he had injured his hand, but noted that Sprewell lived and worked out on his boat all summer. Berman reported that conversation in another article. Berman received a telephone call from a sportscaster for a New York cable channel, who stated that he had suffered an injury similar to the plaintiff's as a result of punching a pole on a basketball court in anger and that such an injury is commonly referred to as a "boxer's fracture." Berman then contacted two physician hand specialists, who explained that boxer's fractures are "caused by a punch, usually by punching a hard object like a wall or a pole" (18). In returning Berman's earlier telephone messages, Gist stated that plaintiff had told him the fracture occurred while "frantically pulling on a rope" to gain control of his boat in rough waters. The *New York Post's* first two editions on October 4 ran Berman's article recounting those details and the fact that the team's general manager had been "peppered with questions regarding how Sprewell broke his pinkie and was even asked if he may have been in a fight" (18).

The court found that, assuming that Berman's statements regarding how the player injured his hand and his alleged attempt to cover up the incident were false, the news corporation and the writer were entitled to summary judgment as the information was not reported as incontrovertible fact, but rather cautioned the reader that it was based on two confidential witnesses and denied by the player. The record demonstrated that the writer subjectively believed the sources, whose partial description of the interior of the player's boat provided additional indicia of reliability. The writer's investigative efforts also demonstrated that the writer did not deliberately fail to seek confirmatory information or otherwise act with reckless disregard for the truth. Thus, the player had not presented any evidence to raise a triable issue of fact concerning actual malice, let alone sufficient evidence to establish actual malice by a clear and convincing standard.

Invasion of Privacy

Invasion of privacy is closely related to the Fourth Amendment's search and seizure clause. It is often found in drug testing and the reporting of suspicion of drug use. The government's interest in the drug testing of athletes is the athletes' health and the maintenance of a level playing field or the natural competitive qualities of the performers. The athletes' interests are in maintaining their privacy. Invasion of privacy, in violation of the First Amendment, has been raised in the context of pat-down searches conducted as a condition of entry to sporting events.

While balanced against the overall interest in safety of the public at large, individual legal challenges to the routinely used practice of pat-down searches persist. One high-profile case receiving much media attention was *Sheehan v. San Francisco 49ers, Ltd.* (2009). The case was brought by two season ticket holders challenging the constitutionality of the team's implementation of a league policy requiring all fans at the team's home games to submit to a pat-down search before entering the stadium. The season ticket holders argued that the California state constitution's guarantee of privacy was violated by the pat-down searches.

The court found that "presumably, the league, and ultimately the team adopted the pat-down policy to enhance spectator safety," but the court could not judge the reasonableness of the policy under the circumstances because the record did not establish the circumstances of, or the reasons for, the policy (992). Furthermore, the team had not yet given any explanation or justification for the policy. The court provided interesting guidance in approaching the constitutionality of these actions:

> In reviewing a private entertainment venue's security arrangements that implicate the state constitutional right of privacy, the court does not decide whether every measure is necessary, merely whether the policy is reasonable. The state constitutional right of privacy does not grant courts a roving commission to second-guess security decisions at private entertainment events or to micromanage interactions between private parties.... Private entities that present entertainment events, like the 49ers, necessarily retain primary responsibility for determining what security measures are appropriate to ensure the safety of their patrons, subject, when those security measures substantially infringe on a privacy interest, to judicial review for reasonableness. (480)

A related pat-down case claiming a Fourth Amendment violation was *Johnston v. Tampa Sports Authority* (2008). The pat-down searches were upheld on appeal in the Eleventh Circuit Court of Appeals using a consent theory rationale. Johnston involved an NFL pat-down search policy that was similar to but slightly different from the one in Sheehan. The search policy described in Johnston encompassed only "limited above the-waist pat-down searches" (1323). In Sheehan, plaintiffs alleged that the screeners "ran their hands around the [plaintiffs'] backs and down the sides of their bodies and their legs" (996). The court in *Johnston* noted "the government had no role in formulating or mandating the pat-down policy. The policy exists solely because of the NFL's mandate" (1329). "Because the condition for entry was imposed by a private party, Johnston was not forced by the government to choose between his constitutional rights and obtaining a benefit to which he was entitled," namely entry to the stadium and sporting event (1329). The court held that, in considering the totality of the circumstances, Johnston voluntarily consented to the pat-down searches each time he attended a football game at this stadium.

Fourth Amendment

The Fourth Amendment to the Constitution states that the "right of the people to be secure in their persons, houses, papers, and effects, against unreasonable searches and seizures, shall not be violated, and no warrants shall issue, but upon probable cause, supported by oath or affirmation, and particularly describing the place to be searched, and the person to be seized."

The system for analyzing Fourth Amendment violations is the same as the system used in analyzing First Amendment facts: balancing of the participant's interest in privacy against the agency's right to maintain order in an environment in which others can safely participate. In order to establish or maintain order, it may be necessary to suspend or discipline a participant; however, valid evidence must be obtained before a complaint can be filed.

Searches

In *New Jersey v. T. L. O.* (1985), a case involving teenage students who lied about smoking in a school bathroom, the United States Supreme Court established that searches could be conducted by persons other than law enforcement officers. The ruling stated that the "Fourth Amendment is applicable to the activities of civil as well as criminal authorities" (740). The Court also attempted to establish a standard that could be used to govern school searches. The question of balance in this situation was identified as an analysis of the individual's expectation of privacy and personal security versus the government's need for an effective method of dealing with breaches of order (741). In this case, order meant to maintain an environment in which learning can occur.

The Court noted that the school setting required restrictions on searches different from those needed by other public authorities in the following ways:

> The warrant requirement, in particular, is unsuited to the school environment; requiring a teacher to obtain a warrant before searching a child suspected of an infraction of school rules would unduly interfere with the maintenance of the swift and informal disciplinary procedures needed in the schools.

The legality of a search of a student should depend simply on the reasonableness, under the circumstances, of the search. Determining the reasonableness of any search involves a twofold inquiry: first, one must consider "whether the ... action was justified at its inception." Second, one must determine whether the search as actually conducted was reasonably related in scope to the circumstances that justified the interference in the first place. (743–744)

In *Gruenke v. Seip* (2000), the court was faced with issues related to both the First and Fourth Amendments. A swim coach suspected one of his swimmers of being pregnant and required her to take a pregnancy test. She and her mother sued, claiming that the requirement of a pregnancy test was an illegal search under her Fourth Amendment rights, interfered with her right to familial privacy, and violated her First Amendment free speech and association rights. Swim team members harassed Gruenke about taking a pregnancy test. Then, they ostracized her after she was found to be pregnant. Medical authorities ruled that swimming competition would not be detrimental to a pregnant person. The district court granted the coach immunity. On appeal, the United States Court of Appeals for the Third Circuit had subject matter jurisdiction over Gruenke's Section 1983 claims. Section 1983:

> imposes civil liability upon any person who, acting under the color of state law, deprives another individual of any rights, privileges, or immunities secured by the Constitution or laws of the United States. This section does not create any new substantive rights but instead provides a remedy for the violation of a federal constitutional or statutory right....
>
> In a typical Section 1983 action, a court must initially determine whether the plaintiff has even alleged the deprivation of a right that either federal law or the Constitution protects.... If the plaintiff 's allegations meet this threshold, we must next determine whether, as a legal matter, the right that the defendant's conduct allegedly violates was a clearly established one, about which a reasonable person would have known. If so, then the defendant is not entitled to qualified immunity. If, in contrast, the plaintiff's allegations fail to satisfy either inquiry, then the defendant is entitled to summary judgment. Until the question of qualified immunity is addressed, a court cannot reach the underlying merits of the case.
>
> It is not sufficient that the right at issue be clearly established as a general matter. Rather, the question is whether a reasonable public official would know that his or her specific conduct violated clearly established rights.

Under a Fourth Amendment analysis, the court held that the swimming coach was not entitled to legal immunity for his actions because the coach should have known that his conduct would violate a clearly established right. The fact that the swim coach, without a medical background, had forced the swimmer to take a pregnancy test was the issue. "His responsibilities can be reasonably construed to include activities related to teaching and training. They cannot be extended to requiring a pregnancy test. Moreover, a reasonable swim coach would recognize that his student swimmer's condition was not suitable for public speculation" (302). Thus, the court found the swimmer's Fourth Amendment rights were indeed violated.

Drug Testing

Drug testing of athletes continues to be a popular deterrent mechanism utilized in professional, collegiate, and high school sports and in maintaining eligibility in maintaining a level playing field. Not only can drug use by athletes result in serious health problems, but organizers of athletic events are also interested in maintaining a level playing field or avoiding an unfair advantage to athletes on performance-enhancing drugs. Court decisions involving drug testing programs in employment routinely find the courts upholding preemployment testing, while random testing has not been upheld. For tests to be upheld among veteran employees, there has to be reason or some suspicion, to believe that the employee is using drugs.

Mary Decker Slaney, a world-class runner accused of a drug doping offense in the 1996 national trials for the Atlantic Olympics, faced a series of confusing decisions affecting her eligibility to compete. Her urine sample was tested for prohibited substances including exogenous testosterone. The court reported:

> Because current technology cannot detect the presence of prohibited testosterone in the body, testing programs measure the ratio of testosterone to epitestosterone ("t/E") in the body. ... Factors which may influence t/E ratio include an individual changing birth control pills, age, menstrual cycle, bacterial contamination of the urine sample, and alcohol use [Slaney tested significantly higher than the accepted ratio].
>
> Slaney claimed that her elevated level was the result of (1) her menstrual cycle, and (2) her changing of birth control pills. Furthermore, Slaney posited that there was no scientific validity to the hypothesis that a t/E ratio above six to one was not normal for female athletes. Nonetheless... the iAAF adopted the investigating doctor's recommendation and found Slaney's specimen positive for the prohibited substance. (586)

The IAAF suspended Slaney just prior to the National Track and Field Championships. The hearing Board, unpersuaded by the testimony of the investigating doctor, unanimously determined that no doping violation had occurred. Satisfied with the USATF hearing Board's finding that the IAAF's rules regarding the use of the t/E ratio test were vague and inconsistent, Slaney withdrew her complaint with the USOC. The IAAF was unsatisfied with the USATF Hearing Board's findings and invoked arbitration. Slaney withdrew from the arbitration and filed a lawsuit in federal court in Indiana. After some negative initial court rulings for Slaney, she appealed her case. The Seventh Circuit affirmed the earlier decision of the district court, finding that Slaney participated in a valid arbitration with the IAAF, which the court was obligated to recognize.

University of Colorado v. Derdeyn (1991, 1993, 1994) involved the constitutionality of the university's drug-testing policy. The policy, created to prepare athletes for NCAA mandatory drug testing, included a range of tests from random testing of athletes' urine samples obtained under direct visual observation to the use of rapid-eye movement examinations. The trial court found that the program violated the students' Fourth Amendment and rights under the Colorado Constitution. Following a bench trial, the court found that "obtaining a monitored urine sample is a substantial invasion of privacy" (*University of Colorado v. Derdeyn*, 1993). Also, "the trial court found that there is no evidence that the university instituted its program in response to any actual drug abuse problem among its student athletes. There is no evidence that any person has ever been injured in any way because of the use of drugs by a student athlete while practicing or playing a sport" (933).

The trial court concluded that "CU's random urinalysis drug testing of athletes without individualized suspicion violates the Fourth Amendment's guarantee that persons shall be secure against unreasonable searches and seizures conducted by the government" (934). The trial court's decision was affirmed by the Colorado Supreme Court, which stressed that because student consent was not voluntary, it could not be used to validate an otherwise unconstitutional search.

Acton v. Vernonia (1995) was the Supreme Court decision that upheld the right of public schools to randomly test athletes for drugs. Vernonia, a small Oregon town, had experienced an increase in drug use among young people; athletes appeared to be the leaders in the drug culture. In response to this change in drug use, the school created a policy. Acton's parents refused to consent to the drug-testing policy, thus denying him an opportunity to play football. His parents filed suit against the school district for declaratory and injunctive relief on the grounds that the Student Athletic Drug Policy violated their son's Fourth Amendment, Fourteenth Amendment, and Oregon Constitutional rights.

The district court found for the school district; the United States Court of Appeals, Ninth Circuit reversed, finding that the policy violated the Fourth and Fourteenth Amendments and the Oregon Constitution. The Supreme Court of the United States granted certiorari. This court's emphasis was on the reasonableness of the search as it balanced the rights of the individual required to take the test with the interests of the government. The U.S. Supreme Court reversed the Ninth Circuit and found the drug testing policy to be constitutional under the Fourth and Fourteenth Amendments. In reaching this conclusion, the high court found the search to be reasonable, as student-athletes have a "lesser privacy expectation with regard to medical examinations and procedures than the general population. Student athletes have even less of a legitimate privacy expectation, for an element of communal undress is inherent in athletic participation, and athletes are subject to preseason physical exams and rules regulating their conduct" (2387, 2388).

In the 2002 decision in *Board of Independent School District, No. 92 of Pottawatomie County et al. v. Earls,* a drug testing policy without suspicion of actual drug use was held not to violate the Fourth Amendment. The Student Activities Drug Testing Policy required all middle and high school students wishing to participate in an extracurricular activity to consent to urinalysis testing for drugs. Students' parents sued under 42 USC 1983, claiming that the policy violated the Fourth Amendment. The Supreme Court used *Vernonia* as a model for a number of issues. In reversing the appellate decision, the Supreme Court stated, "[w] ithin the limits of the Fourth Amendment, local school boards must assess the desirability of drug testing schoolchildren. In upholding the constitutionality of the policy, we express no opinion as to its wisdom. Rather, we hold only that [the drug testing] policy is a reasonable means of furthering the school district's important interest in preventing and deterring drug use among its schoolchildren" (749–750).

Fourteenth Amendment: Due Process

Procedural due process is the opportunity to be heard. It is a system to assure people of fair treatment when a "life, liberty, or property" right is challenged. No right is to be taken prior to due process. The Fifth and Fourteenth Amendments to the United States Constitution guarantee life, liberty, and property rights. Federal rights are embedded in the Fifth Amendment, while state's rights are found in the Fourteenth Amendment. While the "life" right is complex, it does not create the legal confusion that the "liberty" and "property" rights create. "Liberty" rights are, for example, privileges essential to the pursuit of happiness and safe working conditions. "Property" rights include claims of entitlement, termination of benefits or status, and exclusion from state or federal opportunities without cause.

Sport professionals may be called upon to craft some due process systems such as country club membership rights, employment termination agreements, and for various other reasons or circumstances. Requiring a hearing or chance to be heard is usually part of the due process system created. The system is to include the written charge or complaint and detailed reasons for the charge or complaint, adequate time for the defendants to prepare for a hearing and to retain representation, an opportunity for the defending party to present evidence and arguments, including witnesses; and ample time for each party to confront adverse witnesses, are important elements to any process created. Further, the hearing and decision should be made by an impartial decision maker with the ruling based strictly on the evidence provided in the hearing and not based on personal motivations or agendas. A clear and comprehensive statement giving the reasons for the decision is to be provided to all parties in order to satisfy constitutional due process requirements.

Fourteenth Amendment claims have also been raised in the school setting by students and parents of students who have been disciplined for some form of speech critical of the school or its personnel. In *J. S. v. Blue Mountain School District* (2011), a high school student was suspended for ten days for "creating, on a weekend and on her home computer, a [social media] profile making fun of her principal, which contained adult language and sexually explicit content" (920). The student and her parents sued the school district, claiming First Amendment free speech violations, unconstitutionally overbroad and vague policies, and violation of the parents' due process rights under the Fourteenth Amendment to raise their child in the manner that they saw fit. Specifically, they argued that, in disciplining J. S. for conduct that occurred in her parents' home during non-school hours, the school district interfered with their parental rights, and punishing the student for out-of-school speech was outside the district's authority.

Under *Tinker,* the court found the school district violated J. S.'s First Amendment free speech rights when it suspended her for creating the profile, citing the fact that "J. S. was suspended from school for speech that indisputably caused no substantial disruption in school and that could not reasonably have led school officials to forecast substantial disruption in school" (920). On the due process claims, J. S.'s parents alleged that the school district interfered with their ability to determine what out-of-school behavior warranted discipline and what form that discipline took (934). The court found this was not an accurate description of the impact that the school district's actions had upon J. S.'s parents' ability to make decisions concerning their daughter's upbringing because the school district's actions in no way forced or prevented J. S.'s parents from reaching their own disciplinary decision, nor did it force her parents to approve or disapprove of her conduct. Further, there was no triggering of the parents' liberty interest due to the subject matter of the school district's involvement; a decision involving a child's use of social media on the internet is not a "matter of the greatest importance" (934). The court ultimately affirmed that the school district did not violate the parents' Fourteenth Amendment substantive due process rights.

At the time it was handed down, the decision in *Blue Mountain School District* raised questions about how the boundaries of student speech, as delineated in *Tinker,* would be applied by future courts (and in schools) in the context of evolving social media use by students to "speak" about a variety of subjects related to daily life at the school, the teachers, or decisions made by school administrators that affect them. Questions including whether students have the right to make malicious comments about school personnel, so long as the speech takes place off campus, were raised as a result of the court's decision (Bemiller & Trendafilova, 2011). *Mahanoy,* the Supreme Court cheerleader Snapchat case discussed above, demonstrates the need for schools to have clear social media policies for students that are respectful of free speech protections found in the Constitution and policies to address vulgar or even hate speech, as well as comments that may be perceived as online bullying. This is especially true when it involves high school and elementary school level students' speech, when speakers are often minors, and when such speech likely occurs off-campus but is still accessible online to the wider student audience. The most recent student free speech litigation should send a strong reminder to school districts (and possibly their athletic departments) to tread lightly, in a legal sense, in crafting any social media or student speech/protest policies that may be viewed by plaintiffs' lawyers as potentially chilling student speech. School districts should always seek guidance from lawyers well-versed in education law and First Amendment jurisprudence when crafting policies that regulate student speech, consistent with the free speech principles.

Summary

The First Amendment to the United States Constitution includes freedom of religion, freedom of speech, freedom of the press, and defamation. Freedom of religion separates church and state and prohibits the government from enacting laws that aid a church or religion. Freedom of speech is the freedom to speak, remain silent, discuss with others, advocate, and communicate ideas. Freedom of the press is the freedom to write, draw, and create models. Ideas can be published and conveyed. Defamation is influenced by the status of the person—whether he/she is a public figure or an ordinary person. Sport seems to have many cases in defamation; athletes and coaches meet the status of a public figure.

The Fourth Amendment of the Constitution of the United States covers searches and drug testing. It guarantees the rights of people to be secure in their persons and homes against unreasonable searches and seizures. As in the First Amendment, the system for analyzing violations is to balance the rights of the individual with the rights of society.

The Fourteenth Amendment (Due Process Clause) of the United States Constitution is the right of people to be treated fairly when a life, liberty, or property right is challenged. No right can be taken away without providing due process.

Discussion Questions

1. Many of the student speech cases involved schoolchildren who were minors. Why must colleges and universities be cautious in trying to regulate speech by college students at sporting events? Why are the constitutional issues less of a concern when the speaker is a minor?
2. How can stadiums effectively balance the security needs to protect the general public against terrorism with the constitutional protections guaranteed to each citizen at sport venues in the United States?

Activities

1. Locate and review the fan code of conduct policy for your college or university's stadium or arena. Now, locate a similar policy for the venue when hosting an NBA team's games. Are the policies similar? Do you think the policy sufficiently protects the rights of sports fans to "speak" during the event?
2. Locate news articles about the drug testing policies used at the most recent Olympic Games. Are these testing policies effective to ensure fair competition? Now, locate the NCAA policies about drug testing of student-athletes and how polices need to be updated, given technological advances and new substances that may be deemed performance enhancing.

References

Acton v. Vernonia School District, 66 F. 3d 217 (1995).

Bemiller, J., & Trendafilova, S. (2011). Criticizing the coach, social media, and the First Amendment. SEVT conference: Columbia, SC.

Board of Education of Independent School District No. 92 of Pottawatomie County v. Earls, 536 U.S. 822 (2002).

Calvert, C., & Richards, R. D. (2004). Fans and the First Amendment: Cheering and jeering in college sports. *Virginia Sports & Entertainment Law Journal, 4*, 1.

Curtis Publishing Co. v. Butts, 388 U.S. 130 (1967).

Diepenbrock, G. (2009, Oct. 9). Joe-College.com argues judge's ruling would mean end to tshirt company. *KU Sports*. http://www2.kusports.com/news/2009/oct/09/joe-collegecom-argues-judges-ruling-would-mean-end/.

Donnelly v. Univ. of North Carolina, 236 N.C. App. 32 (2014).

Elk Grove Unified School District and Gordon v. Nedow, 542 U.S. 1 (2004).

Gertz v. Robert Welch, Inc., 418 U.S. 323, 94 S. Ct. 2997, 41 l. Ed. 2d 789 (1974).

Good News Club v. Milford Cent. Sch., 533 U.S. 98; 121 S. Ct. 2093 9 (2001).

Grady, J., & Moorman, A. M. (2008). "Muck Fizzou," "Vick 'em," & "I've been ejected!:" Emerging First Amendment issues in sport. North American Society for Sport Management Conference: Toronto, Canada.

Gruenke v. Seip, 225 F. 3d 290 (2000).

Higgins v. Kentucky Sports Radio, 951 F.3d 728 (2020).

Hill v. NCAA, 865 P. 2d 633 (1994).

Hudson, D. L. (2021). Mahanoy Area School District v. B. L. (2021). *The Supreme Court Encyclopedia*. https://mtsu.edu/first-amendment/article/1947/mahanoy-area-school-district-v-b-l.

J. S. v. Blue Mountain School District, 650 F. 3d 915 (2011).

Johnston v. Tampa Sports Authority, 530 F.3d 1320 (2008).

Lee v. Weisman, 505 U.S. 577 (1992).

Liptak, A. (2021, June 23). Supreme Court rules for cheerleader punished for vulgar Snapchat message. *New York Times*. https://www.nytimes.com/2021/06/23/us/supreme-court-free-speech-cheerleader.html.

Mahanoy Area Sch. Dist. v. B. L., 141 S. Ct. 2038 (2021).

Marcum v. Dahl, 658 F. 2d 731 (1981).

Morse v. Frederick, 551 U.S. 393 (2007).

New Jersey v. T. L. O., 105 S. Ct. 733 (1985).

New York Times Co. v. Sullivan, 376 U.S. 254 (1964).

Nystrom, T. (2007, Aug. 30). Battle over unlicensed T-shirts proceeds. *The University Daily Kansan*. https://www.kansan.com/news/battle-over-unlicensed-t-shirts-proceeds/article_0df8a9c6-36c7-5cc1-8289-278de5489c38.html.

Santa Fe v. Doe et al., 530 U.S. 290 (2000).

Sheehan v. San Francisco 49ers, ltd., 45 Cal. 4th 992 (2009).

Slaney v. the International Amateur Athletic Federation, 244 F. 3d 580 (2001).

Sprewell v. NYP holdings, 43 A.D. 3d 16 (2007).

Tinker v. Des Moines School District, 393 U.S. 503 (1969).

University of Colorado v. Derdeyn, 863 P. 2d 929 (1993).

University of Nevada et al. v. Tarkanian, 879 P. 2d 1180 (1994).

Van Orden v. Perry, 545 U.S. 677 (2005).

Vernonia School District v. Acton, 515 U.S. 646 (1995).

Wasserman, H.M. (2006). Fans, free expression, and the wide world of sports. *University of Pittsburgh. Law Review, 67*, 525.

Recommended Reading

Hudson Jr., D. L. (2020 - 2021). First Amendment: Mahanoy Area School District v. B. L.: The Court protects student social media but leaves unanswered questions. *Cato Supreme Court Review.*

Holtzman. E. (2016). "I am Cait," but it's none of your business: The problem of invasive transgender policies and a Fourth Amendment solution. *Florida Law Review, 68,* 1943.

Kaufman, C. J. (2009). Unsportsmanlike conduct: 15-yard penalty and loss of free speech in public university sports stadiums. *Kansas Law Review, 57,* 1235.

Ketter, C. (2020). The NFL player, the schoolchild, and the entertainer: When the term "free speech" is too freely spoken, exactly "who's on first?" *Cleveland State Law Review, 68,* 421.

Miller, J. J., Wendt, J. T., & Young, P. C. (2010). Fourth Amendment considerations and application of risk management principles for pat-down searches at professional football games. *Journal of Legal Aspects of Sport, 20,* 107.

5

Fourteenth Amendment and Title IX

OBJECTIVES

Upon completing this chapter, you will be able to,

- recognize that constitutional law uses a balancing system that recognizes the rights of the individual in relation to the rights of society;
- identify the relationship between the Fourteenth Amendment to the United States Constitution, Equal Protection Clause, and Title IX;
- explain the concept of equity by enrollment;
- identify how the courts view retaliation under Title IX;
- discuss the types of sexual harassment, including hostile work environment and quid pro quo; and
- discuss the legal rights of transgender athletes seeking opportunities to participate in sport.

Introduction

Public schools served as the agencies for race integration in the 1970s; collegiate and scholastic athletics became the agencies for sex integration beginning in the 1990s and remain so today. A review of laws, legal theories, governing structures, and court decisions will enable the professional to understand the factors that influence today's gender equity court decisions. This chapter will also consider sexual harassment under Title IX and cases involving athletes.

Law and Legal Theory

Laws governing equity in athletics are the Equal Protection Clause of the Fourteenth Amendment to the United States Constitution, Title IX, the Civil Rights Restoration Act of 1987, the Civil Rights Act of 1991, the Equity in Athletics Disclosure Act, the 2011 changes in the implementing guidelines of Title IX, and the Title IX regulations regarding sexual harassment, published in 2021. Disparate treatment and disparate impact (equity by enrollment) are found in many cases. These laws and theories were strengthened by the *Franklin v. Gwinnett* (1992) decision.

The Equal Protection Clause of the Fourteenth Amendment

The Equal Protection Clause of the Fourteenth Amendment to the United States Constitution states that "no state shall make or enforce any law which shall ... deny to any person within its jurisdiction the equal protection of the law." An equal protection challenge must show that groups of people are being treated differently without justification. An equal protection challenge in scholastic and collegiate sport is a complaint by a group of people (women) that its members are being treated differently from others (men) in athletics and that no justification exists to warrant the difference in treatment. One woman or a group of women (class) may retain an attorney and bring a legal action against any public institution (including public elementary or secondary schools, or public universities) for sex discrimination under the Fourteenth Amendment.

Oregon's Jerry Hunter is believed to have filed the first Fourteenth Amendment discrimination case in sport. Her filing was a defense to the crime of participating in competitive wrestling (*State of Oregon v. Hunter*, 1956). The court denied her constitutional claim, stating "that there should be at least one island on the sea of life reserved for men that would be impregnable to the assault of women" (458).

The following cases paved the way for Title IX of the Education Amendments of 1972. Note that the dates reported for these cases are settlement dates and that the impetus for the original filing occurred prior to the implementation of Title IX. *Brenden v. Independent School District* (1972, 1973), *Hollander v. Connecticut Interscholastic Athletic Conference, Inc.* (1972), *Reed v. Nebraska* (1972), and *Haas v. South Bend Community School Corporation* (1972) were cases that involved high school women requesting an opportunity to participate on men's teams when women's teams were not available. In many of these cases, the school district was merely enforcing a league rule. In the *Brenden* case, the Eighth Circuit invalidated the association's policy of prohibiting women from participating in cross-country skiing, running, and tennis when no team existed for women. In the *Connecticut* case, Susan Hollander was denied an opportunity to run on the cross-country team. The court in the

Reed case granted her request to play golf. Haas, also a golfer, won her case appeal at the Indiana Supreme Court, which decided the prohibition was discriminatory in its effect because a women's program did not exist and thus, there was no opportunity for interscholastic competition.

Also in the 1970s, a number of young women attempted to gain membership in Little League Baseball and community recreation programs. Ten-year-old Pamela Magill sought injunctive relief to be permitted to participate with males in Little League Baseball (*Magill v. Avonworth Baseball Conference et al.*, 1973, 1975). Despite the absence of an alternative program for girls, the court dismissed the case. Success was finally achieved in a similar situation in which the Essex County National Organization for Women filed a class action suit on behalf of all girls eight to 12 years of age who wanted to play baseball (*National Organization for Women v. Little League Baseball, Inc.*, 1974). In another case, Pookie Fortin received tremendous publicity as she gained entry to Little League (*Fortin v. Darlington Little League*, 1974, 1975).

Title IX of the Education Amendments of 1972

After considerable debate in Congress, Title IX became part of the Education Amendments of 1972. Title IX states,

> No person in the United States shall, on the basis of sex, be excluded from participation in, be denied the benefits of, or be subject to discrimination, under any educational program or activity, receiving federal financial assistance. (20 USC Section 1681 [a])

Title IX, a federal statute, extended the principles articulated under the Fourteenth Amendment to all schools, both public and private, that rely upon federal and/or state funds. Title IX is enforced by the Department of Education. The penalty for institutions in violation of Title IX is to have all federal funds withheld. Although institutions have been fined, no institution has lost all federal funding as a result of a Title IX violation. The Supreme Court decision in *Cannon v. University of Chicago* (1979) enabled individuals to bring a cause of action under Title IX.

In 1975, the U.S. Department of Education's predecessor, the Department of Health, Education and Welfare, issued final regulations implementing Title IX. Then, in 1978, the Office of Civil Rights prepared a policy interpretation of Title IX that was published the following year. Under the topic of effective accommodations, the policy interpretation provided a three-part test that recommended the following:

1) Whether intercollegiate level participation opportunities for male and female students are provided in numbers substantially proportionate to their respective enrollment; or

2) Where the members of one sex have been and are under-represented among intercollegiate athletes, whether the institution can show a history and continuing practice of program expansion that is demonstrably responsive to the developing interests and abilities of the members of the sex; or

3) Where the members of one sex are under-represented among intercollegiate athletes, and the institution cannot show a continuing practice of program expansion such as that cited above, whether it can be demonstrated that the interests and abilities of the members of that sex have been fully and effectively accommodated by the present program. (44 Fed. Reg. at 71,418)

Complaints in the early days of Title IX were usually resolved within a school district or by the Office of Civil Rights. *Yellow Springs Exempted Village School District v. Ohio High School Athletic Association* (1981) and *Petrie v. Illinois High School Association* (1979) were among the few complaints filed in court. In the *Yellow Springs* case, a school district brought an action against the Ohio High School Athletic Association, claiming that the rule prohibiting females from playing contact sports was unconstitutional and violated Title IX. When middle-school girls successfully made the boys' basketball team, the school district was forced by the athletic association to eliminate the qualified girls or withdraw from the league. The federal district court ruled under the Equal Protection clause for the female student athletes, but the court of appeals reversed. The court refused to rule on Title IX. This case contains a rich history of women's athletics. *Petrie* (1979) involved men petitioning the courts under Title IX to be permitted to play on girl's interscholastic volleyball teams. Petrie, a 16-year-old male high school junior, was practicing with the women's volleyball team when he was informed by school officials that the league rules barred him from competition. The trial court "reasoned that the prohibitions against boys were classifications based on sex but were justified because they preserved, fostered, and increased athletic competition for girls and prevented unfair competition that would arise from male dominance from the game" (*Petrie v. Illinois High School Association*, 1979, 857).

Three cases—two in athletics (*Othen v. Ann Arbor School District*, 1981, 1982; *Bennett v. West Texas State University*, 1981, 1983, 1986) and one general college case (*Grove City College v. Bell*, 1982, 1983, 1984)—successfully petitioned the courts to make Title IX "program specific." The phrase "program specific" meant that only those programs receiving direct federal funding were under the purview of Title IX enforcement. High school and college athletics, seldom financed with federal dollars, would no longer be under Title IX jurisdiction. The *Othen*, *Bennett*, and *Grove City* rulings brought the Title IX investigations of athletics and other areas other than those directly receiving federal funding like reading programs and financial aid to a halt.

Disparate Treatment and Disparate Impact

Disparate treatment and disparate impact are employment discrimination legal theories that have influenced "equity in athletics" cases. These theories have been used in court decisions under the Fourteenth Amendment, Equal Protection Clause. They involve practices that appear neutral in their treatment of different groups but fall more harshly on one group than another (*Teamsters v. United States*, 1977). Disparate treatment is identified when evidence exists that there was discriminatory intent or that persons acted pursuant to a policy that is discriminatory on its face. The *Hazelwood* case provides a method of analysis for use in identifying patterns and practices of discrimination under disparate impact. The patterns and practices include history, statistics, procedures, and specific instances. Disparate impact theory in sport is "participation by enrollment" (*Hazelwood School District v. United States*, 1977). Disparate impact theory is the basis for analysis of sport participation legal violations under the Fourteenth Amendment to the U.S. Constitution and prong one of the Title IX statute.

To achieve equity in athletics under the theory of disparate impact, an institution of higher education or secondary school must show that the percentage of females and males given the opportunity to play in sport is the same as the percentage of males and females attending the institution. For example, the figures for an institution with a student body of 16,000 students (9,600 females and 6,400 males) with 600 berths in competition (with 300 under scholarship) are noted in Table 5.1.

TABLE 5.1. PARTICIPATION RATE UNDER FOURTEENTH AMENDMENT AND PRONG ONE OF TITLE IX

	ENROLLMENT	PARTICIPATION	BERTHS	FULL SCHOLARSHIPS
Males	6,400	40%	240	120
Females	9,600	60%	360	180
Total	16,000	100%	600	300

Under a disparate impact theory, all opportunities are to be equal for the athletes. Budgets are to reflect the cost of supporting teams of equal levels of competition. If it costs less to maintain a synchronized swimming team at an elite level of competition than to maintain a football team at the same level, the budgets required to keep each team at an elite level of competition are considered the comparable budgets. Trainers, choreographers, assistant coaches, and others are to be provided to enable males and females to achieve an elite level of recognition in their respective sports.

The Civil Rights Restoration Act of 1987

The Civil Rights Restoration Act of 1987 restored Title IX to its original strength and removed the "program specific" status, reversing the rulings of *Othen*, *Bennett*, and *Grove City*. Title IX was once again applied to an entire institution and to all programs, including athletics.

The Civil Rights Act of 1991

Disparate impact theory was strengthened by the Civil Rights Act of 1991, which places the burden of proof on those who practiced discrimination, not on those who suffered discrimination. Proponents of the act stated: "Plaintiffs must first prove intentional discrimination, then must provide actual injury or loss arising there from to recover compensatory damages, must meet an even higher standard (establishing that the employer acted with malice or reckless or callous indifference to their rights) to recover punitive damages" (House Report, 102 Congress, 72, 1995).

For example, when discrimination is alleged in a university athletic department, the athletic department and the university jointly have the burden of proof (or must show evidence) of equitable participation in all forms of intercollegiate, intramural, and club sports. The athletic department and the university, not the person alleging discrimination, must demonstrate that no discrimination occurred or currently exists, and provide those who incur intentional discrimination with the right to recover compensatory and punitive damages. Punitive damages are based on a deliberate or intentional theory. Attorney fees are to be paid by the losing party.

Historically, many colleges claimed that they did not intend to discriminate as their legal defense. However, it should be noted that in 1992, the United States Office of Education sent a letter of warning about the Civil Rights Act of 1991 to all educational institutions, informing them of their responsibilities under the law. Failure to heed that warning was considered intentional discrimination.

The *Franklin* case, a U.S. Supreme Court sexual harassment decision, allows individuals experiencing discrimination to be compensated under Title IX (*Franklin v. Gwinnett*, 1990, 1991, 1992). Justices "held that a money damage remedy is available for an action brought to enforce Title IX" (208). Prior to this case, civil rights complaints in athletics had requested increases in the number of sports and opportunities for participation, and prohibition from dropping women's sports. This decision changed the law in a significant way so plaintiffs could now also request monetary compensation for lost athletic opportunities.

Equity in Athletics Disclosure Act

The 1994 reauthorization of the federal Elementary and Secondary Education Act contained a provision requiring colleges and universities to collect and disclose information concerning gender equity in intercollegiate athletics. The disclosure component required schools to publish the male-to-female ratio data for school enrollment and athletic participation data. Schools were to list varsity team membership, operating and recruiting expenses, and the number and gender of all coaches. All student aid that is provided to athletes, the revenue that is generated by the teams, and the coaching salaries was to be disclosed and such data was to be published yearly. Legislation introduced in 1997 as the Fair Play Act requires the Department of Education to publish financial and other information about sports and is to be available to prospective college students to assist in making informed choices about athletics.

The Impact of Athletic Governance on Equity

Early collegiate and scholastic athletic programs were governed by men's and women's physical education departments. As more institutions joined the NCAA or other national governing bodies such as the NAIA or NJCAA, colleges created athletics departments to administer men's athletics. Collegiate women's sports typically remained with women's physical education departments and operated more like student-run club sports. Athletic directors, the leaders of men's sports, soon answered only to the university or college presidents; leaders of women's athletics remained an integral part of the university or college and answered to department chairs and deans (the regular line of administrators at the university level). In some secondary schools, athletic departments were formed but their ties were always close to the physical education department.

In 1967, the American Alliance for Health, Physical Education, Recreation, and Dance (AAHPERD), Division of Girls and Women in Sport—the agency that had created, interpreted, and disseminated rules for women's sports for years—established a governance system for collegiate women's athletics. This governance system was the Commission on Intercollegiate Athletics.

In 1971, the DGWS Commission became the Association for Intercollegiate Athletics for Women (AIAW). The AIAW had 278 members and seven national championships in 1971. By 1980–1981, the membership had grown to 961 colleges and universities and 39 championships were staged (*AIAW v. NCAA,* 1983, 490). The AIAW played the same role in athletics for women that the NCAA played in athletics for men—with one exception: the AIAW refused to include athletic scholarships in its programs (Hult, 1980). The AIAW members believed that the scandals in men's athletics were a result of scholarships and the "big business" approach to sport and that scholarships also gave athletics programs too much control over student-athletes. Two different models for collegiate athletics existed at that point in time: a scholarship ("big business") NCAA men's model and a non-scholarship (educational student-athlete) AIAW women's model. For a detailed discussion of today's "big business" men's model of athletics, as predicted by AIAW members, see the articles by Kuznik and Ryan (2008) and Koller (2010) cited below.

The National Collegiate Athletic Association (NCAA) filed a lawsuit in 1976, asking the court to rescind the Title IX regulations related to athletics based on the presumed harm that the operating regulations and the named organizations might cause in the future (*NCAA v. Califano,* 1978, 428). The NCAA's main complaints were that Title IX should not cover athletics because collegiate athletics was privately funded; that the requirement of treating males and females equally was arbitrary and capricious; that the requirement of providing athletic scholarship equally to men and women violated 20 USC 1681 and the Fifth Amendment to the U.S. Constitution; and that the regulations violated the "due process" requirements of the Fifth Amendment (NCAA v. Califano, 1978, 429). The NCAA's case was dismissed for a lack of standing and thus the substantive legal issues were never litigated.

As the AIAW and women's participation in athletics grew, the National Collegiate Athletic Association (NCAA), wishing to maintain control of athletics, created sport championships for women in 1982 and offered current members the opportunity for their female athletes to compete without any additional membership fees. Because the NCAA only offered a few post season championships for women compared to the 39 championships offered by the AIAW, NCAA member colleges and universities were allowed to enter NCAA and AIAW events for the first few years (Uhlir, 1982). In just three years the AIAW lost members, sponsors, and television interests. The AIAW then sued the NCAA, alleging Sherman Act violations involving antitrust laws. In ordering judgment for the NCAA, the court stated that "even if defendant's conduct were avowedly anticompetitive in purpose, this record would not support a finding that its effect on plaintiff was the product of anything but direct competition" (*AIAW v. NCAA*, 1983, 506). The AIAW appealed the decision, which was affirmed, finding no Sherman Act violation (*AIAW v. NCAA*, 1984). With this decision, the NCAA officially took over governance of women's athletics.

Leading Cases in Collegiate and Scholastic Athletics

The leading cases following the implementation of Title IX were *Haffer v. Temple University* (1988) at the collegiate level and *Ridgeway v. Montana High School Athletic Association* (1988) at the scholastic level. Historically speaking, of the 36 early cases reviewed, the following themes appeared: women seeking equitable participation; elimination of sports; athletes seeking membership on opposite-sex teams; facilities; roster management; and the three-prong test.

Collegiate

Haffer v. Temple University (1988) was a class action suit against Temple University by women who were participating in athletics and those who had been deterred from participating in athletics due to sex discrimination. Their claims focused on the extent to which Temple University afforded women students fewer opportunities to compete in intercollegiate athletics, the alleged disparity in resources allocated to the men's and women's intercollegiate athletic programs, and the alleged disparity in the allocation of financial aid to male and female students. Their class action complaint alleged discrimination in opportunities to compete, expenditures, recruiting, coaching, travel and per diem allowance, uniforms, equipment, supplies, training facilities and services, housing and dining facilities, academic tutoring, and publicity. These actions were alleged to be in violation of the Fourteenth Amendment and the Pennsylvania Equal Rights Amendment. With the exception of meals, tutoring, facilities, and scheduling, the court ruled for the plaintiffs in all areas. The case was litigated for over 10 years and provides insight into the changes in civil rights and litigation strategies caused by the Grove City decisions.

Blair v. Washington State University (1989) was similar to the foregoing decisions, except that the trial court chose to exclude football in the equity calculation. The plaintiff appealed the football decision; the Supreme Court of Washington reversed the decision, requiring that football be included in all calculations for finance and participation. While this decision is precedent only in Washington state, it defined the role of football in equity considerations.

Cases litigated in the 1990s changed somewhat as courts began to look at the three-prong test to determine effective accommodation for participation opportunities as published in 1979. Often, schools (particularly universities) failed to recognize the significance of Prong One that had been taken from the Fourteenth Amendment, Equal Protection Clause analysis, and used in many previous cases. It was and is precedent and is therefore an important issue in legal decisions. Prong Two, program expansion for the under-represented gender, and Prong Three, accommodating the interests of students, are Title IX specific. Prong Two was a stop gap for those forced to make radical program changes in a short period of time. However, after 40 years those changes had to occur. Prong Three, meeting the needs and talent of females based on interest surveys has been redefined to be used only as one factor, not the only factor, in determining compliance. Other factors such as participation in club and intramural sports at the institution, as well as high school and club participation in the geographic recruiting area, are also to be considered. Women faced with conforming to the male model of athletics were beginning to speak out.

Considerable resources have been invested, unsuccessfully, by institutions of higher education in litigating their violations of Title IX with the hope of changing the law; however, every court in the country that has addressed these issues has upheld the Title IX regulations and Three-Prong test. *Cohen v. Brown University* (2003) was a class action suit against Brown University, its president, and its athletic director for discrimination against women in collegiate athletics. Women's gymnastics and volleyball team members brought suit on behalf of "all present, future, and potential Brown University women students who participate, seek to participate, and/or are deterred from participating in intercollegiate athletics funded by Brown" (*Cohen v. Brown University*, 1996, 161). They alleged violations of Title IX of the Education Amendments of 1972.

The suit was in response to the 1991 demotion of the gymnastics and volleyball teams from varsity to club status; men's water polo and golf were also demoted. Brown was the Ivy League volleyball champion in 1988 and the gymnastics champion in 1990. The district court in Rhode Island issued a preliminary injunction restoring the volleyball and gymnastics teams to varsity status and prohibiting Brown University from eliminating or reducing the status or funding of any existing women's varsity sport pending the resolution of other Title IX claims (*Cohen v. Brown*, 1992). Brown appealed.

In the 1993–1994 school year, 62% of Brown University's intercollegiate opportunities were for men and 38% were for women. Men constituted 48% of the enrollment, while women made up 52%. A 14% disparity existed between enrollment and participation. The trial court determined that they could not meet Prong One, which is the disparate impact standard of the Fourteenth Amendment. The First Circuit Court of Appeals, affirmed the trial court (*Cohen v. Brown*, 1992). After a lengthy bench trial, the district court found Brown University to be in violation of Title IX and ordered that a compliance plan be submitted. The plan, as submitted, was inadequate and forced the court to maintain varsity status for women's gymnastics, fencing, skiing, and water polo teams.

In *Barrett et al. v. West Chester University of Pennsylvania of the State of Higher Education et al.* (2003, 2006, 2009), eight members of the gymnastics team brought suit against the university when the women's gymnastics and men's lacrosse teams were eliminated in response to state budget cuts. In 1998, 25 years after Title IX became law, West Chester University's "Athletic Department created the Sports Equity Committee to obtain a basic and working knowledge of Title IX in order to begin the task of ensuring that the athletic program was in compliance with the law" (2003, 8). They used the three-prong test. Under accommodations, women were 60.8% of the undergraduate student body and 44.6% of the athletes; they fell short of compliance by over 16%. The fact they had not added a team for women for over 10 years meant Prong Two was violated. It became evident that if they would keep the gymnastics team, it would assist in meeting Prong Three in meeting the interests and abilities of women. Attorney fees and costs were awarded by the court.

The Title IX regulations contain a provision that allows schools to prohibit participation by athletes of the opposite sex on a team if the sport is a contact sport. Heather Mercer, a high school all-state football kicker, tried out as a walk-on player for the Duke University football team (*Mercer v. Duke University*, 1998, 1999, 2001, 2005). Although she failed to make the team, she served as a team manager and practiced with the kickers. Later in the same season, she was selected to play in an intra-squad scrimmage game and kicked a field goal that won the game for her squad. She was then named to the team and the media gave her a great deal of attention. As a result of the attention, the coach became concerned, tried to discourage her from playing, and finally dismissed her from the team.

Mercer brought suit against Duke University, stating that she was discriminated against. The district court dismissed the case because "Title IX did not require Duke University to give a woman an opportunity to play on the men's football team" (2005, 201). Mercer appealed and the United States Court of Appeals for the Fourth Circuit found for Mercer, concluding "that while the contact-sport exemption would have shielded Duke from liability had it refused to allow Mercer to try out for the team, the exception did not give Duke license to discriminate against Mercer because of her sex once Duke decided to allow her to join the team" (2005, 202). Mercer received "one dollar in compensatory damages and two million dollars in punitive damages and attorney fees" (2005, 202). The symbolic compensatory damage award signaled that the court believed that Mercer had not been damaged financially; she had not lost income or potential professional status. The punitive damage award, as explained earlier, was assessed against Duke University for intentional discrimination, at a financial impact the court hoped would stop Duke from committing such behavior in the future.

Choike v. Slippery Rock University (2010) provides a supervised and published settlement, something not found in earlier documents. Plaintiffs were 12 members of the women's swim, water polo, and field hockey teams who filed charges against Slippery Rock University for "intentional discrimination for failure to provide equitable athletic opportunities for [SRU's] female students and equitable treatment of its female students, including its announced elimination of three viable women's athletic teams" (2010, 3). In January 2006, the university announced the elimination of eight varsity sports: men's and women's water polo, women's field hockey, men's golf, men's wrestling, and men's tennis. Soon after the announcement, students formed a committee (Save Our Sports) and met with the athletic administration without success. An audit conducted showed participant opportunities for 2001 through 2005, with the following disparities between the number of undergraduate women enrolled in the university and the number of university women participating in collegiate athletics (Table 5.1) To be in compliance with Title IX, an allowance of plus or minus 1 percent different is allowed under current Title IX application and enforcement.

A formal student survey found that the interests of females had been met. Roster management appeared in this case as a successful means of manipulating Title IX equity. While roster management existed since the first implementation of Title IX, this is the first time it appears as a viable means of addressing equity to a court of law. Roster management is the loading of female teams with all athletes that try out, but only taking a small number of persons on the team to competitions and other events. Some schools have had as many as 40 females on a tennis team, but only eight entered competition. At the same time, the males had a team of 10: eight in competition and two substitutes. Roster management is severe, as demonstrated in this case.

TABLE 5.2. SLIPPERY ROCK UNIVERSITY MALE TO FEMALE SPORT PARTICIPATION DISPARITIES

YEAR	DISPARITY
2001	12.3%
2002	11.2%
2003	8.7%
2004	8.7%

The athletes in *Choike* chose to file a class action suit requiring a preliminary injunction to stop the elimination of the women's teams. The women sued the university's president and athletic director under Title IX for violations in equal participation and unequal coaching and training, disparities in equipment and supplies, publicity, promotional materials, events transportation, uniforms, playing fields, locker rooms, and facilities. The students' claims were successful (*Choike v. Slippery Rock University*, 2006). The parties later returned to the court in 2007, 2008, and 2010 in an effort to resolve ongoing disputes. The case has the contemporary value of the *Temple* case discussed earlier.

In *Equity in Athletics v. Department of Education and James Madison University* (2007, 2008, 2009, 2011), the plaintiff (a nonprofit organization comprised of male student-athletes, coaches, parents, alumni, and fans) challenged the equity by enrollment requirement of Title IX. The appellate court held that the recommended accommodations did not violate the Equal Protection Clause and therefore was legitimate. Equity in Athletics also sought relief against James Madison University, challenging their decision to eliminate 10 sports. Controversy existed over enrollment and scholarships; the court found that women had not achieved equity. The district court dismissed the constitutional, statutory, and procedural claims raised by Equity in Athletics against the Department of Education and James Madison University.

Scholastic Athletics

Ridgeway v. Montana High School Athletic Association (1988), one of the most comprehensive decisions in athletics at the secondary school level, was a class action suit brought on behalf of all Montana high school girls against the Montana High School Athletic Association. The lawsuit alleged violations of Title IX, the Fourteenth Amendment to the U.S. Constitution, and the Montana state constitution. The women claimed that discrimination existed in the number of sports, seasons of play, length of seasons, practice and game schedules, and access to facilities, equipment, coaching, trainers, transportation, the school band, uniforms, publicity, and general support. The parties accepted an agreement that provided for equal opportunity and placed a court-appointed facilitator in charge. The settlement gave specific roles of enforcement to the Montana office of public instruction and to individual schools. The entire state of Montana—not just the three schools represented in the class action suit—were included in the settlement. Although the decision is precedent only in Montana, the case provided a compliance formula secondary schools can use.

Three of the primary scholastic cases involved scheduling. The plaintiffs in *Horner v. Kentucky* (1994, 2000) and *Alston v. Virginia High School League, Inc.* (2000) lost. *Communities for Equity v. Michigan High School Athletic Association* (2003) put together an equity plan. Twelve female high school slow pitch softball players brought suit against the Kentucky State Board of Education and the high school athletic association for discrimination in sanctioning of sports for women and refusing to sanction fast pitch softball (*Horner v. Kentucky,* 1994). Their claims were under the Equal Protection Clause, Title IX, and state law. The district court granted summary judgment for the defendants, finding the female athletes had not been denied equal athletic opportunities. According to the court, the school had offered equal opportunities in accordance with the interest and abilities of students, satisfying Prong Three of the Title IX implementing guidelines. Also, the plaintiffs had failed to prove intentional discrimination. Horner appealed the decision. On appeal, Sixth Circuit reversed the trial court's decision and found for the plaintiffs on their Title IX claim, while they chose to affirm the trial court's equal protection claim. *Alston v. Virginia High School League, Inc.* (2000) was a challenge of intentional discrimination against women in the scheduling of athletic seasons. The court ruled that the Virginia High School League was not an entity subject to Title IX enforcement.

Communities for Equity v. Michigan High School Athletic Association (2008) was a legal challenge of gender discrimination in the planning and scheduling of sport seasons and sport competitions that began in 1998 and was not resolved for ten years. In 2000, the class action was approved, and in 2001, the court determined that the Michigan High School Athletics Association's scheduling of interscholastic athletic seasons violated the Equal Protection Clause (2001). A compliance plan was approved. Plaintiffs continued to return to the court to bring various seasons into compliance. After ongoing litigation spanning almost seven years, the district court in 2008 awarded over $4.5 million in legal fees against the Michigan High School Athletic Association (2008).

High school female ice hockey athletes suing a league for discrimination was first found in *Mason et al. v. Minnesota State High School League* (2004). In *Mason*, female ice hockey players requested a state tournament site equal to that provided the males. The men's team played in Xcel Energy Center in Minneapolis, while the women played at the State Fair Coliseum, a building dedicated mainly to horse shows. In 2000, the women filed a complaint with the Office of Civil Rights (OCR). OCR investigated the difference between the two facilities, identified the University of Minnesota women's ice hockey team facility as a potential arena, and ruled that the women's high school tournament be held there. The high school female athletes decided that the University of Minnesota women's ice hockey facility was not adequate and took their case to the courts, requesting an injunction, which was denied by the judge. On appeal, the defendants were also denied summary judgment.

High school girls complained of discrimination in practice and competitive facilities, locker rooms, training facilities, equipment and supplies, travel and transportation, coaches, and coaching facilities, scheduling of game and practice times, publicity, and funding (*Ollier et al. v. Sweetwater Union High School et al.*, 2010). The school failed all three prongs of Title IX: opportunities were inadequate and a new sport had not been added for years. Further, while lack of interest was demonstrated for field hockey on a survey, it was noted that the team did not have a coach. They also were found to have violated the Fourteenth Amendment to the U.S. Constitution.

Males Complaining of University Systems for Attaining Equity

Gender equity laws and policies have encouraged administrators of athletic programs to increase opportunities so that male-to-female participation levels reflect enrollment ratios. Some administrators have made the decision to reduce male participation opportunities in athletics instead of increasing female participation. This practice is acceptable under a strict reading of the law, and its acceptance has been confirmed by the courts. It does, however, become an issue of ethics and has been condemned as a disfavored practice by the Office of Civil Rights. Nine cases were brought by males since 1994 when they lost competitive opportunities: *Boulahanis et al. v. Board of Regents, Illinois State University et al.* (2000), *Neal et al. v. The Board of Trustees of the California State Universities et al.* (2003), *Chalenor et al. v.*

University of North Dakota (2002). Lichten involved tennis, swimming, and wrestling, while *Boulahanis* involved the elimination of soccer and wrestling.

Five of the cases mentioned above involved athletes who sued their universities because wrestling had been cut in an effort to bring collegiate sport competitive opportunities into compliance with Title IX. Notably, in *all* of the situations, the courts denied the request as there is no legal requirement to sustain men's teams when the institution disproportionately favors men in athletic participation.

In 1993, Drake University cut its wrestling program in response to university budget cuts and lack of support in its athletic conference and community. The scholarships of existing wrestlers were honored until each athlete's graduation. Five of the wrestlers brought a cause of action against the university, its president, and the athletic director for Title IX and the Fourteenth Amendment violations (*Gonyo et al. v. Drake University*, 1995). Drake's Title IX case was legally a weak one, as their 1992–1993 participation data showed a 75.3% male to 24.7% female participation ratio in an institution with female enrollment of 57.2%. In finding against this claim, the court said, "[r]estricting universities from eliminating men's scholarship sports ... while requiring them to expand opportunities for women in athletics ... would make it impracticable to spend less, rather than more, money on their athletic programs. Title IX does not so restrain a university's spending decisions" (1995, 1005).

Roster Stacking in Scholastic and Collegiate Sports

Roster stacking or roster management, a system often used by schools insincere in achieving equity by enrollment, was further discussed in *Biediger et al. v. Quinnipiac University* (2009, 2010), and is still a focus of a number of Title IX lawsuits today. In March 2009, Quinnipiac University decided to cut three sports: women's volleyball, men's golf, and outdoor track teams. At the same time, the university decided to create competitive cheerleading (*Biediger et al. v. Quinnipiac University*, 2009). The volleyball team plaintiffs requested an injunction to stop the elimination of their team. The court granted the preliminary injunction, holding that the university "managed its varsity rosters essentially, by setting artificial ceilings for men's varsity teams and floors for women's varsity teams" (2010, 63). Quinnipiac's practice of requiring individual female members of the cross-country, indoor, and outdoor track teams to be counted as members of all three teams, even though they practiced with only one team, was found to be in violation of Title IX. This case is a classic case for analyzing the possibility of roster management by schools and universities as they attempt to come into compliance with Title IX. One often legally suspect area was the number of athletes on a team that are not included in travel and competition. For example, the *Biediger* court refused to recognize a competitive cheerleading team as a varsity sport for purposes of Title IX, which essentially meant the cheerleaders could not be counted as female varsity athletes. The court's decision to declare that cheerleading wasn't a sport for purposes of gender equity received widespread national visibility. However, the roster management component was equally important to the legal analysis and conclusions made by the court.

Retaliation under Title IX

The United States Supreme Court's first Title IX case, *Jackson v. the Birmingham, Alabama Board of Education* (2005), was a cause of action for retaliation. *Jackson* was a young male women's basketball coach who was dismissed from his coaching position for complaining "that his team was not receiving equal funding and equal access to athletic equipment and facilities" (Jackson, 2005, 1503). The district court dismissed the complaint, ruling that Title IX did not include a claim of retaliation and the court of appeals affirmed the decision. The U.S. Supreme Court reversed, stating that the "private right of action implied by Title IX encompassed claims of retaliation for complaining about sex discrimination as: (1) such retaliation was (a) by definition an intentional act, (b) a form of discrimination; and (c) 'on the basis of sex'" (Jackson, 2005, 1498).

Following *Jackson,* a number of lawsuits were initiated by coaches who had experienced problems in their coaching positions and also had defended equity principles for females. Thus, they sued for retaliation under Title IX for their loss of employment. In many of the cases, particularly among secondary schools, the districts were successful in the courts. They claimed incompetence, insubordination, unethical conduct, and poor competitive records by the coach. Many of the secondary-school personnel lost their contract coaching positions but retained their teaching positions. During that same time, a number of persons who claimed retaliation received successful settlements. Fresno State University awarded Linda Vivas, the university's volleyball coach, $5.85 million after she sued for sex discrimination and retaliation (Lipka, 2007). "Although individuals can't sue public institutions in California for punitive damages, Vivas was awarded the above sum for past and future economic losses and emotional distress" (Redden, 2007a). Five months later, a Fresno jury ordered Fresno State to pay the former basketball coach for $19.1 million. The coach had sued for sex discrimination and retaliation for her advocacy for women's athletics (Redden, 2007b). A similar case was settled by Fresno State with the former associate athletic director, for $3.5 million (Redden, 2007b).

Sexual Harassment

Sexual harassment includes actions of employees, supervisors, teachers, coaches, principals, and students. Litigation has involved same and opposite-sex relationships. Claims are usually filed under Title IX and 42 USC 1983. In these decisions, courts examine the responsibility of the agency (including knowledge or direct involvement in the incident using a negligence or reckless standard), Title VII standards (for hostile environments), and quid pro quo (a strict liability standard). The two major kinds of sexual harassment are hostile environment and quid pro quo.

Hostile Environment

A hostile environment usually involves behaviors of continuous harassment of a sexual nature. It involves repeated, unwanted requests for sex, offensive touching, or threats of a sexual nature. Offensive pictures, stories, and jokes are often evaluated in the context of what is considered appropriate behavior in the community. Quid pro quo, a strict or automatic liability standard, means that certain benefits are conditioned on sexual relationships. Business benefits, high grades, or money are among the conditions.

In *Faragher v. City of Boca Raton* (1994, 1996, 1997, 1998), the U.S. Supreme Court found that employers were vicariously liable for a hostile work environment. The employer was liable to the victim whether the employer knew (or should have known) of the harasser's conduct. Faragher resigned her lifeguard position with the City of Boca Raton, Florida, and brought a cause of action against the city and her immediate supervisors, stating that the supervisors had created a sexually hostile environment, "repeatedly subjecting Faragher and other female lifeguards to uninvited and offensive touching, by making lewd remarks, and by speaking of women in offensive terms, and that this conduct constituted discrimination in the terms, conditions, and privileges of her employment in violation of Title VII and the Civil Rights Act if 1964" (*Faragher v. City of Boca Raton,* 1998, Syllabus). The district court found the City of Boca Raton liable for the harassment of its supervisors. The Eleventh Circuit reversed, holding that the supervisors were not acting within the scope of their employment. The U.S. Supreme Court ultimately agreed.

Female soccer players brought an action under Title IX and 43 USC 1983 against a group of University of North Carolina administrators, alleging hostile environment and sexual harassment against the women's soccer coach and others. The graphic descriptions of hostile environment and sexual harassment in this case enables a reader to recognize such actions in a specialized educational environment like sport. Also, administrators will note that the action was brought against the head and assistant coaches, an athletic trainer, the estate of a former chancellor, an assistant to the chancellor, former and current athletic directors, and an assistant athletic director. Each was sued individually and in their official capacity (*Jennings v. University of North Carolina at Chapel Hill et al.,* 2002, 496). Plaintiffs brought eight claims:

1) 42 USC 1983, violation of constitutional rights under First, Fourth, and Fourteenth Amendments against all defendants;
2) Rights under Title IX against all defendants;
3) Intentional interference with plaintiff one's contractual relationships with the U.S. Soccer Federation against the head coach;
4) For assault by plaintiff one against the head coach;
5) For battery by plaintiff one against the head coach;
6) For constructive fraud by plaintiff two against head coach and University, in general;

7) For negligent retention of head soccer coach by both plaintiffs against the University, in general; and
8) For invasion of privacy by both plaintiffs against the head coach and University. (497)

Defendants stated that all claims should be dismissed for lack of jurisdiction, failure to state a claim upon which relief could be granted, and sovereign immunity (Jennings, 2002, p. 497). The federal district court ruled on each of the above claims as they related to each defendant personally and in their official capacity.

In 2007, the appeals court ruled on many of the detailed facts and remanded the case because,

1) coaches' alleged actions, if proven, constituted sexual harassment based upon sex, as required for liability under Title IX;
2) coach's alleged behavior, if proven, was *sufficiently severe or pervasive* to create hostile or abusive environment (emphasis added); and
3) player alleged report to university's counsel, if proven, provided the university with actual notice of hostile environment, as required for the university to be liable under Title IX. (*Jennings et al. v. University of North Carolina*, 2007)

In 2007, the Fourth Circuit ruled against Jennings on the Title IX and Section 1983 claims and the plaintiffs eventually settled with the university. Dorrance was required to complete Title IX and sensitivity training but is still at UNC Chapel Hill, coaching the women's soccer team to over 22 national championships, and retains the record as the all-time winningest D1 college coach.

Faculty-to-Student Sexual Harassment

A female student in a Texas public high school had a sexual relationship with her male teacher; however, she did not report the incidents to school officials. Later, the police discovered the couple having sex. The teacher was arrested, and the school district terminated his employment (*Gebser et al. v. Lago Vista Independent School District,* 1998). The student filed suit against the school district for sexual harassment under state law, Title IX, and 42 USC 1983. The trial court dismissed the federal claims and remanded the case to state court as a negligence claim. The appellate court affirmed the trial court's dismissal of the federal claims. U.S. Supreme Court review was sought and received. The Supreme Court found that the "student was not allowed to recover for sexual harassment by one of the district's teachers unless an official of the district had actual notice of and was deliberately indifferent to the misconduct" (*Gebser et al.*, 1998, Overview). For a school district to be held liable under *respondeat superior* or constructive notice, they must be aware of the situation. *Respondeat superior* refers to tort liability of the person in charge; constructive notice requires that the individual must be warned of the situation if he/she is to be held liable. Respondeat superior is a tort theory, while constructive notice is a civil rights theory. In *Gebser*, the Supreme Court established a standard for sexual harassment cases in school districts. The plaintiff must prove the abuse occurred, that the school authorities were properly informed, and that they did nothing about it.

Peer Sexual Harassment and Assault by Male Athletes

A female basketball team member alleged sexual assault by three members of the men's basketball team (*Jane Doe v. University of the Pacific*, 2010). She reported the incident to the university, which investigated the incident, expelled one male athlete, suspended the other two male athletes, and suggested that there be no further contact between the men's and women's basketball team members. The female basketball player sued the university under Title IX, stating that the institution did not prevent the assault, failed to respond appropriately to the complaint, and retaliated against both teams through the policy limiting unsupervised social action between team's members. The district court ruled for the university on all claims.

Tiffany Williams' case is an incident of gang rape by athletes involving basketball and football players from the University of Georgia (*Williams v. Board of Regents of the University System of Georgia et al.*, 2007). Williams was invited by one of the male athletes to his room for consensual sex. A second and a third male entered the room and engaged in nonconsensual sex with the defendant. About a year after the rapes, the university held a hearing in which it was decided not to sanction the players. Williams sued. The district court dismissed the Title IX and 42 USC 1983 claims, as well as the request for injunctive relief. Williams appealed. On appeal, the Title IX claims against the UGA Athletics and Athletic Association were reversed and remanded as it was discovered that appropriate persons had knowledge of previous harassment and were deliberately indifferent to these claims. Her request for injunctive relief was also reversed and remanded. All other district court rulings were affirmed. No further information was available.

Plaintiffs Lisa Simpson and Anne Gilmore were sexually assaulted in Simpson's apartment by football players and high school students on a recruiting visit to the University of Colorado, Boulder (*Simpson et al. v. University of Colorado et al.*, 2004, 2005, 2007). Boulder campus officials were aware that sexual assaults could occur on these visits if supervision was not maintained. The local district attorney held a meeting with university officials, warning of such behavior. It was believed that the coaching staff not only knew of but condoned the behavior. Simpson and Gilmore each filed complaints, which were combined. They sought relief under Title IX, claiming that the university knew of the sexual harassment of female students by the football recruiting program and failed to take any action to prevent the assault.

The University of Colorado filed a summary judgment, contending that the Title IX claims were not established. The district court granted the motion, stating that "no rational person could find (1) that CU had actual notice of sexual harassment by CU students, by football players and recruits before Plaintiffs' assaults or (2) that CU was indifferent to such harassment" (*Simpson*, 2005, 1235). There was lack of evidence of notice and indifference. On appeal, the grant of summary judgment to defendants was reversed and remanded for further proceedings. The court stated,

> the evidence before the district court would support findings that by the time of the assaults on Plaintiffs, (1) Coach Barnett, whose rank in the CU hierarchy was comparable to that of a police chief in a municipal government, had general knowledge of the serious risk of sexual harassment and assault during college-football recruiting efforts; (2) Barnett knew that such assaults had indeed occurred during CU recruiting visits; (3) Barnett nevertheless maintained an unsupervised player-host program to show high-school recruits "a good time"; and Barnett knew, both because of incidents reported to him and because of his own unsupportive attitude, that there had been no change in the atmosphere since 1997 (when the prior assault occurred) that would make such misconduct less likely in 2001. A jury could infer that ... the inadequacy [of further training was] so likely to result in [Title IX violations], that [Coach Barnett could] reasonably be said to have been deliberately indifferent to the need. (2007, 1184–1185)

Transgender Individuals' Participation in Sport

As noted by Lenzi (2018), a transgender plaintiff challenging a discriminatory high school athletic policy will likely rely on both the Equal Protection Clause of the Fourteenth Amendment and Title IX of the Education Amendments Act. When assessing a potential equal protection violation, a court must first determine the level of judicial scrutiny: strict scrutiny, intermediate scrutiny, or rational basis review. When a state restricts an individual's access to a fundamental right, the policy must withstand strict scrutiny, meaning the government action must serve a compelling purpose and be the least restrictive means of doing so (*San Antonio Independent School District v. Rodriguez*, 1973). Notably, access to interscholastic sports has not been found by courts to be a constitutionally recognized fundamental right. Due process claims can also be raised about the fairness of eligibility policies applied by high school athletics departments at public schools. There is also the potential for lawsuits by cisgendered plaintiffs claiming equal protection violations if they are forced to compete against trans individuals who have an unfair athletic edge, at least according to their legal arguments. These cases seem to be on the rise.

At the college level, cases involving trans plaintiffs arguing for the right to participate in sports implicates Title IX as possible gender discrimination. "When assessing Title IX claims, courts often rely on Title VII workplace jurisprudence. As mentioned, Title VII protects employees from sex-based employment discrimination" (Title VII, 2012). Like Title

IX and the Equal Protection Clause, Title VII applies to individuals who are discriminated against because they do not conform to stereotypical gender roles" (*Price Waterhouse v. Hopkins*, 1989, 251). Thus, transgender plaintiffs can rely upon this case law's rationale to support their participation and inclusion in sport in their preferred gender, not necessarily their gender at birth (Lenzi, 2018, 872).

While the participation rights of trans athletes is still novel and an emerging legal issue, the parallel eligibility challenges and opportunities for inclusion presents new opportunities to find ways to include trans athletes in the benefits of sport participation, much like was done with individuals with disabilities in the interscholastic and college setting upon passage of the ADA. This is also an area of law in sport that is evolving rapidly, with case law and jurisprudence changing to reflect expectations about how these athletes can and should be included in sport participation, especially at the high school level. Thus, it is best to use the brief introduction to the myriad legal issues presented that barely scratch the surface about how the law and sport are once again being asked to comingle to find the proper balance regarding participation, eligibility, fair competition, and inclusion of all. Updated legal resources, such as case law, legal scholarship, and other sport management subject matter expertise, should be used to develop a better comprehensive understanding of the rights of trans athletes to sport participation but also to understand the legally complex decisions being asked of high school athletic associations, NCAA entities, and now youth sport organizations to ensure a level playing field for all. Finding ways to accommodate the interests and fair competition of all who wish to participate as sport participation has long held a formative role in students' educational and personal development at the interscholastic and collegiate levels.

Summary

Gender equity laws are the Fourteenth Amendment to the United States Constitution, Title IX, the Civil Rights Restoration Act of 1967, the Civil Rights Act of 1991, and the Equity in Athletics Disclosure Act. The Fourteenth Amendment and Title IX identify and give basic rights. The Civil Rights Act of 1987 restored Title IX to its original intent following the "program specific" approach that resulted from the *Grove City* decision. The Civil Rights Act of 1991 provides attorney fees and punitive damages in gender discrimination cases, and requires the defendant to disprove the charge of unlawful discrimination. *Franklin v. Gwinnett* (1992) verified the application of the 1991 statute. Recent cases have helped shape how Title IX is interpreted today.

Disparate treatment and disparate impact (equity by enrollment) have become the bases of many court decisions. Court cases have come from athletes and their parents, coaches, athletic personnel, and others. Significantly, no school that has been sanctioned by the Office of Civil Rights or the courts under Title IX has lost its federal or state funding. Court decisions have been provided under the impact of athletic governance, collegiate and scholastic athletes seeking equity, roster stacking, retaliation, sexual harassment, and eligibility and participation issues for trans athletes in sport.

Discussion Questions

1. What is the difference between a constitutional provision and a statute? Thus, what is the difference between the 14th Amendment, Equal Protection Clause to the U.S. Constitution, and Title IX?
2. Are the majority of high schools and institutions of higher education in compliance with the 14th Amendment and with Title IX?
3. What is roster stacking? Is it now legal or illegal?

Activities

1. Obtain the current NCAA Manual at https://www.ncaapublications.com/p-4630-2021-2022-ncaa-division-i-manual.aspx and identify information on scholarship requirements. Design a program for a typical undergraduate institution of higher education with an enrollment of 60% female and 40% male. Identify sports, numbers of participants or berths on teams, and scholarships. You must include football; no other specific sport is required. The program must be equitable based on gender.
2. Locate gender equity court decisions in Nexis Uni decided in the last five years. Contrast the facts, law, and legal theories found in recent cases with those published ten years ago.
3. Compare and contrast the Fourteenth Amendment Equal Protection Clause with Prong One under Title IX.

References

AIAW v. NCAA, 735 F. 2d 577 (1984); 558 F. Supp. 487 (1983).

Alston v. Virginia High School League, Inc., 108 F. Supp. 2d 543 (2000); 144 F. Supp. 2d 526 (1999).

Atkinson v. Lafayette College et al., 653 F. Supp. 2d 581 (2009)

Barrett et al. v. West Chester University of Pennsylvania of the State System of Higher Education et al., 636 F. Supp. 2d 439 (2009).

Barrs et al. v. the Southern Conference, 734 F. Supp. 1229 (2010).

Bennett v. West Texas State University, 799 F. 2d 155 (1986).

Biediger et al. v. Quinnipac University, 728 F. Supp. 2d 62 (2010).

Blair et al. v. Washington State University, 740 P. 2d 1379 (1989).

Boulahanis et al. v. Board of Regents, Illinois State University et al., 98 F. 3d 633 (1999).

Brenden v. Independent School District, 477 F. 2d 1292 (1973); 342 F. Supp. 1224 (1972).

Cannon v. University of Chicago, 103 S. Ct. 1254 (1983).

Chalenor et al. v. the University of North Dakota, 291 F. 3d. 1042 (2002);

Choike et al. v. Slippery Rock University of Pennsylvania of the State System of Higher Education et al., 2010 U.S. App. LEXIS 23791.

Civil Rights Act of 1991, 42 USC 1981 (2021).

Civil Rights Restoration Act of 1987, 20 USC 1687 (2021).

Cohen et al. v. Brown University et al., 101 F. 3d 155 (1996).

College Sports Council et al. v. Dept. of Education et al., 2007 U.S. App. LEXIS 1420.

Communities for Equity et al. v. Michigan High School Athletic Association et al., 2008 U.S. Dist. LEXIS 62298.

Equity in Athletics, Inc. et al. v. Department of Education et al., 2011 U.S. App. LEXIS 4493.

Equity in Athletics Disclosure Act of 1994, 20 U.S.C. § 1092(g) (2021).

Faragher v. City of Boca Raton, 118 S. Ct. 1115 (1998).

Foltz et al. v. Delaware State University, 269 F.R.D. 419 (2010).

Fortin v. Darlington Little League, 376 F. Supp. 514 F. 2d 344 (1975).

Franklin v. Gwinnett, 111 S. Ct. 949 (1991).

Gebser et al. v. Lago Vista Independent School District, 118 S. Ct. 1206 (1998); 118 S. Ct. 1989 (1998).

Gonyo et al. v. Drake University et al., 879 F. Supp. 1000 (1995).

Grove City v. Bell, 104 S. Ct. 1211 (1984).

Haffer v. Temple University, 678 F. Supp. 517 (1988).

Hass v. South Bend Community School Corporation, 289 N. E. 2d 495 (1972).

Hazelwood School District v. United States, 97 S. Ct. 2736 (1977).

Hess et al. v. Ramona Unified School District et al., 2008 U.S. Dist. LEXIS 102743; 2007 U.S. Dist. LEXIS 67687.

Hollander v. Connecticut Interscholastic Athletic Association, 164 Conn. 654 (1972).

Horner v. Kentucky High School Athletic Association, 206 F. 3d 685 (2000).

House Report, 102 Con., 1st Session at 72 (1995).

Hult, J. S. (1980). The philosophical conflicts in men's and women's collegiate athletics. *Quest, 32*(1), 77–94.

Jackson v. Birmingham Board of Education, 125 S. Ct. 1497 (2005).

Jane Doe v. University of the Pacific, 2010 U.S. Dist. LEXIS 130099.

Jennings et al. v. University of North Carolina at Chapel Hill et al., 482 F. 3d 686 (2007).

Koller, D. L. (2010). Not just one of the boys: A post-feminist critique of Title IX's vision for gender equity in sports. *Connecticut Law Review, 43*, 401.

Kuznick, L., & Ryan, M. (2008). Changing social norms? Title IX and legal activism. *Harvard Journal Law & Gender, 31*, 367.

Lederman, D. (1982). U.S. draft memo on sex equity in college sports. *The Chronicle of Higher Education*, 38(22), 1.

Lenzi, M. J. (2018). The trans athlete dilemma: A constitutional analysis of high school transgender student-athlete policies," *American University Law Review, 67*(3), Article 4. http://digitalcommons.wcl.american.edu/aulr/vol67/iss3/4.

Lipka, S. (2007). Jury orders Fresno State U. to pay ex-coach $5.85-million in discrimination case. *The Chronicle of Higher Education, 53*(46), A30.

Magill v. Avonworth Baseball Conference et al., 516 F. 2d 1328 (1975).

Mason et al. v. Minnesota State High School League, 2004 U.S. Dist. LEXIS 13865.

Mercer v. Duke University et al. 401 F. 3d 199 (2005).

National Collegiate Athletic Association (NCAA) v. Califano, 444 F. Supp. 425 (1978).

National Organization for Women v. Little League Baseball, Inc., 338 A. 2d 198 (1974).

Neal et al. v. the Board of Trustees of California State University, 51 Fed. Appx. 736 (2002).

Ollier et al. v. Sweetwater Union High School District et al., 267 F.R.D. 338 (2010).

Othen v. Ann Arbor School District, 699 F. 2d 309 (1982).

Petrie v. Illinois High School Athletic Association, 394 N. E. 2d 855 (1979).

Price Waterhouse v. Hopkins, 490 U.S. 228 (1989).

Redden, E. (2007a, July 11). Big payday for Title IX advocate. *Inside Higher Ed.*

Redden, E. (2007b, December 10). Fallout from Fresno State's multi-million dollar case(s). *Inside Higher Ed.*

Reed v. Nebraska Athletic Association, 341 F. Supp. 258 (1972).

Ridgeway v. Montana High School Association, 858 F. 2d 579 (1988).

San Antonio Independent School District v. Rodriguez, 411 U.S. 1, 16–17 (1973).

Simpson et al. v. University of Colorado, 500 F. 3d 1170 (2007).

State of Oregon v. Hunter, 300 P. 2d 455 (1956).

Teamsters v. United States, 431 U.S. 324 (1977).

Title IX of the Education Amendments of 1972, 20 USC 1681–1688 (2021).

Title VII of the Civil Rights Act of 1964, 42 USC 2000e-2(a) (2012).

Uhlir, A. (1982). The wolf is our shepherd: Shall we not fear? *Phi Delta Kappa, 64*(3), 172.

United States Dept. of Education, Office of Civil Rights. (2021, July). Questions and answers regarding the Title IX regulations for sexual harassment. https://www2.ed.gov/about/offices/list/ocr/docs/202107-qa-titleix.pdf.

Williams v. University of Georgia, 477 F. 3d 1282 (2007).

Yellow Springs Exempted Village School District v. Ohio High School Athletic Association, 647 F. 2d 651 (1981).

Recommended Reading

Anderson, P. (2008). A historical review of Title IX litigation. 18 *J. Legal Aspects of Sport* 127.

Brown, K. D. (2014). The transgender student-athlete: Is there a Fourteenth Amendment right to participate on the gender-specific team of your choice? *Marquette Sports Law Review,* 25, 311. http://scholarship.law.marquette.edu/sportslaw/vol25/iss1/14.

Hefferan, J. (2007). Changing seasons, changing times: The validity of nontraditional sports seasons under Title IX and the Equal Protection Clause. *Vanderbilt Journal of Entertainment & Technological Law, 9*, 861.

Katz, R. S., & Luckinbill, R. W. (2017). Changing sex/gender roles and sport. *Stanford Law & Policy Review, 28*, 215. https://law.stanford.edu/publications/changing-sexgender-roles-and-sport/.

Staurowsky, E., & Wright, E. A. (2013). Discovering dysfunction in Title IX implementation: NCAA administrator literacy, responsibility, and fear. *Journal of Applied Sport Management, 5*(1), 1–30. https://trace.tennessee.edu/jasm/vol5/iss1/9.

6

Americans with Disabilities Act (ADA) and Stadium Accessibility

OBJECTIVES

Upon completing this chapter, you will,

- understand the relationship between various laws applicable to accommodating people with disabilities in sport settings;
- explain what a plaintiff is required to establish to bring a claim for violation of the ADA;
- apply the steps necessary to make a determination about modifying sport rules or eligibility for people with disabilities;
- discuss the detailed requirements for stadium accessibility; and
- conduct an individualized inquiry assessment of a person with a disability requesting a modification of an organization or venues' policies or procedures.

Introduction

Providing equal opportunity for people with disabilities is the fundamental principle of the Americans with Disabilities Act (ADA) of 1990. Sport opportunities for people with disabilities have expanded since passage of the ADA. With the enactment of the ADA, efforts have been focused on including people with disabilities in sport, as both participants and spectators. Historically, full participation and equal opportunity in sport and recreation services have been a challenge for people with disabilities (Fay & Wolff, 2000). This can be attributed to barriers to participation, such as sport and recreation facilities not being accessible to individuals with disabilities, as well as a lack of understanding by non-disabled people of the needs of people with disabilities while participating in sport or attending sporting events as spectators or in employment.

Providing an inclusive environment for people with disabilities has been a priority in physical education and sport management and "is now (or should be) an integral part of any discussion when making programming decisions or facility renovations" (Grady & Andrew, 2003, p. 231). While substantial progress has been achieved, sport managers continue to face challenges in implementing the access provisions of the ADA into their facilities (Grady & Andrew, 2003). Grady and Moorman (2016) commented on this progress since the ADA's inception and noted that implementation of the ADA has yielded significant improvements in physical access and attitudinal awareness of the needs of individuals with disabilities in sport settings, yet still provides a challenge for sport professionals to meaningfully integrate people with disabilities into their operations. This can be attributed, in part, due to the complex patchwork of laws, regulation, and guidelines that comprise "disability laws" within the United States. While the ADA is the most recognizable law mandating access for people with disabilities in public service and educational environments in the United States, the legal precursors to the ADA are also applicable to certain segments of the sport industry.

Section 504 of the Rehabilitation Act

As awareness of the need to educate children with disabilities grew, the United States Congress enacted federal legislation and provided funding to assist school districts in educating children with disabilities. In 1973, Congress passed the Rehabilitation Act. Section 504 of the Act states,

> No otherwise qualified handicapped individual in the United States, as defined in section 7(6), shall solely by reason of his handicap, be excluded from the participation in, be denied the benefit of, or be subjected to discrimination under any program or activity receiving federal financial assistance. (45 CFR 84)

The scope of Section 504 of the Rehabilitation Act includes schools that educate children, as well as entities that receive federal funds. Importantly, this includes almost all colleges and universities, as well as cultural venues such as performing arts centers, which often rely on federal funds to support operations. While similar to the purpose and goals of the ADA in ensuring access to programs and services, a working knowledge of Section 504 of the Rehabilitation Act requirements may be necessary depending on the types of sport programs or services being offered. For example, a high school athletic director would likely need an awareness of Section 504.

Americans with Disabilities Act of 1990 (ADA)

President George H. W. Bush signed the Americans with Disabilities Act (ADA) into law on July 26, 1990. The ADA was enacted to provide a national mandate to eliminate discrimination faced by people with disabilities on a day-to-day basis (42 USC 12101[b]). That lofty goal remains elusive today, although much progress has been made in improving access to programs, services, and places of public accommodation (Grady & Moorman, 2016). Per the Office of Civil Rights (OCR), discrimination is defined as "denial of services, aids, or benefits, provision of different service or in a different manner, and segregation or separate treatment" based on disability (U.S. Department of the Interior, n.d., para. 4). The ADA supplements existing federal and state statutes designed to accommodate individuals with one or more disabilities. The ADA is a remedial statute (meaning its goal is to remedy the effects of past discrimination) and is modeled after the Civil Rights Act of 1964 and the Rehabilitation Act of 1973. It provides civil protection in employment (meaning the ability to file a private lawsuit against the employer for money damages or injunctive relief), in government services (including transportation and schools), and in public accommodations.

To establish a prima facie case of discrimination under the ADA, the plaintiff must prove:

(1) that she has a disability;

(2) that she is a qualified individual; and

(3) that she was subject to unlawful discrimination because of her disability.
(*Morisky v. Broward County*, 1996)

ADA Titles

The ADA contains five titles that detail legal rights provided to persons with disabilities:

Title I: Employment

Title II: Public Services

Title III: Public Accommodation

Title IV: Telecommunications

Title V: Miscellaneous Provisions

Title I protects people with disabilities from employment discrimination in businesses with 15 or more employees. Businesses that fall within the scope of ADA are required to provide reasonable accommodation so that the individual with a disability may perform the required tasks of his/her job. For example, an arena that provides a ticket taker who has chronic back pain with a chair to take periodic breaks while taking tickets may constitute a reasonable accommodation.

Key provisions of the ADA applicable to sport management, physical activity, and the provision of recreation services are Title II and Title III (Grady & Andrew, 2003). Title II mandates public entities, including state and local governments, give people with disabilities an equal opportunity to benefit from all of their programs, services, and activities (42 USC 12132). Title II incorporates aspects of Section 504 of the Rehabilitation Act, is enforced in schools, and is a factor when sport and physical activity facilities are municipally owned. Title II is relevant in creating individualized educational programs (IEPs) for students with disabilities that include or should include physical activity.

Educational components of Title II are also addressed under the Individuals with Disabilities Education Act (IDEA). IDEA requires public schools to develop an individualized education program (IEP) for each child that reflects her individualized needs (U.S. Department of Justice [U.S. DOJ], n.d.).

Title III provides protection for individuals with disabilities seeking access to places of public accommodation (42 USC 1282). Title III specifically mentions sport, recreation, and play facilities and is usually the area of greatest concern in accessing sport and physical activity. "Title III of the ADA outlaws not just intentional discrimination but also certain practices that have a disparate impact upon persons with disabilities even in the absence of any conscious intent to discriminate," also known as de facto discrimination (*Indep. Living Res. v. Oregon Arena Corp.*, 1169). With respect to de facto violations, places of public accommodation under Title III are only required to "take remedial measures that are (a) effective, (b) practical, and (c) fiscally manageable" (*Ass'n for Disabled Am., Inc. v. Concorde Gaming Corp.*, 1362).

Title IV addresses telecommunication and telephone services with the Federal Communication Commission (FCC) and individual states. Title V involves retaliation, nondiscrimination in service benefits, and attorney fees for prevailing parties in actions brought to enforce the ADA. The Equal Employment Opportunities Commission (EEOC) is responsible for providing technical assistance for Title I. The Department of Justice (DOJ) is to provide technical assistance for Titles II and III.

Definition of Disability

The term "disability," for the purposes of the ADA, means that an individual has,

1) a physical or mental impairment that substantially limits one or more of the major life activities of such individual;
2) a record of such an impairment; or
3) been regarded as having such an impairment. (42 USC 12101, Section 3[2])

Purpose of the ADA

The purpose of the Act is:

1) to provide a clear and comprehensive national mandate for the elimination of discrimination against individuals with disabilities;

2) to provide clear, strong, consistent, and enforceable standards addressing discrimination against individuals with disabilities;

3) to ensure that the Federal Government plays a central role in enforcing the standards established in this act on behalf of individuals with disabilities; and

4) to invoke the sweep of congressional authority, including the power to enforce the Fourteenth Amendment and to regulate commerce, in order to address the major areas of discrimination faced day-to-day by people with disabilities. (42 USC 12101, Section 2[b])

Title I

Title I is "an antidiscrimination statute that requires that individuals with disabilities be given the same consideration for employment that individuals without disabilities be given" (29 CFR 1630.1[a] Purpose). It reaffirms Title VII of the Civil Rights Act of 1964 and Section 504 of the Rehabilitation Act of 1973. The phrase "qualified individual with a disability" refers to a person who is able to perform the essential functions of a job with or without reasonable accommodations. Under the ADA and Section 504, no employer can discriminate against a qualified individual with a disability in the application and interview process, hiring, assignments, evaluation, promotion, and termination. Compensation, training, disciplinary action, leaves, in-service opportunities, and other terms, conditions, and privileges of employment must be the same. Employers have the same obligations to current employees who become disabled while employed.

The ADA requires that reasonable accommodations for the physical or mental limitations of a qualified applicant be made. Reasonable accommodations include facility access, restructuring job tasks with accommodations in mind, modifying work schedules, and providing readers, special computers, and interpreters. While the ADA's role is to remove barriers and to force employers to examine perceived barriers, the ADA does not relieve an employee or applicant with a disability from the obligation to perform the essential functions of the job. The purpose is to enable persons with disabilities to compete in the workplace and be measured on the same performance standards as all employees.

Accommodations are required unless the accommodation places an undue hardship on the employer. Factors to be considered in determining undue hardship:

- nature and cost of accommodation;
- overall financial resources of agency;
- size, budget, and profitability of business; and
- financial impact of the recommended accommodation.

An undue hardship defense is also available under Title II (discussed below). These decisions are made by the Equal Employment Opportunity Commission (EEOC) on a case-by-case basis.

The ADA does not require an employer to hire an applicant or retain an employee who poses a "direct threat" to the health or safety of other employees or clients or themselves that cannot be eliminated. A "direct threat" means a significant risk to the health or safety of others that cannot be eliminated by reasonable accommodations. Direct threat situations in sport and physical activity nearly always involve safety (i.e., the safety of the clients, participants, and employees). In these situations, safety requirements are based on real risks—not speculations, stereotypes, or generalizations about persons with disabilities.

Title I enforcement is similar to the enforcement of Title VII of the Civil Rights Act of 1964. The investigation is conducted by the EEOC. Furthermore, a right to file a civil lawsuit exists.

Title II

Title II of the ADA, entitled Nondiscrimination on the Basis of Disability in State and Local Government Services, prohibits discrimination in services, programs, and activities provided or made available by state and local governments or their instrumentalities. The receipt of federal financial assistance is not required for enforcement of rights protected under Title II. The statute extends the provisions of Section 504 of the Rehabilitation Act of 1973 to state and local governments, including schools and municipal recreation facilities. The sport professional employed in Title II environments should inform individuals of their rights regarding access to programs and services. In addition, the professional must analyze facilities, programs, policies, and procedures for physical and psychological barriers. Lastly, the sport professional should assess for violations and retain written documentation.

Title III

With Title III of the ADA (public accommodations and services operated by private entities), sport and physical activities are specifically covered in Section 301(7). Included in this section are the following:

> 1) a park, zoo, amusement park, or other place of recreation;
>
> 2) a nursery, elementary, secondary, undergraduate, or post-graduate private school, or other place of education;
>
> 3) a daycare center, senior citizen center, or other social service center establishment; and
>
> 4) a gymnasium, health spa, bowling alley, golf course, or other place of exercise or recreation. (Title III, Section 301[7])

Title III requires that all privately operated, nonresidential buildings become accessible to and usable by individuals with disabilities. Title III prohibits discrimination against persons with disabilities in the full and equal enjoyment of goods, services, facilities, privileges, and advantages of any public accommodation provided by private individuals or organizations. Discrimination under Title III would include provision of different services or benefits to people with disabilities, as well as providing services and benefits in a different manner to people with disabilities. A place of public accommodation is a facility operated by a private entity (as opposed to operated by a government entity) whose operations affect commerce and fall into one of the following categories: lodging, eating, entertainment, recreation, service, and education. Public accommodations include restaurants, hotels, shopping malls, grocery stores, museums, and recreation centers, among others.

Under Title III, facilities must comply with the required approach, entry, and use standards. Use standards are programs, policies, and procedures. Accommodations for people with mobility impairments, visual impairments, hearing impairments, and mental capacity issues are to be made. When strict compliance is not possible, minor deviations are permitted. However, no deviation that is a safety risk is allowed.

The Department of Justice (DOJ) recommends a detailed written plan that establishes a good faith effort to be prepared. Plans are to include goals, objectives, programs, services, evaluations (including assessment tools), and methods of integrating results. As mentioned, the U.S. Attorney General, Office of Civil Rights, investigates violations of the ADA. When violations are identified, a compliance review is initiated.

The DOJ's Civil Rights Division is responsible for Titles II and III compliance reviews and complaints. The Equal Employment Opportunities Commission (EEOC) is responsible for Title I complaints. States with laws similar to the ADA and cities with building codes that mirror the ADA standards also play a role in the resolution of violations of the ADA.

Defenses to Disability Discrimination

While the ADA creates numerous obligations for the sport business, there are several defenses available to a service provider that can be used to deny a policy modification request or to protect the health and safety of other patrons (Grady & Andrew, 2003). Under Title II, a public entity is not required to take actions that would result in undue hardship, including undue financial and administrative burdens (42 USC 12111). Undue hardship refers to "an action requiring significant difficulty or expense" when considered in light of several factors (42 USC 12111[10]). The factors considered are the same as an undue hardship defense under Title I in the employment context and include the nature and costs of the accommodation requested, the overall financial resources of the facility providing reasonable accommodation, the number of employees at the facility, the effect on expenses and resources resulting from providing the accommodation, the overall financial resources of the covered entity, and the type of operation of the covered entity (42 USC 12111[10, A]).

Under Title II, the public entity is "required to make reasonable modifications to policies, practices, and procedures where necessary to avoid discrimination, unless the service provider can demonstrate that doing so would fundamentally alter the nature of the service, program, or activity being provided" (U.S. Department of Justice, 2002). The fundamental alteration defense was raised by the PGA Tour, where the Supreme Court held that allowing Casey Martin to use a golf cart during PGA qualifying tournaments would not fundamentally alter the nature of the golf tournaments (*PGA Tour v. Martin*, 2000, 690). Similarly, Title III requires "reasonable modification of policies, practices, or procedures of a public accommodation unless doing so would fundamentally alter what is offered" (*PGA Tour v. Martin*, 2000, 668).

Title III also requires the removal of architectural or structural barriers that prevent access to public accommodations, when their removal is readily achievable (42 USC 12182[b]). If barrier removal is not readily achievable, the public accommodation must make its goods or services available to people with disabilities through alternative methods, if such alternative methods are readily achievable (42 USC 12182[b]). For example, if a stadium only sells tickets online, the facility must establish an alternative sales method, such as calling on the telephone or buying tickets in person, to accommodate patrons who cannot purchase tickets online because of their disability.

While Title III does not allow for an undue hardship defense for the failure to construct new facilities in accordance with the ADA's implementing regulations and ADA Accessibility Guidelines (28 CFR 36.406, Appendix A), an undue hardship defense can still be raised related to policies and procedures using an administrative burden theory (Grady & Andrew, 2003). In *PGA Tour v. Martin* (2000), the PGA Tour asserted that if their organization had to review numerous appeals by other golfers with disabilities requesting accommodations, the administrative process would constitute an undue hardship since it would create an administrative burden (1002). The court referred to *Washington v. Indiana High Sch. Athletic Association* (1999, 852), where the court analyzed the individualized assessment requirement for a learning-disabled student athlete waiver from an eight-semester limit on competition. The court in *Washington* stated that the few case-by-case analyses that the athletic association "would need to conduct hardly can be described as an excessive burden" (852). Citing the rationale adopted by the Seventh Circuit in *Washington*, the Ninth Circuit rejected the undue burden defense, finding that an individualized determination would not impose an intolerable burden on the PGA (*PGA Tour v. Martin*, 2000, 1002). Anecdotally, no sudden anticipated wave of disability accommodation requests ever flooded the PGA Tour, as they had feared.

As mentioned earlier in the context of Title I, the "direct threat" exception can be raised as a defense when there is concern about health or safety of others given the nature of the person's disability or due to the auxiliary aid that the person uses, such as a wheelchair. "Direct threat" is often an issue in the context of emergency evacuation of people with disabilities (Grady & Andrew, 2007). For example, seating patrons in wheelchairs in a path designated as the emergency evacuation route used by able bodied patrons would raise "direct threat" concerns, as other patrons may not be able to evacuate quickly and efficiently in an emergency due to the presence of the wheelchairs, as well as the potential inability of patrons in wheelchairs to evacuate quickly. To utilize the direct threat defense, the service provider must conduct an individual assessment of the risk to the health and safety of others (McGovern, n.d.). "The assessment must include a consideration of how reasonable accommodations such as rule changes or adaptive equipment would eliminate or minimize the risk and enable participation in the activity" (McGovern, n.d.).

Cases

The following cases have examined the application of the ADA in sport: *PGA Tour v. Martin,* 2000; *Anderson v. Little League Baseball, Inc.,* 1992; *Bowers v. the National Collegiate Athletic Association et al.,* 2003; as well as several cases involving age eligibility issues of high school athletes with learning disabilities.

Modifications of Rules and Policies

Casey Martin's decision from the United States Supreme Court is the most often mentioned court decision in sport related to the Americans with Disabilities Act. The PGA Tour uses uses a three-stage qualifying tournament as the most popular means of gaining entry into its tour. Stages one and two permit a participant to use a golf cart while playing; players must walk the course in the third stage. Martin, a professional golfer, has a degenerative circulatory disorder that meets the ADA definition of a disability. He petitioned the PGA Tour requesting an accommodation under Title III to use a golf cart during the third stage of qualifying, which was denied.

Martin filed an action against the PGA Tour under Title III of the ADA. The District Court of Oregon entered a preliminary injunction permitting him to enter the tournament. After a trial, the injunction became permanent. An underlying issue in the case was whether Title III, which includes public accommodations, could be applied in professional sport. The Ninth Circuit affirmed the lower court's decision, stating that the golf course was a place of public accommodation and that the use of a cart during the tour would not fundamentally alter the tournament. The United States Supreme Court affirmed the decision, finding in favor of Martin.

In another high-profile case, Arizona judge Lawrence Anderson, a wheelchair user, was selected to coach a 1992 All-Star National Little League competition (*Anderson v. Little League Baseball, Inc.,* 1992). However, the president of Little League Baseball adopted a policy stating that a coach in a wheelchair could coach from the dugout but not from a coach's box, citing the safety of the players. Judge Anderson had been an on-field coach of his son's team for three years without incident. Coach Anderson saw the policy as a way to eliminate him from coaching if his team made the finals. In 1991, Judge Anderson's team was eliminated early in the competition. During 1992, the local branch of Little League Baseball allowed him to continue to assume his preferred coaching position. When it appeared that his 1992 team was going to be successful in the national tournament, he filed an injunction to stop enforcement of Little League's policy (or, in the alternative, asked the court to allow him to participate fully by coaching on the field), requesting that he be "involved to the full extent of his responsibilities as a coach" (344). Anderson petitioned the court to stop Little League Baseball from intimidating or threatening players, parents, coaches, officials, umpires, and other participants in the game. Anderson also requested that the court forbid the league from attempting to induce a boycott of the game. The restraining order was granted. Anderson coached his team from the field in the national tournament.

Eligibility

Bowers v. the National Collegiate Athletic Association et al. (2003) involved a high school football player who had been recruited by several premier educational institutions. Bowers was denied eligibility to play by the NCAA Clearinghouse based on a rule that, in order for athletes to be eligible to play at the collegiate level, they must have satisfactorily completed 13 core courses in secondary schools. A diagnosed learning disability prevented Bowers from taking several of the core courses. Instead, he took special education classes, which did not satisfy the core courses requirement.

Bowers' action was against the NCAA, its clearinghouse, and others for violation of the ADA and the Rehabilitation Act. His request for a preliminary injunction to be declared eligible to play was denied. He then added the universities to the complaint. The district court granted summary judgment for the clearinghouse and, in part, for the NCAA and a number of the individual colleges and universities. Claims were subsequently made against other universities, which claimed Eleventh Amendment and sovereign immunity. The Third Circuit dismissed some of the universities' appeals but also found that Temple University had a valid claim for contribution and remanded the case back to the district court. The protracted litigation in *Bowers*, which lasted over a decade and produced twelve court opinions, demonstrates the complex issues raised, often involving numerous defendants, and highlights a need to provide a system that protects the legal rights of athletes with learning disabilities.

A novel case that even the court admitted "push[ed] the margins of federal disability discrimination laws" was *Shepherd and Hollonbeck v. USOC* (1075). The consolidated case was filed by elite Paralympic athletes who challenged their exclusion from financial and other support from the USOC through their Athlete Support Programs (2006) in violation of the ADA, as well as violation of the Rehabilitation Act. Plaintiffs claimed "it is discriminatory for the USOC to provide them programming, privileges, and financial support inferior to that provided nondisabled athletes under the Olympic program" (1075–1076). The district court ruled against the Paralympic athletes, finding it "irrelevant that the USOC chooses to provide Olympic programming only to Olympic athletes as long as the gateway to that program operates in a nondiscriminatory manner.... Plaintiffs are afforded a participation opportunity defined by their disability, the benefits of which are lesser based not an additional layer of discrimination but by operation of eligibility criteria beyond the reach of the ADA and Rehabilitation Act" (1095). The court effectively concluded that "Paralympic athletes' expectations for the equitable allocation of benefits between Paralympians and Olympians competing on behalf of the United States under the auspices of the USOC is not a matter that courts, through the ADA, may mandate or enforce" (1095). The Court of Appeals ultimately affirmed the decision.

Stadium Accessibility

Stadium accessibility is an area that has experienced much high-profile litigation, generated the most backlash by stadium owners and operators, and required legally complex interpretations about what level of accessibility is required in sport facilities, which to most sport industry professionals still seems like a constantly moving target by the federal government. Guidelines and standards used in meeting the laws related to accessibility include the Americans with Disabilities Act Accessibility Guidelines for Buildings and Facilities and the Uniform Federal Accessibility Standards, as well as the 2010 Standards for Accessible Design. Two distinct architectural standards related to accessibility exist, depending on the year of construction and date of first occupancy of the facility. For "existing" facilities (those constructed prior to 1993), Title III requires the removal of existing architectural barriers in facilities considered places of public accommodation where removal is "readily achievable," meaning without much difficulty or expense. Facilities intended for first occupancy and building alterations started after January 1993 (referred to as "new" facilities) are required to be in full compliance with all accessibility requirements. A comprehensive listing of "stadium accessibility" requirements is published by the Department of Justice (U.S. DOJ, n.d.).

As large-scale renovations to old college stadiums are contemplated, such as adding luxury suites or expanding the existing seating bowl, when do such renovations trigger additional obligations under the ADA (Grady & Andrew, 2008)? There are specific rules set forth in the ADA and related standards for facilities that undergo renovations. Under Title III, renovations (referred to as "alterations" in the ADA) made by places of public accommodation after January 26, 1992, must be "readily accessible to and useable by individuals with disabilities" to "the maximum extent feasible" (42 USC 12183[a]; 28 CFR 36.402). The facility must also ensure that the area of modification or alteration or expansion complies with the ADA Accessibility Guidelines (ADAAG) for new construction (Hymas & Parkinson, 2003). For facilities that fall within the scope of Title II, public entities must ensure that the altered portions of the facility are accessible but have a choice in applying either the ADAAG or the Uniform Federal Accessibility Standards (UFAS) to the altered portion of the facility (28 CFR 35.151). "Alterations" refer to any additions, programmatic changes, or major renovations (not routine painting and decorating). These alterations include exterior approaches, entries, and uses of buildings. "A public entity that undertakes alterations ... must take that opportunity to make the facilities accessible" (*Association for Disabled Americans v. City of Orlando*, 2001, 1319). In addition, the sport facility must ensure that the area of modification or alteration or expansion complies with the ADAAG regulations for new construction (Hymas & Parkinson, 2003).

Determining whether a renovation is significant enough to trigger the accessibility guidelines for new construction was the main issue in a lawsuit brought by the Michigan Paralyzed Veterans of America against the University of Michigan regarding a planned $226 million renovation of Michigan Stadium, commonly known as "the Big House." The initial renovation plans called for increasing the seating capacity to over 108,000, including adding 28 luxury boxes and 3,200 indoor and outdoor club seats, while only increasing the number of accessible seats from 90 to 282. The university classified the extensive and costly project as necessary to "repair" severe crumbling of the concrete base of the bowl, not to change or alter the stadium or its seating. The U.S. Department of Education Office of Civil Rights (OCR), which joined as a coplaintiff in the case, believed the scope of the project constituted a "renovation." If deemed a renovation, this would trigger the updating of various sections of the stadium, including the seating bowl, to meet the one percent of accessible seating requirements for "new" sport facilities (U.S. Department of Justice, n.d.). In defense of its position, the university phrased the issue as follows: "the principal issue in this case presented by OCR is whether a phased concrete project ... constitutes an 'alteration' of the stadium, which would trigger ... the establishment of a percentage of wheelchair places (of all seats) in the alteration, as well as a requirement for dispersion of these places" ("University's Response," 2007). The university's position was that, as a public institution, the university is required to provide accessibility to wheelchair users to the stadium when viewed in its entirety ("University's Response," 2007). The Department of Education disagreed, finding that the changes to the physical structure of the stadium constituted an alteration. The university entered into a settlement with plaintiffs in exchange for dropping the lawsuit in which the university agreed to implement a plan for enhancing access that required the university to provide at least 329 wheelchair-accessible seats when the renovation project concluded, at a cost of about $2 million (Nelson, 2008).

As ADA litigation has evolved and become more nuanced, so has the nature of the claims raised by plaintiffs. In *Feldman v. Pro Football, Inc.*, (2011) plaintiffs included deaf people and people with hearing impairments who regularly attend Washington Redskins football games. Plaintiffs argued that the Washington Redskins and FedEx Field failed to provide them with equal access to the information and announcements broadcast over the stadium's public address system, in violation of the ADA (699). The team and stadium offered assistive listening devices to fans with hearing impairments. However, these devices did not benefit these individual plaintiffs. In 2003, plaintiffs requested the team make all announcements on the Jumbotron available with closed captioning. By 2006, when the case was filed, the only captioning that occurred was an emergency evacuation video. Some aural (audio) content also began to be captioned but not all that plaintiffs had requested. The captioning was placed on LED boards that were not within the line of sight of the Jumbotron, and the stadium music was not captioned. The district court ruled for plaintiffs, finding the Redskins could provide auxiliary access to the music lyrics without undue burden. However, the appellate court declined to require captioning because the ADA does not dictate a particular auxiliary aid must be utilized. Defendants appealed and asked the court to decide "whether the deaf and hearing-impaired game spectators require access to music lyrics in order to fully and equally enjoy defendants' goods, services, privileges, and facilities" (383). The appellate court agreed Title III required the Redskins to provide fans equal access to the aural information broadcast over the public address system, as "part of the football game experience" (384). This case signaled that future courts may be willing to adopt a broader application of the ADA to all aspects of managing stadium accessibility to create an enjoyable fan experience.

Another recent case, challenging the equivalent sight lights provisions of Title III, provides a window into how courts interpret and apply the relevant ADA standards to the context of a stadium. In *Landis v. Washington State Major Baseball Public Facilities District Baseball of Seattle* (2021), the case challenged inadequate sight lines over standing spectators at T-Mobile Park, home of MLB's Seattle Mariners. At issue was Section 4.33.3 of the 1991 ADA Accessibility Guidelines (ADAAG), dealing with comparable lines of sight for wheelchair users to ensure similar views of the action. This standard requires that a person using a wheelchair has comparable sightlines over standing spectators only when two requirements are met. First, a person using a wheelchair must be able to see the playing surface between the heads and over the shoulders of the persons standing in the row immediately in front. Second, a person using a wheelchair must be able to see the playing surface over the heads of the persons standing two rows in front. At the appellate level, this case turned into largely a procedural one, focused on administrative deference to federal agency's interpretations of its own guidelines, known as *Auer* deference. Thus, on the merits, the impact of this case on ADA stadiums case law may be limited, focused primarily on proper application of administrative deference issues and analysis. However, *Landis* is notable as the most recent ADA stadium case to reach appellate review by the Ninth Circuit and further refines ADA guidance.

2010 Revisions to the ADA (Ticketing Regulations)

The most significant changes to the ADA since its inception with application to sport facilities were enacted in 2010. The 2010 revisions provided specific guidance for sport facilities in the areas of ticket sales for wheelchair spaces, ticket prices, ticket transfers, hold and release policies, the secondary ticket market, and the number of accessible and companion seats that must be sold together. According to DOJ guidance, "as of March 15, 2011, venues that sell tickets for assigned seats must implement policies to comply with the new ticketing requirements" (U.S. DOJ, 2011, 1). The updated regulations were necessary because "over the past 20 years, some public and private venues, ticket sellers, and distributors have not provided the same opportunity to purchase tickets for wheelchair-accessible seats and non-accessible seats" (1). These regulations were designed to offer guidance to sport facilities about the terms of ticket sales and seating for wheelchair users. The 2011 regulations apply to selling tickets for assigned seats at events such as concerts, plays, and sporting events (U.S. DOJ, 2011). The requirements are identical for Title II and Title III entities/facilities and apply to tickets sold for single events, as well as tickets sold as season tickets.

Summary

The ADA has five titles, three of which have a direct connection to and impact on sport and physical activity professionals. Title I covers employment discrimination. Title II prohibits state and local governments from discriminating against people with disabilities. Title III, the public accommodations and services area provision, is most relevant to stadium accessibility and impacts how stadiums and other sport facilities provide access to people with disabilities so they may experience the stadium in an equivalent manner as patrons without disabilities.

Discussion Questions

1) How can the legal requirement to provide accessibility become a genuine opportunity for a sport facility to enhance the stadium experience for its current fan base? Explain your ideas in the context of a response to the general manager of a medium size sport facility who always argues to their professional staff that complying with the ADA is just "too costly."
2) As stated in the chapter, the ADA is a remedial statute (meaning its goal is to remedy the effects of past discrimination) and is modeled after the Civil Rights Act of 1964 and the Rehabilitation Act of 1973. Through cases and legal issues discussed, can you see this remedial nature in action? Does the law do enough to "remedy" past discrimination?
3) How do the defenses provided in the ADA legislation give sport organizations sufficient protection to operate without fundamentally altering the nature of sport competition?

Activity

1. Review the 2010 ADA updated ticketing regulations: (https://www.adapacific.org/assets/documents/ticketing_doj.pdf). Design a ticket sales policy for an event at a specific sports venue that complies with the 2010 ADA requirements for ticket sales (capacity, seating levels, accessible seating disbursement, etc.).

References

Americans with Disabilities Act of 1990, 42 USCS § 12021-1213 (2021).

Anderson v. Little League Baseball, 794 F. Supp. 342 (1992).

Association for Disabled Americans v. City of Orlando, 153 F. Supp. 2d 1310 (2001).

Association for Disabled Americans v. Concorde Gaming Corp., 158 F. Supp. 2d 1353 (2001).

Bowers v. National Collegiate Athletic Association et al., 346 F. 3d 402 (2003).

Fay, T., & Wolff, E. (2000). Critical change factors model: Understanding the integration process of sport opportunities for athletes with disabilities into national governing bodies and the United States Olympic Committee. *Proceedings of the 2000 Pre-Olympic Congress: International Congress on Sport Science, Sports Medicine and Physical Education.*

Feldman v. Pro Football, 579 F. Supp 2d 697 (2008); 419 Fed. Appx. 381 (2011).

Grady, J., & Andrew, D. P. S. (2003). Legal implications of the Americans with Disabilities Act on recreation services: Changing guidelines, structures, and attitudes in accommodating guests with disabilities. *Journal of Legal Aspects of Sport, 13,* 231.

Hymas, R. D., & Parkinson, B. R. (2003). Architectural barriers under the ADA: An answer to the judiciary's struggle with technical non-compliance. *California Western Law Review, 39,* 349.

Indep. Living Resources v. Oregon Arena Corp., 1 F. Supp. 2d 1159 (1998).

Individuals with Disabilities Education Act (IDEA), 20 USC 1400–1491 (2021).

Landis v. Wash. State Maj. Baseball Stadium Pub. Facilities Dist. Baseball of Seattle, Inc., 2021 U.S. App. LEXIS 26365 (9th Cir. 2021).

Morisky v. Broward County, 80 F.3d 445 (1996).

McGovern, J. N. (n.d.) Recreation access rights under the ADA. https://www.multibriefs.com/briefs/wpra/recreationaccess.pdf

Mills v. Board of Education for the District of Columbia, 348 F. Supp. 866 (1972).

Nelson, G. (2008, March 9). University reaches settlement in Big House lawsuit. *The Michigan Daily.* https://www.michigandaily.com/uncategorized/university-reaches-settlement-big-house-lawsuit/.

PGA Tour, Inc. v. Martin, 532 U.S. 661 (2001).

Shepherd and Hollonbeck v. United States Olympic Committee, 513 F.3d 1191 (2008).

U.S. Department of the Interior. (n.d.). About the Office of Civil Rights. https://www.doi.gov/pmb/eeo/about-office-civil-rights.

U.S. Department of Justice (n.d.). Accessible stadiums. https://www.ada.gov/stadium.txt.

U.S. Department of Justice (2011). Ticket sales. https://www.adapacific.org/assets/documents/ticketing_doj.pdf.

Recommended Reading

Anderson, P. M. (1999). Spoiling a good walk: Does the ADA change the rules of sport? Virginia. *Journal of Sports & Law, 1,* 44.

Cottingham, M., Gearity, B., Goldsmith, A., & Kim, W. (2015). A comparative analysis of factors influencing spectatorship of disability sport: A qualitative inquiry and next steps. *Journal of Applied Sport Management, 7*(1), 20-39.

Grady, J., & Andrew, D. P. S. (2007). Equality of access to emergency services for people with disabilities under the Americans with Disabilities Act. *Journal of Legal Aspects of Sport, 17*, 1.

Grady, J., & Moorman, A. (2016). The Americans with Disabilities Act 25th anniversary: Assessing progress, opportunities, and challenges. Introduction to the special issue. *Journal of Legal Aspects of Sport, 26*, 1.

Hums, M. A., Schmidt, S. A., Novak, A., & Wolff, E. A. (2016). Universal design: Moving the Americans with Disabilities Act from access to inclusion. *Journal of Legal Aspects of Sport, 26*, 46.

Moorman, A. M (2021). Planning and accessibility issues in venue/event operations. In L. Sharp, A.M. Moorman (Ed.), & C. Claussen, *Sport Law: A managerial approach* (4th edition), pp. 542–580. Routledge.

Race, P. A., & Dornier, S. M. (2009). ADA Amendments Act of 2008: The effect on employers and educators. *Willamette Law Review, 46*, 357.

Schoepfer, K. (2017, December 7). Levi's stadium case illustrates "associational discrimination." *Athletic Business.* https://www.athleticbusiness.com/operations/legal/article/15152118/levis-stadium-case-illustrates-associational-discrimination.

U. S. Department of Justice (2005). A guide to disability rights laws. https://www.ada.gov/cguide.htm#anchor65310.

Part III: The Business of Sport

Laws in the business of sport include contracts, business organizations, labor and antitrust, intellectual property, and risk management. Sales agreements, leases, warranties, employment contracts, physician statements, and releases are addressed in Chapter 7. Chapter 8 separates employment into the two categories: self-employment and working for others. Independent contractor status is explained as are the various models one needs to investigate before selecting a business organization. Chapter 9 reviews Antitrust law and covers four major acts (Sherman, Clayton, Norris LaGuardia, and National Labor Relations) as well as Article One of the U.S. Constitution in the context of professional sport athletes and team owners. The increasing impact of Antitrust law on college sport as a result of several high-profile cases involving the NCAA will also be reviewed.

Trademarks, service marks, patents, copyrights, and right of publicity are the topics of Chapter 10. These types of intellectual property may be licensed, sold, loaned, or given to others. An athlete has property rights in his name, image, and likeness, referred to as the right of publicity. These rights are now being extended to college athletes. Chapter 11 is concerned with risk management, a critical area of importance to sport facility and event managers as well as other sport professionals. The risk management process involves identification, evaluation, and control of loss to personal and real property, clients and students, employees, and the general public. A risk management program includes a systematic and strategic analysis of all aspects of a business The COVID-19 pandemic has brought much focus to the process of risk mitigation at sporting events and other mass public gatherings at sport and entertainment facilities.

7

Contracts and Representation

OBJECTIVES

Upon completing this chapter, you will be able to,

- analyze a contract to determine if there has been an offer, acceptance, and consideration;
- understand the process of forming a contract in sport contexts;
- recognize the significance of various provisions commonly included in contracts in sport; and
- understand the importance of contracts in establishing and maintaining business relationships in sport between teams, athletes, and ticket holders.

Introduction

A contract is a legally enforceable promise or set of promises between two or more people. A breach of the promise or set of promises results in a remedy, usually money, or a demand for performance. Contracts in sport include employment agreements, vendor agreements, sponsorship, naming rights agreements, leases, and warranties. Furthermore, releases and hold-harmless documents may be contracts. An important element of athlete representation is the contract.

Contracts can be express or implied. Express contracts are written or oral agreements, while implied contracts result from conduct. Courts do not distinguish between express and implied contracts. The court's role is to assist the parties in retaining the original or intended agreement. Written agreements are easier to prove than oral agreements. Implied contracts can be difficult to prove. Only adults may enter into contracts; minors are not held to such agreements. The Uniform Commercial Code (UCC) and state and federal regulations require that certain agreements be in writing. Contract law and how courts interpret agreements differ from state to state. Contracts should be drafted and reviewed or updated annually by legal counsel.

Contracts

A contract is an agreement between two or more parties in which at least one party has made a promise, a second party has accepted the first party's promise, and the element of consideration has been determined. The required elements of a contract are:

(1) Offer,

(2) Acceptance, and

(3) Consideration.

Required Elements of a Contract

The offer is a promise or expression of intent. The offer, as made, must be accepted by another person to whom it was made to constitute an acceptance. An offer may be withdrawn prior to acceptance unless the offer contains exact dates or a period of time in which the offer is open. The offer must be accepted within the period of time designated or within a reasonable period of time if no specific period of time has been designated. Consideration is the third component of the contract. While consideration is often the payment of money, consideration can also be an agreement to do something or not to do something. For example, I offer you a position as a head lifeguard for $65,000 for one year. You accept the position and agree to begin work on January 1, 2012. The offer was the offer of the position and the acceptance was your stating that you would take the position. The consideration was the $65,000. Additional terms of the contract that may also serve as consideration could include the fact that you are required to not pursue other full-time employment during the term of the contract (so, in effect, you are agreeing to not do something that you would otherwise legally be entitled to do). This entire process is often referred to as manifestation of mutual assent. When the agreement is put in writing, it becomes a written contract. Oral contracts are also enforceable but establishing the existence of a contract and the terms of the contract becomes more difficult for the party trying to enforce an oral contract.

A contract may also be accepted with conduct that amounts to acceptance of the offer. An example of this would be if I offer you $20 to mow my lawn. When I arrive home from work, I notice that the lawn has been mown. Your conduct of mowing the lawn, rather than directly accepting my offer to mow the lawn, constituted acceptance of the offer. Twenty dollars was the consideration.

Consideration may be required before the accepting party carries out the task or is paid following completion of the work. The timing of the consideration is to be understood by both parties in written and oral agreements. If the accepting party (the offeree) refuses to accept the promise exactly as the promise was made by the offeror and requests that the offer be altered, the original offer is "dead" and cannot be accepted. Changing the original terms is a counteroffer, not an acceptance. When a counteroffer is made, the entire process is repeated with the parties exchanging positions (the original offeror now becomes the offeree; the original offeree becomes the offeror by making a counteroffer).

Agreements with Merchants

When the agreement is with a merchant, contract concepts and negotiation processes can be altered to meet the unique needs of the industry. Agreements with merchants usually fall within the scope of the Uniform Commercial Code (UCC) and are described in the law of sales. The offer may be through a wide range of marketing documents, such as through television, newspaper, and internet advertisements, with the formal bill of sale being the element most resembling the offer. Advertisements and circulars are not offers but invitations to the public to make an offer. Preliminary negotiations are not offers. Advertisements, circulars, and preliminary negotiations become important, however, when the accepting party relies on their content in entering into a deal.

Consideration in a contract with a merchant is the price. If the price is acceptable to the industry, the price can be stated or left open until the date of delivery. The ability to leave the price open is important for orders placed three to six months in advance of delivery in a market where prices shift rapidly.

Shipping and designation of the time of the product's transfer from the manufacturer (or vendor) to the purchaser are unique to sales, including the sale of sport equipment such as would be necessary in starting a fitness center. Depending on the terms of the contract, the purchaser takes ownership at the time the product leaves the manufacturer's (or retailer's) loading dock or at the time the product arrives at the door of the purchaser. The payment of freight, insurance coverage, and obligation to trace lost products are the responsibilities of the owner. Purchasers who have agreed to pay freight on delivery often ignore other potential aspects of ownership until problems occur. Transfer of ownership needs to be clearly understood by all parties at the time of contract formation.

Acceptance of a product often includes inspection prior to acceptance. Although most freight handlers require a signature of acceptance, the signature merely records the location of the product on a particular day. If, after inspection of the product, the purchaser finds that the product does not meet the expectations of the agreement, the purchaser must notify the manufacturer or seller. Alterations in the product, substitutions, and any other changes not acceptable to the purchaser are to be rejected immediately. Contracts should contain the period of time the purchaser has to inspect and accept (or reject) the product and a designation of freight and insurance coverage of a returned product.

Manufacturers and sellers of products should become familiar with the laws regulating commercial paper or negotiable instruments. These transactions (shipping, inspecting, accepting, and paying for merchandise) are governed by the Uniform Commercial Code (UCC). While the contents of negotiable instruments are beyond the scope of this book, manufacturers and sellers need to be aware that what they believe to be a contract may have additional meaning and obligations in sales.

Breach of Contract

A contract is breached when one of the parties fails to live up to one or more of the promises within the agreement or fails to perform the expected service. A failure to perform or to live up to an agreement is not legally excused. When a party breaches a contract, the non-breaching party may take the breaching party to court. The court will determine whether the agreement or contract was valid as drafted. If the agreement is found to be valid, the court has a number of choices, including directing the parties to carry out the agreement or providing a damage award to the person harmed. Specific performance is directing the parties to carry out the agreement. Courts will assess damage awards to the breaching party in order to restore the injured party to the position the injured party held prior to the agreement.

Contracts can specify liquidated damages to be paid in the event of a breach of contract. For example, renovations to a stadium could contain financial penalties for the contractors for every day beyond the promised date of completion of all construction. Also, a financial penalty or a form of punitive damages can be specified in the written agreement. Making the elements of a breach of contract part of the written agreement enables parties and the court to understand the ramifications of a breach. On occasion, it may become impossible to carry out a contract. For example, if the building necessary to carry out the activities is destroyed by fire or a natural disaster, employment and participant contracts may be breached. If the promise or service has not begun, money may easily be returned. When the disaster occurs after the event has commenced, it may be difficult to ascertain the appropriate return and payment of monies.

Reliance

In addition to express and implied contracts, there are times when a party can enforce an agreement because he/she relied on a promise. Although a formal agreement is incomplete, courts will consider the fact that one of the parties relied on the agreement, usually to their detriment. When one party to the agreement has relied on the agreement to their detriment or has been harmed because of reliance on the promises made, the courts will consider the following in examining the agreement: What kind of loss has the party experienced? How can that loss be quantified in dollar figures? A promise is binding as a contract when it has been relied upon by one of the parties and when the reliance has caused substantial harm to that party. A promise is also binding when the promisee can foresee the harm created by a breach of promise. An agreement in which one party has been unjustly enriched as a result of the contract may be examined by the courts to remedy the injustice.

Written Agreements

When the contract is in writing and the parties have agreed to the written statements, the courts will use a standard interpretation of the agreement. The standard is the ordinary meaning of the writing to the parties at the time and place of the initial agreement and under the circumstances of its construction. Contracts may be vague, containing only broad general agreements, or be drafted in greater detail. A court will interpret a vague contract with emphasis on what the parties thought they were agreeing to at the time of the agreement and will interpret a detailed contract using the exact wording of the agreement.

All agreements are to be made in good faith. When the contract's terms involve terminology or practices of a specific industry or business, the court will examine the contract in light of the customs in that industry and in terms of expected performance. Fraud, misrepresentation, and nondisclosure are factors that do not meet the good faith element and can cause a contract to be void. In some situations, the agreement may be so unfair to one of the parties that, even though the parties signed the contract, the court may choose not to enforce the contract.

Merchant forms are forms created by sellers to be used in ordering equipment and arranging for service contracts. If changes are made in the forms, the changes must be in writing and be identified in the first page of the form.

Employment contracts usually list starting and completion dates. Wages, major job duties and responsibilities, and the kind of relationship that will exist between the employer and employee are listed in the agreement. Employee handbook policies and regulations are often incorporated into written and verbal employment agreements. When an employment contract requires a party to have certain licenses or certificates and the person signing the contract does not have the required credentials within a specified period of time, the contract is not binding.

Misunderstandings about employment contracts are frequent in schools and universities, in which contracts must be ratified by a board. For example, when a teacher signs an offered contract that has not been signed by the school district and returns it to the school system, he/she assumes the agreement is complete. For the agreement to be complete, however, the returned contract must be approved or ratified at the next school board meeting. On occasion, the school or university may choose not to ratify the agreement. If this decision is made, the person no longer has a contract or a job. When prospective employees have sued, the courts have maintained that the agreement signed by the employee was not a valid contract until it was ratified by the appropriate board.

Agreements in spas, sport and fitness clubs, team or individual sports (e.g., part-time coaching positions), and any other sport or physical activity environment may establish the employee as an independent contractor. Chapter 8, Legal Entities and Employer-Employee Relationships contains a discussion on the subject of independent contracting and reviews the system for analyzing such a contract.

Minors

A person must be 18 years of age, or the age of majority, to enter into a contract. Contracts cannot be negotiated with minors. If a minor enters into a contract, the minor may ratify or accept the agreement once the minor turns 18. The supposed contract, entered into with a minor, is also voidable by the minor but not by the party contracting with the minor. there is no obligation to ratify a contract entered into as a minor.

Warranties

Warranties were discussed in detail in Chapter 3, Product Liability. The failure of a warranty is the failure of an agreement or contract. Warranty failure requires proof of injury that the warranty was made, that goods did not conform to the warranty, that the injury was the real cause of the failed warranty, and that damage exists. Disclaimers to warranties are also contracts and are treated as contracts by the courts.

Physician Statements as Agreements

A physician's statement to a sport professional is an agreement. It should delineate the role and duties of the person who is making the statement. According to Gallup (1995), "A letter of agreement that sets forth the [team] physician's duties and responsibilities, rather than a formal contract, is sufficient to create contractual obligations and protection" (p. 11).

Leases

According to the Statute of Frauds, leases are required to be in writing. Agencies should consider negotiating written leases with groups that use their facilities. In addition to the routine agreements about duration of the rented space, keys, and opening and closing schedules, the elements of safety, maintenance, and insurance are to be identified. The retaining of a positive image for the facility is to be considered when drafting a lease. For example, will the leasing party supply its own lifeguards on the 1-to-75 participant ratio that satisfies the local health code or will it maintain the leasing agency's more stringent ratio of 1-to-25? The building owner may require that the building safety or security personnel be named as part of the lease agreement.

Releases

A release, waiver, or consent form is a contract when it is signed by an adult and meets the elements (offer, acceptance, and consideration) of a valid contract. A release used with a minor or a release that does not meet elements of a contract is a document used to inform patrons of the risks involved in participation. While such a document should more properly be called a risk information form, many people call it a release. The following checklist is to be used in identifying the elements of a release for adults:

1) Terminology of release, waive, covenant not to sue, forever discharge, etc., is used in the construction of the release.
2) The company, officers, directors, etc. and anyone else who might be sued are listed in the release.
3) The release clearly states what is to be released.
4) Releases can be drafted for negligence only, and some negligence releases with adults may not be upheld by the courts. Courts seldom honor a release that is considered against fair public policy.
5) The release must be for both death and injury.
6) The party executing the release must not only release himself/herself but release any and all parties, including creditors, dependents, etc., that might have a cause of action.
7) The release is to acknowledge the risk of the activity. The risk is described so that an ordinary person understands the chances one takes in participating in the activity. These statements are best created by the professional in physical skills.
8) The signing party must clearly acknowledge an understanding of the risk, a willingness to accept the risk, and proof that no pressure existed to force the person to accept the agreement.

The verbiage of offer, acceptance, and consideration is to be part of the written statement. For example, in consideration of being allowed to participate in rafting, an individual would agree to ("I accept...") all the requirements of the release. The courts will look at the release to determine that it is clear, explicit, and unequivocal.

Influence of Court Decisions

The acceptance of a release as a contract differs from state to state. In *O'Connor v. The United States Fencing Association* (2003), the level of acceptance of such releases in California, Colorado, and New York is compared. Erin O'Connor, a fencer with aspirations for national recognition, severely injured her knee while performing in a competition held in California. O'Connor reported that "she lost her footing when executing this maneuver because the [fencing] strip was not properly anchored" (548). The injury required surgery and extensive rehabilitation. O'Connor's suit alleged a severe injury as a result of a negligently prepared competitive surface.

The United States Fencing Association (USFA) requested summary judgment on the basis of the following waivers. The first one was signed by O'Connor and her mother, as she was a minor at the time. She was an adult at the time she signed the second waiver. The first waiver stated,

> You must sign waiver of liability or membership will be null and void.
>
> Upon entering events sponsored by the USFA and/or its member Division, I agree to abide by the rules of the USFA, as currently published. I understand and appreciate that participation in a sport carries a risk to me of serious injury, including permanent paralysis or death. I voluntarily and knowingly recognize, accept, and assume this risk and release the USFA, its sponsors, event organizers, and officials from any liability. (547)

All participants must read and sign each of the following statements:

> Waiver of liability: Upon entering this tournament under the auspices of the USFA, I agree to abide by the current rules of the USFA. I enter this tournament at my own risk and release the USFA and its sponsors, referees, and tournament organizers from any liability. The undersigned certifies that the birth date of the individual is as stated on the entry form and that the individual is a current competitive member of the USFA. (548)

The USFA reported that it was not responsible for the incident as it did not provide the fencing strips. Illinois Fencing, a third party, was responsible for the placement of the floor strips. When the waiver became the primary point of contention, the state law to be used became significant. The plaintiff was a resident of New York, while the incident occurred in California, and the USFA had its principal place of business in Colorado. "New York had a longstanding policy disfavoring contracts [waivers].... indeed, the New York legislature passed a statute specifically disclaiming the legitimacy of exculpatory contracts in the context of recreational activities" (549).

In New York, waivers are considered against public policy. By contrast, California law favors waivers of liability, and when the waivers meet the requirements of a contract, they are considered valid and are enforced. Colorado law, while not as specific as New York law, appears to be closer to New York than California. Colorado law speaks to the issue of a "contract of adhesion," one in which the person accepting the agreement has no alternative to accomplish his/her goal but to sign the contract. If O'Connor wanted to compete in a competition sponsored by the USFA, she had no other option than to sign the release. If her ambition were to be an Olympic fencer, no other form of fencing competition would prepare her for that goal. "In this case, Ms. O'Connor was not in a position to negotiate a less onerous contract with [the] USFA, as the waiver of liability was a prerequisite to participation in the National Championship Competition" (552).

The court mentioned the release was too broad and failed to identify specific risks that she was waiving. Therefore, "it is difficult to see how a person signing the agreement involved in this case would have been able to foresee the risk of inappropriate or defective flooring. This is not an inherent risk in the sport of fencing (nor a common or expected risk) and it would not be particularly obvious to an inexperienced amateur fencer like O'Connor, who was competing in her first national tournament" (553).

The United States District Court for the Eastern District of New York denied the United States Fencing Association's summary judgment and motion to dismiss. O'Connor was successful.

On occasion, minors participate in activities unaccompanied by their parents or guardians. Usually the agencies sponsoring such activities obtain blanket releases from the parents prior to the trip. When an event on a trip requires the signature of a parent or guardian, the persons chaperoning the young people usually sign.

Johnson et al. v. New River Scenic Whitewater Tours, Inc. (2004) identifies the problems that can occur in such a situation. Fourteen-year-old Lindsey Gillespie traveled to West Virginia with a church-sponsored youth group. The culminating activity was a whitewater rafting trip on the New River. The associate pastor of the church planned and accompanied the group on the trip. On the day of the rafting event, he was asked to sign the following releases on behalf of each minor:

> In consideration for Lindsay Gillespie ("minor") being permitted by NEW River Scenic Whitewater Tours to participate in its recreational events and activities, I agree to this waiver, release, AND indemnification; the undersigned parent and/or guardian of the minor, for themselves and on behalf of the minor, join in the foregoing waiver AND release and stipulates and agrees to save AND hold harmless, indemnify, AND forever DEFEND NEW River Scenic Whitewater Tours from and against any claims, actions, demands, expenses, liabilities (including reasonable attorneys' fees), and negligence made or brought by the minor or by anyone on behalf of the minor, as a result of the minor's participation in NEW River Scenic Whitewater Tours sponsored recreational events and activities and the use of the facilities of NEW River Scenic Whitewater Tours.
>
> I understand this rafting trip, which has been arranged by NEW River Scenic Whitewater Tours, Inc. is a participation sport that involves certain hazards and risks. The risks and hazards involved may include, but are not limited to,

> traveling in rough waters in a rubber raft, having medical emergencies in remote areas, unexpected weather conditions, as well as risks involved in transportation by cars, buses, and other vehicles.
>
> By signing this form, I indicate I am aware of the above dangers and that, furthermore, I release New River Scenic Whitewater Tours, Inc. from liability, claims, debts, and actions of all kinds both now and in the future, as a result of my participation in this trip. It will also serve as a release for my heirs, executors, administrators, and any minor accompanying me (Parents or Guardian must sign for all persons under age 18).
>
> I hereby assume all risks and dangers and all responsibility for any losses and/or damages whether caused in whole or in part by the negligence or other conduct of the owners, agents, officers, or employees of New River Scenic Whitewater Tours, Inc., or by any other person.
>
> I, on behalf of myself, my personal representatives, and my heirs hereby voluntarily agree to release, waive, discharge, hold harmless, defend, and indemnify ... and its owners, agents, officers, and employees from any and all claims. (624–625)

During the trip, Gillespie's raft flipped over and "she was pinned against a rock beneath the water and drowned before she could be rescued" (625). Gillespie's mother, Ms. Johnson, filed suit against the rafting company, claiming the "raft operator's conduct was reckless, intentional, and in contravention of the standard of care imposed by the West Virginia Whitewater Responsibility Act" (627). New River, the rafting company, filed a third-party complaint against the church and the associate pastor, "alleging that the two documents the [pastor] signed operate as indemnity agreements, requiring the third-party defendant to pay any damages for which New River Scenic or Scott [employee] may be held liable" (625). Fortunately for the parties involved, the court could not find language in the release to support a conclusion of third-party indemnification. West Virginia law was the controlling law. The court found for the plaintiff, as the whitewater rafting company had violated the West Virginia Whitewater Responsibilities Act.

Contracts Involving Student-Athletes

As colleges and universities engage in competitive recruiting of top high school athletes, certain promises (either oral or written) are likely to be made by the coaching staff or university representatives. When relied upon by the student-athletes, these promises can form the basis of a lawsuit for breach of contract. *Giuliani v. Duke University* (2010) involved a case focused on representations made during recruiting by the former golf coach at Duke. As a junior in high school, Andrew Giuliani was recruited to play varsity golf at Duke University by then-head varsity golf coach Rod Myers. During the recruitment, Myers told Giuliani that if he came to Duke, he would be given "life-time access" to Duke's "state-of-the-art" training facilities as an alumnus of the Duke Golf Program, as well as "have the opportunity to compete with his teammates to earn spots in the most competitive tournaments against the most talented players in the NCAA" (2). Giuliani alleged that these inducements were material to his decision to enroll at Duke (2). He further alleged that, in exchange for roughly $200,000 in tuition and fees, as well as forgoing numerous opportunities at other colleges and universities, Duke "promised to provide [Mr. Giuliani] with various educational services, lodging, and a right of access to the Athletic Department's varsity program and facilities" (3).

In the spring of 2007, Coach Myers passed away, and Coach O. D. Vincent took over Duke's golf program. Coach Vincent cut the size of the golf squad in half and "announced to the team that he was unilaterally cancelling [Giuliani's] eligibility to participate in the University's Athletics Program immediately and indefinitely," citing several incidents involving Mr. Giuliani that allegedly occurred in early February. Coach Vincent indicated that Mr. Giuliani's suspension would become permanent unless all 12 of his teammates wrote a letter supporting his reinstatement to the team. Giuliani alleged that his teammates generally supported his return to the team but that Coach Vincent instructed players to "back off" and "was instilling new fears in his teammates that their positions on next year's roster were also in jeopardy." Coach Vincent required Giuliani to participate in a qualifier to rejoin the team for the upcoming season even though Coach Vincent had indicated earlier that those who participated as a member of the varsity team in a 2007–2008 tournament, as Giuliani had done, had already qualified for the team (4). The coach then told Giuliani that he could maintain his status on the team without re-qualifying if he agreed to certain "parameters" that were included in a written agreement. Giuliani refused to agree to these conditions. He alleged the coach then retaliated against him and did not inform him that he had been kicked off the golf team.

In July 2008, Giuliani sued Duke and Coach Vincent for breach of contract, breach of the covenant of good faith and fair dealing, and tortious interference with contract. The United States Magistrate Judge for the United States District Court for the Middle District of North Carolina recommended that the defendant's motion be granted because Giuliani failed to establish the elements of a breach of contract claim. Giuliani filed objections to the recommendations. Duke and Coach Vincent then filed a motion to dismiss Giuliani's claim.

In analyzing the breach of contract claim, Giuliani argued, in part, that Coach Myers' oral recruiting statements were contractual terms "binding on Duke by operation of ordinary principles of contract law" (14). He specifically alleged that Coach Myers's recruiting offer included an opportunity to compete, a promise of a right of access to the Athletic Department's programs and facilities while he was a student, and life-time access to Duke's training facilities. Giuliani further alleged that when he enrolled at Duke, the recruiting offer was converted into a binding promise enforceable under long-held principles of North Carolina contract law. Duke and Coach Vincent, meanwhile, argued that Myers had not alleged facts that establish the elements of an oral agreement between Coach Myers (on behalf of Duke) and Mr. Giuliani. They pointed to the fact that in his complaint, Giuliani identified four documents rather than the oral communications between Coach Myers and himself as the specific provisions of the contract at issue. The four documents were the Duke University Student-Athlete handbook, the Duke University Athletic Department Policy Manual, the Duke University Student Bulletin, and the NCAA Division I Manual.

The court stated that a valid contract is formed when two parties manifest an intent to be bound. "A contract does not exist if 'one party simply believes that a contract exists, but there is no meeting of the minds'" (17). In addition, the terms of the contract must be "definite and certain or capable of being made so" such that the parties "assent to the same things, in the same sense" (17). In analyzing his breach of contract claim, the court found that Coach Myers's oral statements made during recruiting did not constitute a valid contract because the statements did not show a meeting of the minds, nor did they establish definite and certain terms (17). Rather than manifesting an intent to be bound, Coach Myers's statements to Mr. Giuliani described the potential benefits available if Mr. Giuliani enrolled at Duke, earned a spot on the golf team, and maintained that spot on the team (17–18). The court found that the statements were, at best, ambiguous as to the circumstances under which Mr. Giuliani would acquire any rights. In the court's view, the statement regarding inclusion in tournaments was framed as an "opportunity to ... earn spots" to compete, and the statement regarding life-time access was conditioned on Mr. Giuliani being an "alumnus of the Duke Golf Program' (18). These statements are not certain and definite as to what constitutes an "opportunity" or how one may become an "alumnus of the Duke Golf Program" (18). Therefore, the court held that the alleged representations of Coach Myers did not create an enforceable contract (20).

On Giuliani's claims that the handbooks and policy manuals established a valid contract, the court found that "although plaintiff has alleged the statements of Coach Myers and the existence of the handbooks, plaintiff has not produced or alleged a contract specifically incorporating Duke's handbooks and policy manuals into a contract." Thus, his claim for breach of contract was denied.

More recent interpretations of contracts involving student-athletes have focused on the use of image and likeness in video games. One argument, under contract law, is that requiring amateur student-athletes to waive certain rights, specifically their right of publicity, in order to be eligible to compete under NCAA rules is unconscionable. For a detailed discussion of the unconscionability arguments and how consent theory could cure some of these issues for member institutions and the NCAA, consider Baker, Grady, and Rappole (2012). Significant cases, including *Keller v. NCAA* (2010), are discussed in further detail in Chapter 10, Intellectual Property.

Appearance Contracts

Litigation related to athlete appearance contracts for promotional purposes has become more frequent as celebrity athletes build their own unique commercial brands. *FrontLine Promotions & Mktg., Inc. v. Mayweather Promotions, LLC* (2009) involved a promotional appearance by Floyd Mayweather during the 2008 NBA All Star Weekend in New Orleans. In 2008, Insights and Front-line entered into a partnership agreement to produce two boxing events in New Orleans. They each agreed to procure the attendance of certain celebrities and musicians to appear at the events. Front-line agreed to secure Mayweather to host a Sunday night event. A representative of Front-line purporting to be Mayweather's talent representative signed an agreement for Mayweather to appear at the NBA All Star Weekend in exchange for a $25,000 fee, half of which was to be paid within 24 hours of executing the contract. At the top of the agreement was the heading "Mayweather Promotions, LLC." The "talent" is identified as "Floyd Mayweather of Mayweather Promotions, LLC." The final paragraph of the supposed contract stated, "This agreement is confidential between the promoter named Front-line Promotions and the talent named Floyd 'Money Mayweather' of Mayweather Promotions, LLC." A second page of the fully executed version of the agreement contains signature lines for "Promoter" and for "talent Representative." Mayweather ultimately did not appear at the event.

Plaintiffs subsequently filed a lawsuit seeking damages for financial loss and reputational injury due to defendants' alleged breach of the agreement, as well as consequential damages for defendants' bad faith failure to perform under the agreement. Defendants filed a motion seeking dismissal of all claims against Mr. Mayweather and dismissal of all claims by Insights. The defendants argued that Mayweather was not a party to the contract and therefore could not be liable for any breach of that contract. The plaintiffs contended, however, that Mayweather was a proper defendant for the following three reasons: Robinson-White was his agent and she bound him to appear at the event when she signed the contract on his behalf; that Mayweather's obligation to appear was strictly personal, under the Louisiana civil code, and that he could not escape personal liability; and, that the contract was vague and ambiguous as to the identity of the obligor and that it should, therefore, be construed against the drafter Mayweather Promotions. Under 12 Louisiana Civil Code article 1766:

> An obligation is strictly personal when its performance can be enforced only by the obligee, or only against the obligor.
>
> When the performance requires the special skill or qualification of the obligor, the obligation is presumed to be strictly personal on the part of the obligor. All obligations to perform personal services are presumed to be strictly personal on the part of the obligor.

> When the performance is intended for the benefit of the obligee exclusively, the obligation is strictly personal on the part of that obligee.

The district court ruled since "[a] party cannot breach a contract to which it is not a party," determining whether Mayweather was indeed a party to the contract was key and found that "in construing contracts, it is well established that ... the contract itself is the best evidence of the relationship existing between the parties and the true intention of the parties is to be sought and determined by the language of the contract when the wording is clear" (9). The court found that the agreement identified two parties to the contract: 1) Front-line, as promoter; and 2) "Floyd 'Money Mayweather' of Mayweather Promotions, LLC" as talent. This plain text suggests that this agreement intended to make Mr. Mayweather a party. Defendants still emphasized that Mr. Mayweather never signed the agreement, as it was initialed and signed instead by Robinson-White as his "talent Representative." She testified about signing similar agreements as talent representative of Mr. Mayweather, which were part of her job duties for Mayweather Promotions.

The plantiffs argued that since Robinson-White was acting as Mayweather's agent when she signed the agreement, Mayweather was bound to perform the obligations that Robinson-White, acting on his behalf, agreed he would perform. There was also conflicting testimony about whether Robinson-White was indeed his agent with authority to book appearances on his behalf. Mayweather testified that Robinson-White lacked the "ability to sign appearance agreements" on his behalf, notwithstanding the facts in this case. Because of the conflicting testimony about whether Robinson-White was indeed acting as Mayweather's agent, the district court denied Mayweather's claims and found for plaintiffs.

Contracts Involving Tickets

As personal seat licenses become the norm and season ticket holders gain ownership rights to seats and season tickets at professional and college sporting events, litigation involving tickets becomes inevitable. In *Brotherson v. Professional Basketball Club, LLC* (2009), former season-ticket holders of the Seattle Supersonics sued after the team moved to Oklahoma City. Plaintiffs' claims for breach of contract involved the "Emerald Club Contract." The contract that the team ownership group, Professional Basketball Club (PBC), offered to virtually all Sonics 2007 season-ticket holders, let them renew their tickets for the 2008 season at 2007 season prices, and, notably, gave them the option to renew at the same price for the 2009 and 2010 seasons. The contracts were allegedly formed in the spring of 2007, although there was a high probability the team would leave Washington. As noted by the court, the Emerald Club was created out of "concern that uncertainty over the team's future would hurt ticket sales" (1276).

In the meantime, PBC described the Emerald Club in several publications, most notably in a brochure mailed to 2007 season-ticket holders. The brochure provided details of an "unprecedented offer" to Sonics season-ticket holders and an "unprecedented commitment" to provide "three-year cost certainty through the 2009–10 season" (1280). While the brochure did include a message about uncertainty in reaching an agreement with the state and local government to finance a new arena, "nowhere in the Brochure did PBC suggest that the Sonics might play home games at a location other than Key Arena before the 2011 season" (1281). The court found that "PBC deliberately declined to acknowledge the possibility of relocation before 2010 in the Emerald Club Brochure or any other communication sent to potential Emerald Club members" (1281). Furthermore, "whatever uncertainty surrounded the team, PBC marketed the Emerald Club to 'move forward with business models and business practices to promote and sell the team in a go-forward basis in Seattle.' Even when the chairman of Professional Basketball Club, the owners of the Seattle Supersonics, learned that the NBA itself was concerned with PBC's 'messaging relative to renewals,' PBC made no change to the Emerald Club terms" (1281).

In analyzing the breach of contract claims, the court found the existence of a contract. On the question of whether the parties mutually assented to a contract, the court found that the brochure sent by PBC and season-ticket holders had "all the hallmarks of an offer," including 1) containing the word "offer," 2) stating a fixed price and material terms, and 3) giving the option to purchase future tickets at a set price (1284). PBC instead claimed that the brochure was not an offer, relying upon cases holding that certain advertisements are not offers. The court found PBC's argument that the brochure was not an offer "mystifying," ruling that "the brochure itself was an explicit promise that it could provide seats for all renewing season ticket holders" (1284). The court went on to find that "having received the Emerald Club offer, there is no dispute that each Plaintiff accepted PBC's offer by paying the price stated in accordance with the Brochure's instructions. Moreover, no one disputes that Plaintiffs' payments were adequate consideration for the Emerald Club Contract" (1284).

The court then considered whether PBC breached the contract as a matter of law by refusing to honor the option to renew tickets for 2009 and would breach the contract again as a matter of law by not honoring the option for the 2010 season. According to the court, "nowhere in the Emerald Club Contract does PBC mention that the tickets it was selling are revocable, much less revocable at will. Given this omission, PBC finds no support for the notion that the revocable nature of the tickets is disclosed within the four corners of the Contract. Any reasonable person entering the Emerald Club Contract would have understood that the tickets were licenses, in the sense that he or she would have understood that the tickets did not create a property interest in a seat or access to Key Arena" (1286–1287). The court opined, "if a reasonable consumer understood that he or she was buying nothing other than the right to be subject to the unfettered whim of PBC, the court queries why anyone would have entered the Emerald Club Contract" (1287). Thus, the court found that PBC had no absolute right to revoke tickets it sold to Emerald Club members, and thus could not avoid damages on that basis (1285). Furthermore, the court determined that uncertainty over PBC's future in Seattle or its decision to move to Oklahoma City created a condition precedent that would relieve PBC of its contractual obligations to Emerald Club season-ticket holders (1289).

In analyzing the option to purchase tickets for the 2009 season and 2010 season, the court was unable to determine as a matter of law whether plaintiffs had exercised their option in a timely manner. If it was found that PBC breached the Emerald Club option, then plaintiffs had the right to prove expectation damages. Plaintiffs also sought specific performance of the option to purchase 2010 season tickets. Specific performance would compel the sale of the tickets under the agreed-upon terms. They asked the court to order PBC to sell tickets to them on the terms of the option. The court found they were not entitled to specific performance and dismissed these claims. "Even if specific performance were available as a matter of law, the court would not exercise its equitable power to award Plaintiffs tickets that they do not want" (1294).

Other pending cases involving rights owed to season-ticket holders include a suit by the Rosen family against the University of South Carolina (Shain, 2011). The Rosen family claimed they were promised free parking near the football stadium if they became lifetime Silver Spur members of the Gamecock Club, the university's booster organization. The family said they were told when they agreed to become lifetime members in 1987 that they would not have to pay for parking. But the university, as part of a wide-ranging effort to raise more money to improve facilities, started charging for parking around the stadium. Richland County, South Carolina Judge Joseph Strickland dismissed the Rosens' case in 2009 after ruling that the University of South Carolina did not breach the written contract because it did not promise that parking would be free. The Rosen family appealed. A three-judge panel of the South Carolina Court of Appeals agreed with the Rosens.

Another lawsuit was filed by a fan who sued her sister over their family's season tickets for Duke basketball (Brooks, 2011). Katina Dorton, the daughter of a longtime Duke basketball season-ticket holder, is seeking unspecified damages and asking a North Carolina superior court to invalidate the "fraudulent transfer" of a pair of Duke basketball season tickets to her sister, Sophia, and her sister's husband. Dorton's father, a Duke graduate and dentist who treated athletes and coaches, paid his dues over the years and earned season tickets by contributing to the Iron Dukes booster club. When Sophia Caudle's then-fiancé Gordon transferred the tickets into his name in July 2008, Mr. Dorton was ill and unable to act for himself and eventually died in 2010. The lawsuit alleged Caudle was not a member of the Dorton family at the time of the transfer and therefore had no authority to repossess the season tickets. In other words, the sum and substance of the family's legal argument was, "he was just my sister's fiancé, your Honor!"

A more recent ticketing case implicating contract law involves ticket resale policies, especially on the secondary market. In *Smile for Kids, Inc. v. Madison Square Garden Co.* (2016), this case was a legal challenge brought by ticket brokers that sued Madison Square Garden (MSG) over MSG's ticketing policy to restrict the number of season tickets someone could buy or hold for Knicks or Rangers games. The contract law case challenged application and reference to a New York state statute that restricts sports and entertainment venues from interfering with ticket resale. The court found that the statute refers to tickets as licenses subject to operator's terms and does not govern season tickets and decided that MSG could not cancel plaintiffs' season ticket renewals but could add additional terms and conditions.

Employment Contracts

Bires v. Waltom, LLC involved a complaint between an auto-racing team that runs a rookie development program and NASCAR Nationwide Series driver Kelly Bires. In 2005, Bires signed an agreement that prohibited him from negotiating for a driving position on another team for a period of forty-five days. He claimed that he had no choice but to sign the agreement based on the surrounding circumstances and as a result, forfeited opportunities to secure other employment. Later that month, Bires received a call from the team's owner that purportedly included a formal offer to drive for the team during the following season. Bires claimed that subsequent phone conversations solidified the terms of that offer and all together resulted in an oral contract to drive for the racing team in 2006, in which he would be paid a salary, bonuses, and a percentage of race winnings. According to Bires, the team never indicated that its promises would not be binding until a written agreement was signed or that he would have to make future royalties' payments.

Bires later claimed he was subsequently forced to enter into a written agreement with substantially different contract terms. Specifically, he challenged enforceability of a royalty clause that required the driver to pay the team 25% of his gross race earnings for 10 years. The court held that the royalty provision was not a wage assignment covered by Illinois law regarding wage and hour. In addition, the court found paying the driver for less than one year of employment constituted insufficient consideration by the team to support their claim to the new royalty clause. On adequacy of consideration, the court stated, "Any act or promise that benefits one party or disadvantages the other is sufficient consideration to support the formation of a contract," noting further "the agreement makes these purported payment obligations entirely optional to Waltom to perform or not perform" (1028). Bires argued Waltom's contract promises were illusory and that, because it could terminate the contract at its sole discretion, the agreement lacked mutuality (1028).

Athlete Representation

In general, athlete representation is similar to representation in the business world in that it requires the representative to understand the person or project and the environment in which the person or project exists. That foundation is in contract, accounting, labor, and intellectual property law. What is complicated about athlete representation is the understanding of the business of sport. It involves a thorough knowledge of the sport, including the business of a particular sport (i.e., it is essential to understand the rules of the National Collegiate Athletic Association [NCAA]). The agent is expected to understand the particular sport's collective bargaining agreement and bylaws, draft system and other means of gaining entry to a team, salary caps, and value of a particular playing position. The athlete's situation in terms of rules related to interscholastic and intercollegiate governance must be understood. A sincere respect for the athlete is a must.

Representation of athletes in organized team sports and in individual sports varies considerably. In organized team sports, the athlete is usually selected through a draft and is governed by league rules; the collective bargaining agreement and bylaws govern the job. The representative's first task is to explain the collective bargaining agreement and contract to the athlete. At the same time the agent negotiates all additional terms (beyond the collective bargaining agreement) that will meet the needs of the athlete. This combination of accepting the collective bargaining agreement and negotiating contractual terms is unlike any other type of employment. Employees are either members of a union and work under the union's collective bargaining agreement or are management and bargain for the terms of their individual contracts. Team sport athletes have both. Representation of the team sport athlete may be full support, partial support, or only contractual assistance. In addition to the contract, the full-term support includes obtaining a portfolio of sponsorship and speaking engagements, intellectual property, financial and investment advice (including trusts and wills), real estate guidance, and any support agreed to in the representative/athlete agreement. Partial support usually includes contract, sponsorship, and intellectual property representation. Contract negotiation is the third area.

Individual sport representation is different in that one of the representative's biggest tasks is the identification, selection, and obtaining of the athlete's acceptance to a range of tournaments or events. These tournaments or events must meet the athlete's goals and schedule yet bring the greatest revenue and future opportunities possible. The logistics of travel, car rentals, applications, and hotels are among the basic tasks. Training, practice, equipment maintenance, and schedules at home and in tournaments are arranged. Player contracts are usually agreements for individual performance and events.

Athlete representatives or agents are required to have state licenses and league certifications. They are also expected to have experience in contract negotiations and leads for endorsements. They will help the athlete obtain equipment for the athlete's use, equipment and product endorsements, personal appearances (i.e., speeches, autograph sessions), select volunteer and charitable opportunities, summer camp presentations, trading cards, and other opportunities. Financial guidance is extremely important as an athlete usually makes considerable money in a very short period of time. A representative's skill in guiding the athlete in understanding how that large sum of money can enable the athlete to be financially secure for life is paramount.

The scandals that have plagued professional athletes created a need for licensing of sport agents. Many states have statutes requiring agents to be licensed and post a substantial security bond. Often, this legislation has been in response to specific state problems. As the number of states that licensed agents grew, confusion existed among agents as to the merits of seeking licenses in multiple states. There was a cry for reciprocity across state lines, which is the recognition of an agent's license in one state by another state. This prompted the creation of the Uniform Athlete Agents Act (UAAA). The UAAA has been passed in 40 states, the District of Columbia, and the U.S. Virgin Islands. In most cases, the UAAA requires an athlete agent to register with a state authority, typically the Secretary of State, in order to act as an athlete agent in that state. During the registration process, an athlete agent must provide important background information, both professional and criminal in nature. It also provides reciprocity of registration across state lines for an agent certified in a neighboring state. Penalties and remedies for violation of components of the act are provided.

Cases in Representation

Cases that describe two very typical situations in the representation of athletes include the provision of cars and other impermissible benefits to NCAA athletes (*Black, et al. National Football League Players Association, Inc.*, 2000) and the problems that athletes might encounter with recommended financial advisors (*Clark v. Weisberg, et al.*, 1999). The National Football League Players Association (NFLPA) brought disciplinary proceedings against Black for allegedly providing NCAA athletes with cars, stocks, and bribed coaches. Black brought suit against the NFLPA, describing the disciplinary proceedings as unlawful and affecting his livelihood. Specifically, his complaint was an antitrust conspiracy. The NFLPA then revoked Black's contract advisor certificate for three years. Black filed an amended complaint, removing the antitrust complaint and adding new claims.

The United States District Court for the District of Columbia ruled that the plaintiff could gather additional evidence through discovery on the discrimination claims, but that the defendant was entitled to judgment as a matter of law on the claims of tortuous interference and violation of the Federal Arbitration Act (2). In 2001, William (Tank) Black was sentenced to nearly seven years in prison followed by three years' probation and a fine of $15,000 for money laundering charges (Suhr, 2001). A similar legal case, involving agent contracts, yet much less high profile than the protracted legal saga involving Tank Black was *United States v. Person* (2019), where defendants had agreements to send college players to specific "service providers" when they decided to go to the pro leagues.

A case involving former Duke basketball phenom Zion Williamson also involved the contractual claims of a former marketing agent who claimed to have an agreement to exclusively represent Williamson once he went pro. North Carolina courts had already begun to consider the original claims of a contract, made by the marketing agent Gina Ford and Prime Sports Marketing, as well as debate the counter arguments made by Williamson's team in analyzing whether he could legally agree to this type of marketing and legal representation at the time he did. The most recent development in the case was a 2021 decision by a North Carolina judge, who determined the supposed agreement violated North Carolina law over requirements found in the state's Uniform Athlete Agent's Act, designed to protect student athletes from unscrupulous agents; Williamson was a student when he signed the supposed agreement (Gordon, 2021).

Summary

Contracts are legally enforceable agreements containing a promise (or set of promises) accepted by another (through signature, verbal agreement, or conduct) for consideration. Consideration can be either a promise to do something, a promise not to do something, or money. Sales agreements, leases, warranties, employment contracts, and releases may be contracts. Contracts can be express or implied. Express contracts are facilitated either verbally or in writing. Implied contracts are agreements accepted as a result of the conduct of the accepting party.

Discussion Questions

- How can contract law be used to protect the rights of a range of sport businesses? Under what circumstances would a lawsuit for breach of contract become necessary?
- Given the evolution of the internet and digital communications, how can professional athletes protect their commercial interests using contract law?

Activities

1. Retrieve the coaching contracts of the head coach in any sport at your college or university, if publicly available. Determine what provisions of the contract are included and analyze whether the specific provision benefits the coach or the school, or both.
2. Do an internet search for a personal appearance contract. Review the terms of the agreement. Now, consider what terms would be necessary for a similar appearance contract between a professional athlete and a sponsor, such as a beverage company.

References

Bires v. Waltom, 662 F. Supp. 2d 1019 (2009).

Black et al. v. National Football league Players Association, 87 F. Supp. 2d 1 (2000).

Brooks, M. (2011, July 15). Duke basketball family lawsuit: Fan sues sister, school over Blue Devils season tickets. *Washington Post*. http://www.washingtonpost.com/blogs/early-lead/post/

duke-fan-files-lawsuit-against-family-members-university-over-bluedevils-basketball-tickets/2011/07/15/giQAsbZaGi_blog.html

Brotherson v. Professional Basketball Club, l.l.C, 604 F. Supp. 2d 1276 (2009).

Front-line Promotions & Marketing Inc. and Insights Marketing & Promotions, Inc. v. Mayweather Promotions, LLC and Floyd Mayweather, Jr., 2009 U.S. Dist. lExiS 27136 (2009).

Gallup, E. M. (1995). *Law and the team physician.* Human Kinetics.

Gordon, M. (2021, January 20). Judge voids contract Zion's contract with Florida firm, crippling $100m lawsuit against player. *Charlotte Observer.* https://www.charlotteobserver.com/sports/college/article248640865.html.

Guliani v. Duke University, 2010 U.S. Dist. lExiS 32691 (2010).

Johnson et al. v. New River Scenic Whitewater Tours, Inc. et al., 313 F. Supp. 2d 621 (2004).

Keller et al. v. Electronic Arts, Inc.; National Collegiate Athletic Association; and Collegiate Licensing Company, 2010 U.S. Dist. LEXIS 10719; consolidated as in re NCAA Student-Athlete Name & likeness licensing litigation, 2010 U.S. Dist. LEXIS 139724.

National Conference of Commissioners on Uniform State Laws (2000). Uniform Athlete Agents Act (2000). https%3A%2F%2Fwww.uniformlaws.org%2FHigherLogic%2FSystem%2FDownloadDocumentFile.ashx%3FDocumentFileKey%3Dc2695d74-b116-667e-e58b-9473df056d21%26forceDialog%3D0%23%3A~%3Atext%3DThe%2520act%2520specifics%2520terms%2520which%2Cmust%2520be%2520retained%2520by%2520the&clen=351056&pdffilename=UAAA_FinalAct_2000.pdf

O'Connor v. the United States Fencing Association, 260 F. Supp. 2d 545 (2003).

Ruxin, R. M. (2010). *An athlete's guide to agents* (5th ed.). Jones & Bartlett.

Shain, A. (2011, July 7). Court: Gamecock fan family can continue fight for free parking. *The State.* https://account.thestate.com/paywall/subscriber-only?resume=18148517&intcid-ab_archive

Shropshire, K. C., & Davis, T. (2008). The business of sports agents (2nd ed.). University of Pennsylvania.

Smile for Kids, Inc. v. Madison Square Garden Co., 32 N.Y.S.3d 866 (2016).

Suhr, J. (2001, June 14). Tank Black jailed 6+ years. *CBC News.* http://www.cbc.ca/sports/story/2001/06/14/black010614.html

United States v. Person, 373 F. Supp. 3d 452 (2019).

Recommended Reading

Baker, T. A., Grady, J., & Rappole, J. M. (2012). Consent theory as a possible cure for unconscionable terms in student-athlete contracts. *Marquette Sports Law Review, 22.*

Carfagna, P. A. (2018). *Representing the professional athlete* (3rd edition). West Academic. https://faculty.westacademic.com/Book/Detail?id=245967.

Deubert, C. (2011). What's A "Clean" Agent to Do? The Case for a Cause of Action Against a Player's Association. *Villanova Sports & Entertainment. Law Journal, 18,* 1.

Sahl, J. P. (2020). The changing landscape of intercollegiate athletics—The need to revisit the NCAA's "no agent" rule. *Santa Clara Law Review, 61,* 1.

Recommended Reading

8

Legal Entities and Employer-Employee Relationships

OBJECTIVES

Upon completing this chapter, you will,

- describe a number of ways to organize a business;
- compare the status of an independent contractor with a regular employee;
- explain the role of vicarious liability; and
- recognize the role of the Fourteenth Amendment of the United States Constitution, Equal Protection Clause, procedural due process, in terminating an employee.

Introduction

Sport managers have responsibilities that require an understanding of a wide range of business-related laws. Independent contractors play a significant role in sport and physical activity. Coaches can be considered independent contractors. This chapter begins with a description of business organizations, including sole proprietorships, partnerships, "C" and "S" corporations, and limited liability companies and partnerships. Self-employment or working for others becomes a legal concern as the reader compares regular and leased employees with independent contractors. Vicarious liability is the liability of administrators for the torts of their employees. Procedural due process is the major legal theory in employment, evaluation, and termination of personnel.

Business Organizations

A person starting his/her own business has a number of decisions to make in selecting the organization most appropriate to his/her needs. Businesses are organized under state law. Liability and tax consequences play a primary role in the decision-making process.

Sole Proprietorship

A sole proprietorship is a business owned and operated by one person. The business is started by opening a bank account and obtaining requisite licenses and permits. The sole proprietor is liable for the debts of the business and pays them from the business or personal resources. When the business needs credit or the ability to obtain a loan, a sole proprietor uses his/her personal credit to obtain resources. If the business hires employees, the owner is personally liable for their wages and for federal and state employment taxes. The sole proprietor's personal assets will be used to satisfy debts the business encounters, including a judgment following litigation. Income from the business—after deductions for money spent to make the income—is taxed at the sole proprietor's individual income tax level. If the business goes bankrupt, the owner covers the bills. If the owner cannot cover the bills, the owner goes bankrupt. Should the owner die or not be able to work, the business may fail.

The advantages of a sole proprietorship are its informality and ease of establishment. Decisions can be made in a short period of time, and the individual is not required to share profits. Profits and losses are part of the owner's personal income tax statement. Sole proprietorships are popular with people starting a business. Often, persons who start as sole proprietors move to a more sophisticated organization as the business grows.

Partnership

The Uniform Partnership Act (UPA) defines partners as two or more co-owners in a business for profit. A written agreement is recommended but not required. Partners need to identify the financial, material, and managerial contributions of each partner. The law considers all partners equal. If partner contributions are not equal, the differences must be identified in writing. The death of a partner is a problem to be addressed in the agreement. Will the partnership fold, with the assets going to the next of kin of the deceased partner, or will the partnership go to the living partner with no assets to the deceased partner's family and/or next of kin? Often, insurance is used to offset the damage that might occur to the business and/or the partner's next of kin at the time of death.

Advantages of a partnership are ease of creation, direct award of profits, more capital than the sole proprietorship, freedom from direct government control, and flexibility in decision-making. If people work together effectively, partnerships can provide a business with little bureaucracy. The disadvantages of a partnership are that one partner can be liable for the expenses of both partners, that one partner can speak and/or obtain credit or loans for both partners without the other partner's knowledge, and that capital is difficult to obtain.

Corporation

A corporation is a business formed by the authority of state government through the filing of articles of incorporation with the secretary of state. In addition to obtaining a charter from the state, a corporation must hold annual meetings and adhere to government regulations. Regular "C" and subchapter "S" are the two basic types of corporations. A corporation is a legal entity that is separate and distinct from the shareholders who own the corporation. A corporation can be sued and can sue. It has the same rights and privileges as a person. Shareholders indirectly control corporation activities by electing a board of directors, which in turn elects the officers responsible for the day-to-day operations of the business. All assets are owned by the corporation, not by the shareholders. Owners of the corporation are stockholders and can be held liable only for the extent of their investment in the corporation. The legal ramifications are that shareholders in a corporation can lose only the investment they have in the corporation; their personal assets cannot be attached for corporate debts unless the court can find that the corporation was a sham. Stocks and bonds issued by the corporation must satisfy the federal Securities Act of 1933, the Securities and Exchange Act of 1934, and the policies of the Securities and Exchange Commission (SEC). A corporation pays taxes at a predetermined level. Shareholder dividends are taxed at the shareholder's personal tax rate. Shareholder profits are taxed twice, at the corporation level and at the personal income level.

Subchapter "S" Corporation

A subchapter "S" corporation has all of the characteristics of a corporation. The difference is that profits and losses pass through to the shareholders—as they do in the sole proprietorship and partnership—and become a part of each shareholder's individual taxable income. Thus, shareholders pay taxes once on the profits of the corporation. Limitations of a subchapter "S" corporation are that shareholders are limited to 75 shareholders. Shareholders have only one class of stock and must be United States citizens; corporate status has to be attained as well. The advantages of a subchapter "S" corporation are the limited liability of stockholders to their investment, the status as a legal entity, and the ease of ownership and transfer. In addition, the organization is not affected by the death of participants, and it has a base for securing capital from investors. The disadvantages are governmental control, laws, charter activities, and expenses associated with the forming of a corporation.

Limited Liability Company (LLC)

A limited liability company (LLC) is an organization that is accepted in most states and treated as a partnership for federal (not state) income tax purposes. The LLC has the limited liability of a corporation. It is formed by two or more persons who file articles of organization with the secretary of state. Business elements, including management systems, are in the agreement. The number of partners is unlimited, which permits other corporations and partnerships to become shareholders. The LLC operating agreement resembles a partnership agreement. A limited liability company is not as complex as a subchapter "S" corporation. An advantage is that owners have the liability of a corporation, as it is a separate entity. Owners are called members, not partners, and no formal minutes or resolutions are required. Disadvantages are that an LLC is dissolved when members die or file for bankruptcy, whereas corporations go on forever.

Limited Liability Partnership (LLP)

Limited liability partnerships (LLPs) are often public service partnerships that retain partnership tax benefits while obtaining corporate liability benefits. Again, similar to the information noted above concerning the LLC, each state is unique in its requirements for an LLP. Therefore, the regulations for an LLP differ from state to state.

Not-for-Profit Corporation

A not-for-profit corporation is a corporation that does not distribute income to its members, directors, or officers. It is organized for charitable, benevolent, educational, religious, social, athletic, scientific, or trade association purposes. The basic organization is the same as any other corporation; it is only the purpose of the organization that differs. While members of the board are not paid, the organization has a staff that is paid.

Employer-Employee Relationships

Employment relationships are regular employee (working for another); independent contractor; self-employed; or leased employee (a combination of regular employee and independent contractor). The leased employee is a regular employee of a business that serves as an independent contractor on the work site. Labor unions are addressed in Chapter 9, Antitrust and Labor Law. The major differences in these relationships are in the various parties' responsibilities for legal, financial, and social obligations.

Regular Employees

A regular employee works directly for the employer. The worker answers to the employer or to a person in the employer's chain of command. In a regular employment relationship, the employer has the right to control the employee and to direct the employee's work. How and what the work will be is controlled by the employer. Employers are responsible for the actions of their employees. In regular employment, the employer has an equitable hiring process and safe working environment, evaluates only the tasks of the job, and provides a due process hearing—if appropriate—prior to termination. Employers have financial responsibilities to the employee for wages, unemployment insurance, worker's compensation, benefits, and other negotiated services. Employers also provide supplies and equipment. The employer is legally responsible for all work-related torts committed by the employee. The relationship in the law is often referred to as master/servant.

Independent Contractors

In an independent contractor relationship, the employer has a contract right to the completed task or project. The employer has no control over selection, training, or the means used by personnel to accomplish the tasks. Independent contractors are usually paid in lump sums. The employer is not liable for the torts of independent contractors or their employees. An employer becomes liable for independent contractors and their employees only if the work environment is hazardous or the independent contractor's status is violated as explained in the test of independent contractor status below.

Independent contractors are responsible for their own actions and those of their employees. Independent contractors pay wages, federal and state taxes, and insurance. They are liable for their own injuries. Even though an employer has created an independent contractor relationship through a written agreement, the employer can—by accident—assume control sufficient to end the status. To avoid this situation, the parties should identify, in writing, the party responsible for worker's compensation, withholding taxes, adhering to civil rights legislation (including age, race, and sex discrimination), wage and labor laws, and employee safety. Employers may be personally liable for selecting a contractor with a history of carelessness, permitting a hazardous situation to exist, failing to perform required legal duties, and allowing persons to engage in inherently dangerous work.

When an employer chooses to use an independent contractor, the employer must be confident that the independent contractor understands his/her status. Asking a person to sign an independent contractor agreement may be insufficient. If challenged, the employer must prove that the independent contract was not signed under duress, federal and state taxes were paid, and legal liability was recognized. An employer with both regular employees and independent contractors must treat each according to their status. An independent contractor supplies his/her own materials and equipment; the business supplies materials and equipment for regular employees.

Test of Independent Contractor Status

Over the years, the courts have arrived at a number of questions to guide a party or the court in distinguishing between a regular employee and an independent contractor. It is not necessary to fulfill all of the requirements listed below; however, a majority of affirmative responses is expected.

1) *Control.* Who is in charge? What is the extent of their control? Who hires, evaluates, and fires? Who determines method of work and when the work will be completed? In an unforeseen situation, who becomes the leader? If the independent contractor controls the above, independent contractor status will be retained.

2) *Is work unique?* Does the job require special certificates or licenses? What is the level of specialization of the employees? When the level of specialization is sufficiently unique that few people can control the day-to-day tasks of the employees, the situation lends itself to the independent contractor status. For example, when the administrator of a sports facility is unable to supervise the swimming pool, the pool manager could easily be an independent contractor.

3) *Custom.* Is the selected relationship—regular employee or independent contractor—the one used most often in the industry?

4) *Skills.* Are requisite skills so unique or so advanced that it is difficult to control or supervise employees? A company claiming independent contractor status must avoid all but minimal orientation, in-service training, or other forms of employee control. Requirements that specific progressions be used could void the independent contractor status. Note that an employer who wishes to retain an independent contractor status can, for example, require in the contract that all employees possess an American Red Cross certificate; however, they cannot demand the use of a specific program in accomplishing the task.

5) *Period of employment.* Independent contractors are hired to do specific tasks for an identified period of time. Continuous employment will be examined for violation of an independent contractor status.

6) *Compensation.* Compensation is a lump sum. The money is paid only to the contractor. Employer payments directly to independent contractor employees may void the independent contractor agreement.

Leased Employees

According to Clement (2004), leased employees include the regular employee and the independent contractor. The leasing firm serves as the independent contractor to the employer. The employee becomes an employee of the leasing firm and not the business where they may be assigned to perform work and is given salary, fringe benefits, and liability coverage by the leasing firm. Leasing firms also hire, fire, and evaluate employees. "The employer merely creates a contract for a specific task needed to be accomplished, and the leasing company provides the requested service" (p. 101). Under the Equal Employment Opportunity Commission (EEOC), leased employees, temporary, seasonal, and part-time employees are considered contingent or temporary workers. Interns and volunteers are not covered by these provisions.

Interns and Volunteers

The United States Department of Labor updated its requirements and guidance in 2018 about when internships are required to be paid in the private sector under the Fair Labor Standards Act (FLSA). The fact sheet entitled Internship Programs under the Fair Labor Standards Act (2018) identifies seven criteria that must be analyzed to determine if interns working at the business must indeed be paid for performing work, even if it is part of an educational experience for academic credit.

The FLSA fact sheet (2018) notes that courts have used the "primary beneficiary test" to determine whether an intern or student is an employee under the FLSA. This test allows courts to examine which party is the "primary beneficiary" of the relationship. It is a flexible test and no single factor is determinative. Thus, whether an intern or student is an employee under the FLSA depends on the unique circumstances of each case. If analysis of the factors and work circumstances reveals an intern or student is actually an employee, then he or she is entitled to both minimum wage and overtime pay under the FLSA. On the other hand, if the analysis confirms that the intern or student is not an employee, then he or she is not entitled to either minimum wage or overtime pay (FLSA Fact Sheet, 2018).

In a general sense, the FLSA federal guidance about paid interns has shifted in a fairly significant way to require more traditional college internships to be compensated as opposed to predominantly unpaid. Even if interns have not traditionally been paid in sport and athletics, where gaining new skills and experience have been prioritized over being paid, the FLSA requirements and recent guidance are clear and should not be ignored. This is particularly true if a sport business routinely utilizes interns to administer operations. For example, an organization that runs youth sport tournaments or sport camps may now need to pay interns under this revised guidance, adding to staffing costs of hosting events.

Vicarious Liability

Vicarious liability is the manager's responsibility for the torts of his/her employees. Managers are liable for torts committed in the workplace even though they (the managers) were not present or aware that the tort was committed. The legal theory *respondeat superior* finds administrators responsible for the torts of their employees merely because they are administrators. In addition, administrators may be personally liable for having hired an incompetent employee or incompetent independent contractor.

Torts that are committed beyond the job description or the administrator's supervision are not covered under vicarious liability. The test of vicarious liability, or *respondeat superior,* is the administrator's right to control and direct the work of the employee. An administrator's status as a volunteer does not change his/her vicarious liability status. Intentional torts are not covered by vicarious liability unless the administrator has directed the employee to commit the intentional tort or has ratified the intentional tort after it was committed.

Types of Employees

Employer-employee categories are regular, at-will, contract, or membership in a labor union.

Regular Employee

Regular employee is the type of employment most often found in the work force. The regular employee works at the request of the employer; has income taxes, social security, and Medicare withheld from his/her income; and may be provided with insurance, pensions, and paid leaves. As mentioned earlier, the employer is liable for the torts of a regular employee, for providing a safe working environment, and for honoring the employee's legal rights.

At-Will

At-will employment occurs when an employer has a task to be done, seeks persons capable of doing the task, and offers a wage, followed by the parties' agreeing to the job. When one party no longer wishes to work with the other, the party merely informs the other of his/her wishes. The reason for either party's termination does not have to be given. Today, Florida, Georgia, and Louisiana are total at-will states. Bennett-Alexander and Hartman (2009) list the following as exceptions to the at-will categories: implied contracts, public policy, and good faith. Using information gathered from the Bureau of National Affairs Labor and Employment law, they provide information on each of these exceptions by state (pp. 28, 29).

Contracts

There are two types of employment contracts: written agreements and implied contracts. Written agreements are used universally in certain businesses and industries. Universities tend to use written agreements; therefore, most collegiate athletic department agreements will be in written form. The details of written agreements (contracts) are outlined in the chapter on contracts. Implied contracts are agreements between parties usually based on the practice in the industry, verbal promises of long-term employment, and policies that would lead an applicant to feel secure in taking an offered position. Many states permit an implied-contract relationship through policies, handbooks, and promises.

Labor Unions

Labor unions (agencies that negotiate contracts with businesses) are private associations formed to represent groups of workers with common needs and a common desire to obtain the best wages possible for the entire group.

Employing, Evaluating, And Terminating Employees

A business creates a system for employing each individual that begins with a need, followed by a job description, advertisements, candidate screening, and finally employment. There are several federal employment laws that prevent discrimination in hiring. Evaluation—and on occasion, termination of employees—is influenced by the Fourteenth Amendment to the U.S. Constitution, the Due Process Clause.

Federal Employment Laws

Employers are subject to federal laws created to remedy discrimination on the basis of race, color, sex, age, religion, national origin, and handicap. The federal laws that deal with discrimination include the Equal Pay Act of 1963, the Executive Orders of the 1950s and 1960s, Title VII of the Civil Rights Act of 1964, the Age Discrimination in Employment Act of 1967, the Rehabilitation Act of 1973, and the Americans with Disabilities Act of 1990. The Equal Employment Opportunities Commission (EEOC) is the federal government agency responsible for administrating many of the discrimination acts. Affirmative action, a program designed to remedy past discriminatory practices in hiring minority groups, is used when discrimination has been found. It enables protected groups to receive special attention in employment until such time as their numbers are proportionate to the percentage of employees in the non-protected group. Employees may volunteer or be required to establish an affirmative action program.

Procedural Due Process

The Fourteenth Amendment of the U.S. Constitution states that "No state shall make or enforce any law which shall abridge the privileges or immunities of citizens of the United States; nor shall any state deprive any person of life, liberty, or property, without due process of law." State actions, not private actions, are covered under the Fourteenth Amendment. Procedural due process enables an individual who is about to lose a liberty or property right to present his/her side of the situation and to be assured of fair treatment. Analysis, under procedural due process, is the balancing of the interests of the state against the rights of the individual.

Procedural due process systems are to be tailored to meet the needs of the business or agency. Legal advice is to be obtained before finalizing a system. When an employer is about to remove a liberty or property right (job) from an employee, the employee:

- must know and understand the charge and complaint;
- have a right to a hearing and to be represented by counsel in the hearing;
- be able to prepare and respond to charges; and
- present witnesses and question adverse witnesses.

The system must be in writing and contained in employee handbooks or related documents. The appeal process is to contain the following steps:

- Written notice of charges including dates, times, and details;
- Time and date for hearing;
- Explanation of representation and how it will be used in the hearing;
- Ample opportunity to prepare for hearing;
- Hearing is to give each side an opportunity to present its case;
- The hearing is convened before an impartial panel;
- Effort is made to negotiate a viable settlement among the parties;
- Settlement is made at hearing, if appropriate;
- The decision and rationale for the decision is contained in a written report; and
- Proceedings are recorded and available to the employee.

The employee may bring a lawsuit if not satisfied with the conduct of the hearing or if he/she believes that due process was compromised.

Employing

Search

The following suggestions are based on results in *Griggs v. Duke Power Company* (1971), *Equal Employment Opportunity Commission v. Atlas Paper Box Company* (1989), and *Ward Cove Packing Company v. Atonio* (1989). In preparation for an employee search, supervisors are to learn the labor laws and contracts that cover the job. They are expected to understand the agency or corporation's affirmative action program. The job description is the centerpiece of the employment process. It must contain an accurate and comprehensive description of the significant job tasks. Qualifications essential to success in carrying out the tasks of the job are to be stated. Experience and qualifications unrelated to the job are to be avoided. The job is to be advertised in publications read by potential candidates. If application deadlines are used, they are published and should be enforced. The employer, in conjunction with the search committee, forecasts the worker pool for the newly created position. What will be the extent and magnitude of the pool? Will the talent pool contain a diverse array of candidates for the position? Among those qualified, how many would be inclined to accept, and at what salary?

Screening

Initial screening of candidates is based on objective published criteria. Checklists that use job criteria are recommended for use in the process. Only those meeting the published criteria move into the second level of screening. Each level of screening increases the demands on the candidates. The screening instruments, size of interview pool, and use of recommendations in making decisions are determined prior to the start of the job search. With candidates' consent and authorization, each listed reference and former employer of the applicants is checked.

Interviewing

The interviewing process is designed to provide a detailed assessment of the candidate's knowledge, skills, and abilities. Training may be provided to interviewers to avoid the possibility that an interviewer would ask a discriminatory (or potentially discriminatory) question about such things as age, marital status, sexual orientation, gender identity, pregnancy status, and provisions for childcare. Candidates should leave the interview understanding the employment relationship classification and if it is a contract, the nature and contents of the contract. Interviewers are to submit common form-written evaluations for each candidate. Documentation is the employer's key to the entire process. Each step within the process is outlined and defined prior to instituting the search. The job description is crafted with the needs of the job and requisite skills and credentials in mind. The job description is easy to explain and defend should it be challenged. Screening and interviewing checklists and reports are objective when possible, signed, and dated. They are collected immediately after their use.

Search committees inform candidates of their status throughout the review process. The only legal requirement is that eliminated candidates be informed of their status when the job has been filled. Employers are to create a plan, follow the plan, and carefully document each step in the process.

Evaluating

Employee evaluation is an assessment of the elements of the job description and day-to-day tasks of the position. It is to be made in a fair manner. *Griggs v. Duke Power Company* (1971) established the need for performance evaluation based on identified job requirements. If, for example, in-service training is highly valued in evaluation, evidence must exist that it is essential to successful job performance. Sound business management suggests that employees are to engage in an evaluation assessment dialogue prior to completing an evaluation. Results of an evaluation are to be available to the employee. Serious deficits in work habits and disagreements over the execution of job tasks are to be reviewed. A rehabilitation program to address work deficiencies is to exist and be used appropriately. Continuous monitoring of the success or failure of individuals in the program is to be maintained.

Terminating

The termination process is to be contained in the employee handbook and is to be carried out exactly as it has been described. Legal reasons for termination include a comprehensive poor work record, documented by numerous evaluations over a substantially long period of time; violation of federal or state laws, including possible illegal drug use; or creation of a hazard in the work environment. The due process system is used in termination to ensure the employee has a chance to raise legitimate concerns.

Summary

Business organizations include sole proprietorships, partnerships, "C" and "S" corporations, and limited liability companies and partnerships. A sole proprietor assumes total liability and responsibility for the business, including all of his/her financial assets. Partnerships involve shared responsibility among partners. Corporations are legal entities where owners have only their investments in the corporation at risk. Subchapter "S" corporations have corporate liability status and individual tax status. Limited liability companies and partnerships have corporate liability status and partnership tax status. Regular employee, independent contractor, and leased employee are three potential employment relationships. Vicarious liability is the liability of administrators for the torts of their employees. Due process laws assist an employer in employing, evaluating, and terminating employees.

Discussion Questions

1. You are starting your own business. Analyze the advantages and disadvantages of each of the following business organizations: sole proprietorship, subchapter S corporation, or limited liability company (LLC). Which one would you select and why?
2. What is the most popular business organization among professional team owners?
3. Contrast an independent contractor with a regular employee relationship.
4. What are the requirements for an internship under the Fair Labor Standards Act?

Activities

1. Create a job description for a position in your current organization where you work. In small groups, conduct mock interviews for the position using the proper legal protocols advised.
2. A friend is starting a new business as an entrepreneur. Given the content of this chapter, what advice would you give your friend?
3. You are the owner of a leasing company that provides lifeguards for a local pool. Your contract states that each guard is to work Monday through Saturday from 9 a.m. to 4:30 p.m. Two of the guards report that they have been asked to work until 7 p.m. nearly every night for the past month. What should you do? Is your status as an independent contractor threatened? Advise on a legal and practical course of action to address the human resource issue.
4. Prepare an employee evaluation form for a current employee of the organization.

References

Bennett-Alexander, D. R., & Hartman, L. P. (2021). *Employment law for business,* 10th edition, International edition. McGraw-Hill.

Clement, A. (2004). Sport Law: Product liability and employment relations. In B. L. Parkhouse (Ed.). *The management of sport* (4th ed.; pp. 164–177). Mosby.

Equal Employment Opportunity Commission v. Atlas Paper Box Company, 868 F. 2d 1489 (1989).

Griggs v. Duke Power Company, 401 U.S. 424, 91 S. Ct. 849 (1971).

Internship Programs under the Fair Labor Standard Act, Wage and Hour Division. (2018). https://www.dol.gov/agencies/whd/fact-sheets/71-flsa-internships.

Uniform Partnership Act (1994), 614, Section 34, 300-499.

U.S. Department of Labor, Wage and Hour Division. (n.d.). *Handy reference to the Fair Labor Standards Act.* WH Publications. https://www.dol.gov/agencies/whd/compliance-assistance/handy-reference-guide-flsa.

Ward Cove Packing Company v. Atonio, 104 l. Ed. 2d 733 (1989).

Recommended Reading

Gutman, A. (2012). *EEOC and personnel practices* (2nd ed., published online). Sage. http://dx.doi.org/10.4135/9781452224718

Noe, R. A., Hollenbeck, J. R., Gerharts, B., & Wright, P. M. (2019). *Human resource management* (11th ed.). McGraw-Hill.

Activities

9

Labor Law and Antitrust

OBJECTIVES

Upon completing this chapter, you will,

- appreciate the history of labor law in the United States;
- discuss the role of labor law in professional sport;
- identify how antitrust law has been applied to sport;
- contrast the differences in the antitrust court decisions among a range of sports; and
- understand contemporary antitrust court decisions and recent litigation trends in sport.

Introduction

Black's Law Dictionary (2011) identifies antitrust as "the body of law designed to protect trade and commerce from unlawful restraints, monopolies, price-fixing and price discrimination" (p. 41). Although antitrust issues appear in both the private and public sectors of sport, most antitrust legislation is designed to provide control in the private sector or profit-making businesses. Article One of the U.S. Constitution, the Sherman Act of 1890, the Clayton Act of 1914, the Norris La Guardia Act of 1932, and the National Labor Relations Act (a result of amendments to the Wagner Act of 1935) play a role in the understanding of antitrust. Three U.S. Supreme Court decisions have exempted professional baseball from all antitrust laws. Decisions in other professional and amateur sport have not received the same special treatment. In recent years, litigations surrounding collegiate sports and the governance of sport activities has increased.

Labor Laws

Article One of the United States Constitution

Article One, Section Eight (Number Three) of the U.S. Constitution states that Congress shall have the power "to regulate commerce with foreign Nations, and among the several states, and with the Indian tribes." Section Eight (Number Eighteen) gives Congress the power "to make all laws which shall be necessary and proper for carrying into execution the foregoing powers, and all other Powers vested by this Constitution in the Government of the United States, or in any Department or Officer thereof."

Antitrust

Federal antitrust laws regulate interstate commerce in an effort to prevent the organization of monopolies. The laws cover goods, land, and services. Practices such as price fixing are in violation of these laws. When the courts are asked to examine a potential violation of antitrust law, the courts use a "rule of reason test" in which the illegal practice is balanced against the anti-competitive effect. When analyzing sport in the context of the following laws, sport is viewed as private and operated to make a profit.

Sherman Act of 1890

Section I of the Sherman Act states that every "contract, combination in the form of trust or otherwise, or conspiracy, in restraint of trade or commerce among the several States, or with foreign nations, is declared to be illegal. Every person who shall make any contract or engage in any combination or conspiracy hereby declared to be illegal shall be deemed guilty of a felony."

Section II adds that "every person who shall monopolize, or attempt to monopolize, or combine or conspire with any other person or persons, to monopolize any part of the trade or commerce among the several States, or with foreign nations, shall be deemed guilty of a felony."

Clayton Act of 1914

The Clayton Act is more precise than the Sherman Act and is thought to have further defined the Sherman Act. Sections Four and Six of the Clayton Act are significant to professional athletes, as they negotiate individual contract components and collective bargaining agreements. Section Four states that any person who shall be injured in his business or property by reason of anything forbidden in the antitrust laws may sue therefore in any district court of the United States in the district in which the defendant resides or is found or has an agent, without respect to the amount in controversy, and shall recover threefold the damages by him sustained, and the cost of the suit including a reasonable attorney's fee. The court may award under this section ... simple interest in actual damages for the period beginning on the date of service of such person's pleadings.

Section Six states that the labor of a human being is not a commodity or article of commerce. Nothing contained in the antitrust laws shall be construed to forbid the existence and operation of labor, agricultural or horticultural organizations, instituted for the purpose of mutual help, or to forbid or restrain individual members of such organizations from lawfully carrying out the legitimate objects thereof; nor shall such organizations, or the members thereof, be held or construed to be illegal combinations or conspiracies in restraint of trade under the antitrust laws.

Norris-LaGuardia Act of 1932

The Public Policy provision of the Norris-LaGuardia Act of 1932 defined the liberty of contract and freedom of labor roles of the individual worker who was not part of a formal labor group. He/she gained the freedoms of association, self-organization, and representation granted to the groups in the earlier antitrust laws. The act provided a solid recognition for American labor. This recognition was fine-tuned in the National Labor Relations Act.

National Labor Relations Act

The National Labor Relations Act, a result of amendments to the Wagner Act of 1935, noted that "Employees shall have the right to self-organization, to form, join, or assist labor organizations, to bargain collectively through representatives of their own choosing, and to engage in other concerted activities for the purpose of collective bargaining or other mutual aid or protection, and shall also have the right to refrain from any or all of such activities except to the extent that such right may be affected by an agreement requiring membership in a labor organization as a condition of employment." An employer or a labor organization that restrains or coerces an employee in the exercise of the employee's rights commits an unfair labor practice. It is also an unfair labor practice for a labor organization to refuse to bargain collectively with an employer who is an official representative of their employees.

Unique Characteristics of Professional Sport

Sport is considered "big business"; however, sport has a culture far different from the traditions associated with business and industry. The first distinction is in the definition of sport (the product). Sport competition is the product. For sport competition to be successful in the entertainment market, play must be exciting and lively with a close score throughout the event. The exciting, lively, and highly competitive (i.e., close score) encounter is most assured when a "level playing field" (or equal skills) has been established prior to competition. To create a level playing field, players must be allocated to competing teams on the basis of skill and talent so all teams in a competitive league have an equal start. Such items as drafts, trades, and salary caps are among the systems used to create this equality. Owners within a league work cooperatively to allocate players. Once all players have joined a team, each owner works diligently to win or beat the other league owners. This close working relationship coupled with a passionate desire to beat the very same teams is one of the hallmarks of professional league competition.

In business and industry, employees either join unions and accept collective bargaining agreements or individually negotiate their employment contracts. An employee in professional athletics automatically becomes a member of the players' union (the players' collective bargaining unit) and accepts the work, economic, and other benefits that have been negotiated by the union. Outstanding athletes then bargain individually, usually through an agent, for additional privileges. Thus, the second major difference between professional sports and business and industry is the role and use of labor unions and individually negotiated employment contracts.

Another difference between sport and business/industry is found in client interaction and satisfaction. In most businesses, an unhappy client or customer can search out another source for products or services. Often, the unhappy collegiate and professional sport client (spectator) cannot find another team to support. Gary Roberts (1991) noted that a legal problem in antitrust claims in sport is defining "the relevant market that the plaintiff claims has been monopolized. The market definition must include both a product and a geographic dimension—for example, professional football entertainment in the United States" (p. 138).

Career longevity is another difference between professional sport and business/ industry. Few employers expect a person's entire career to span an average of three to five years. Professional athletes have short timeframes for career success; this difference in length of careers prompts the professional athlete to want instant success and demand the gratification that accompanies such success. Employees in business and industry do not have to establish their value in the workplace in such a short time period. Because of limitations on the potential length of their playing careers, professional athletes want free agency status and the ability to test their skills in the free labor market. They want these opportunities when they are performing at their best, not at the completion of three or five years into a contract. They are also concerned career-ending injuries may shorten their career lifespan. Each of these factors plays a role in professional sport antitrust cases.

Litigation

Antitrust cases in sport include unique decisions awarded in professional baseball, football, basketball, hockey, collegiate sport, and sport organizations. The majority of the litigation in sport has been in professional "big business" team sports. Today, collegiate sport has become a party in antitrust cases, and individuals have used antitrust in defining player rights.

Professional Sport

Baseball

Three U.S. Supreme Court decisions (1992, 1953, and 1972) have exempted professional baseball from antitrust laws. The 1922 Supreme Court, under Justice Holmes, found in *Federal Baseball Club of Baltimore v. National League of Baseball Clubs* (1922) that professional baseball did not meet the Sherman Act "interstate commerce" clause, as its "business is giving exhibitions of baseball, which are purely state affairs" (208). The suit was brought over the "reserve clause" in relation to contracts signed by professional baseball players. As a result, a player was bound to an owner for his entire career unless the owner chose to trade him. This system, designed to create a level playing field for competitive balance, prohibited a team from making an offer to a player who was under contract.

In the case of *Toolson v. New York Yankees* (1953), the plaintiff approached the Supreme Court review believing that the court would find professional baseball part of "interstate commerce" due to the advent of television. Surely, national television broadcasts had turned professional baseball into "interstate commerce." Again, the issue was the "reserve clause" and that the contract clause violated the Sherman Act and Clayton Act. This time the Supreme Court said that baseball had operated successfully under the decision of *Federal Baseball Clubs of Baltimore v. National League of Baseball Clubs,* and as a result, it seemed appropriate to continue to exempt baseball from antitrust law.

Curt Flood, a player traded to another club without his knowledge, filed a cause of action (*Flood v. Kuhn,* 1972) under antitrust law. Again, the U.S. Supreme Court noted that baseball had operated successfully under the antitrust exemption and therefore the antitrust exemption should be maintained. In 1995, the Major League Baseball Players Association (MLBPA), the collective bargaining representative for the players in all 28 clubs at the time, reported their owners' labor law violations to the National Labor Relations Board (NLRB). The employment agreement expired at the end of 1993, and the players went on strike in August of 1994. The action halted the season, resulted in the cancellation of the 1994 World Series, and continued through part of the 1995 season. Owners wanted a salary cap, the elimination of the salary arbitration system, and restricted free agency. The players' counterproposal was a tax system to "deter extravagant wage offers" (*Silverman v. Major League Baseball*, 1995, 252).

The NLRB sought a preliminary injunction pending the outcome of their investigation. At issue were complaints that the owners had violated Section 8(a, 1) of the Sherman Act, which is where the employer seeks "[to interfere with, restrain, or coerce employees in the exercise of guaranteed rights: wages, hours, and conditions of employment] and (5) [to refuse to bargain collectively with representatives of employees] of the Act by unilaterally eliminating, before an impasse had been reached, salary arbitration for certain reserve players, competitive bargaining for certain free agents, and the anti-collusion provision of their collective bargaining agreement" (*Silverman v. Major League Baseball*, 1995, 250).

The issues involved free agency and the "reserve clause." Under free agency, a player with six years or more of play could become a free agent. Once the player signed a new contract, the player had another five years before becoming a free agent. This agreement also limited the number of free agents that each club could sign in two top-performance categories. Reserve players, those with fewer than six years of play, were under the Uniform Players Contract. Each year they were offered a new contract with a salary adjustment. According to the Uniform Players Contract, "if the player refuses the offer, the owner is entitled to 'reserve' the player's services and the player is not permitted to play for other teams. An owner may only reserve a player once under this system" (*Silverman*, 1995, 251). After a three-year period, the athlete could request salary arbitration where the outcome of such arbitration did not affect the player's reserve status.

The court issued an injunction directing Major League Baseball: "(1) to restore the terms and conditions of employment provided under the expired basic agreement, which was effective January 1, 1990, including its free agency/reserve system with salary arbitration for eligible reserve players ... (2) immediately to rescind by written notice to all club members any actions taken ... and (3) to bargain in good faith without unilateral changes to the basic agreement with the Major League Baseball Players Association in compliance with 8(a, 1) and (5) of the National Labor Relations Act" (*Silverman v. Major League Baseball*, 1995, 261).

In 1998, Congress passed the Curt Flood Act, which partially repealed baseball's antitrust exemption. The act by subjected business practices, "directly relating to or affecting employment of major league baseball players ... to the antitrust laws to the same extent such ... practices ... would be subject to the antitrust law of ... persons in any other professional sports business affecting interstate commerce" (15 USC 27A [a]). The Act repealed baseball's antitrust exemption only as it affected labor issues between owners and players. It did not affect franchise ownership, expansion and relocation, existing broadcasting arrangements, the draft, or owner-commissioner agreements.

The case *Major League Baseball et al. v. Crist* (2003) was a response to Major League Baseball's decision to eliminate two teams from the league (Florida Marlins and Tampa Bay Devil Rays). Charlie Crist, Florida's attorney general, began an investigation of Major League Baseball under Florida's antitrust act relating to the proposed contraction and/or relocation of the Tampa Bay Devil Rays and/or the Florida Marlins" (1180). The Eleventh Circuit ruled the federal antitrust exemption preempted any state antitrust law and that the attorney general could not continue with his investigation. The decision provides a comprehensive analysis of antitrust law at the state and federal levels and how it was uniquely applied to baseball.

Football

Football players have long wondered why baseball was exempt from antitrust regulations and football was not exempt. Professional football was denied an antitrust exemption in *United States v. Shubert* (1955) and *Radovich v. National Football League* (1957). In 1974, football players decided to challenge the "Rozelle Rule" under antitrust law (*Mackey v. National Football League,* 1976). The "Rozelle Rule" required a team signing a veteran free agent to compensate the team losing the player with cash or a draft choice. The district court found that the "Rozelle Rule" violated the Sherman Act, which the Eighth Circuit affirmed that determination. As a result, the "Rozelle Rule" was replaced by the "Right of First Refusal," a system found to be less offensive to players. A right of first refusal is a contract right that belongs to the current contract holder, such as the NFL team, to match the offer made to a specific player by another team within or outside of the league, within a designated time. If the offer is not made within the time period stated, the player goes to the new team. If the offer is made in a timely manner, the player stays with their current team.

Powell, the plaintiff in *Powell v. National Football League* (1988, 1989, and 1991), brought a case on behalf of a number of members of the National Football League Players Association (NFLPA) against the National Football League (NFL) for violation of the Clayton and Sherman Acts. The dispute was "over the rights of veteran free agents to play for the NFL clubs of their choosing. For more than a decade, the movement of veteran free agents has been subject to the Right of First Refusal/Compensation System" (*Powell et al. v. National Football League et al.,* 1988, 813). The parties returned to federal district court in Minnesota requesting a preliminary injunction, which the court denied. Granting an injunction would conflict with the purpose of the Norris-LaGuardia Act to bargain in good faith. On appeal, the Eighth Circuit reversed, holding that "the antitrust laws are inapplicable under the circumstances of the case as the non-statutory labor exemption extends beyond impasse" (*Powell et al. v. National Football League* 1989, 1304). Powell returned to court and requested an opportunity to consolidate with the McNeil case (*McNeil v. National Football League,* 1992), which is analyzed below. The request was denied.

In the *McNeil* case, eight NFL players whose contracts had expired brought a cause of action under the Sherman Act against all the NFL team owners. This was not an NFLPA action as presented in *Powell*; it covered only the named players. The complaint was over the wage scale and a plan created by the owners that they called "Plan B." The players' goal was to prevent the enforcement of the first refusal compensation plan. Plan B allowed each team to retain limited rights to 37 players each season. Players classified as unprotected would become unrestricted free agents and would be free to sign with any NFL club. Owners retained a right of first refusal for all protected players. If a protected player signed with a new team, the new team was expected to provide a draft choice to the player's original team. The jury found components of the wage plan in violation of the Sherman Act. Only those players that were found to have sustained injury were awarded money damages.

As a result of the McNeil case, today's existing system was created. It allows teams to have exclusive control over players for their first three years. The players have limited rights of first refusal for years four and five and unrestricted free agency after five years. Once the decision was final, 10 players were granted a temporary restraining order to prevent enforcement of the first refusal compensation (Jackson et al. v. National Football League, 1992).

Two weeks after *McNeil,* Reggie White and five other named plaintiffs representing all professional, college, and other individuals who had played or wanted to play professional football from 1987 onward brought a class action suit against the NFL over "the right of first refusal rules of Plan B, the college draft, the NFL Player Contract, and the preseason pay rule" (*White v. NFL,* 1993[1], 1394). The proposed settlement agreement provided the NFLPA would be the exclusive bargaining agent for the players. A hearing was held in which many players objected to the details of the settlement and the district court overruled their objections. Shortly thereafter, the NFL and the NFLPA entered into a new collective bargaining agreement that included the terms of the initial settlement. The court affirmed the approval of the settlement of the district court. The parties extended the collective bargaining agreements with amendments in 1996 and again in 2006 for the contract through 2012.

In 2008, the NFL asked to be relieved from the current agreement for financial reasons. At the same time, the NFL recognized that in order to achieve their interests, a lockout might be necessary. The players wanted to avoid a lockout. The media rights became the pivotal issue. The broadcast contracts provided about half of the NFL's total revenue. The current broadcast contracts did not require the media to pay television rights fees during a lockout. The NFL decided to extend broadcast rights with any media agencies willing to renegotiate. Critically, this would mean that the players could not use the revenue loss from the media as a bargaining tool in future negotiations. Under the new DirecTV contract, the "NFL could receive substantially more from DirecTV in 2011 if it locks out the players than if it does not" (*White et al. v. National Football League,* 2011, 945). Other deals were negotiated with other networks and media partners. In June 2010, the players sued the NFL for violating the agreement by extending and renegotiating the broadcast contracts without trying to get the greatest revenue. The court eventually awarded the players $6.9 million in damages for the NBC violation and found players had not met the burden of demonstrating damages for other media deals. The players objected.

In March 2011, the players filed a complaint that the lockout threatened by the NFL would violate antitrust laws, state contracts, and tort law. They again asked for an injunction. The league then imposed a lockout of its own players and notified players under contract that they were not permitted to enter team facilities except in connection with a non-team event or a charitable event, they would not receive compensation or health insurance benefits from their teams, and they were not permitted to play, practice, work out, attend meetings, or consult with team medical or training staff at team facilities. The league also filed an amended unfair labor practice charge with the National Labor Relations Board, alleging that the NFLPA's disclaimer was a "sham" and that the combination of a union's disclaimer and subsequent antitrust litigation was a "ploy and an unlawful subversion of the collective bargaining process." The league had filed a previous charge in February 2011, alleging that the union failed to confer in good faith during negotiations (*Brady et al., v. National Football League et al.*, 2011, 788). The Eighth Circuit in *Brady* did not agree with the district court's view in the *White* case, that the "balance of the equities tilts heavily in favor of the Players" (793). *The Brady et al. v. NFL et al.* case was eventually dismissed after the lockout ended in the summer of 2011.

The issue in *American Needle, Inc. v. National Football League* (2008, 2010) was whether the NFL was a single entity or a group of separate teams. The day of the filing of the suit, the NFL had 32 separately owned and operated football teams. They played a series of games throughout the season with the Super Bowl as the finale. The NFL defined "the product that teams produced jointly—NFL football—requires coordination and integration between the teams" (*American Needle, Inc. v. National Football League*, 2008, 737). In the early 1960s, the individual teams pooled their intellectual property rights and the NFL granted licenses to a number of different vendors, including American Needle, to create products. In 2000, the NFL requested bids from vendors with the decision to select an exclusive licensee. The contract, for 10 years, went to Reebok; none of the licensees were renewed. American Needle, one of the former vendors, sued under antitrust, a "contract, combination, ... or conspiracy in restraint of trade" (738). American Needle claimed that the NFL's requirement to pool individual team trademarks under one license vendor was a conspiracy in violation of antitrust and felt that each team should hire their own vendors.

The NFL claimed it was a single entity and not a collection of different entities in the various pro teams. American Needle responded that they did not have enough information to know if the NFL was a single entity. After much discovery, the court determined the NFL was a single entity. American Needle's claims failed as a matter of law. The court of appeals affirmed the district court's decision. The United States Supreme Court reversed and remanded under the "rule of reason" test. Under this test, the course examined whether there was a contract, combination, or conspiracy among the individual teams? Was there concerted action?

The Court found that "the NFL teams do not possess either the unitary decision-making quality or the single aggregation of economic power characteristic of independent actions. Each ... is a substantial, independently owned, independently managed business whose general corporate actions are guided or determined by separate corporate consciousness, and whose objectives are not common" (*American Needle, Inc. v. National Football League*, 2010, 2205). The court therefore reversed the earlier court's decision and remanded the case back to the lower courts.

Basketball

The National Basketball Association (NBA) negotiated a contract in 1988 that expired in 1994 (*NBA et al. v. Williams et al.*, 1995). In the 1994 contract negotiations, the players demanded the elimination of three provisions in the 1988 Collective Bargaining Agreement (CBA): the "College Draft," the "Right of First Refusal," and the "Revenue Sharing/Salary Cap System."

- The College Draft is the process by which exclusive rights to negotiate with eligible college players are apportioned among the NBA teams.
- The Right of First Refusal permits a team to match any offer made to one of its current players by another team and thus to retain the player's services.
- The Revenue Sharing/Salary Cap System establishes an overall wage framework that provides that the: (i) total player salaries and benefits paid by all NBA teams will be no less than a specified percentage of revenues; and (ii) the total salary paid to players by each team is subject to both a maximum and a required minimum.
- The Right of First Refusal and the present version of the College Draft have been incorporated in all the CBA's signed by the parties since 1976; the Revenue Sharing/Salary Cap provision has been included in every CBA since 1983. (*NBA et al. v Williams et al.*, 1995, 685)

In 1994, a New York federal district court judge granted the NBA's request for relief and dismissed the case. The players soon appealed. The Second Circuit affirmed, holding "the antitrust laws do not prohibit employers from bargaining jointly with a union, from implementing their joint proposals in the absence of a CBA, or from using economic force to obtain agreement to those proposals" (693).

Hockey

In 1977, McCourt signed a three-year National Hockey League (NHL) Standard Player Contract to play hockey for the NHL's franchise located in Detroit. In an effort to gain a new player, the Detroit Red Wings gave McCourt to the LA Kings. Instead of going to Los Angeles, McCourt sued the NHL, LA Kings, National Hockey League Players Association, and the Detroit Red Wings (*McCourt v. California Sports, Inc. et al.*, 1979). He alleged that the reserve system violated the Sherman Act. McCourt received a preliminary injunction restraining defendants from enforcing the arbitration award and his reassignment. The NHL appealed. On appeal, the Sixth Circuit vacated the injunction and remanded the case, holding that the non-statutory labor exemption applied since the reserve system was collectively bargained in good faith.

The value of a professional sport league and team brands has increased measurably over the last two decades. The NHL decided to grow hockey by improving the strength of the league brand. They had plans to to achieve the entertainment successes experienced by

MLB and the NFL. To attain such visibility, they considered enticing the individual NHL Clubs to assign their trademarks to the league so that the league could be marketed on a collective basis. In 1994, member clubs granted the NHL exclusive rights to use or license trademarks for advertising and for the sale and distribution of products and services. The clubs also agreed the right to develop and exploit the online marketing tools resided in the league" (*Madison Square Garden, L.P. v. National Hockey League et al.*, 2007, 5).

In 2000, the clubs decided to change the internet approach to a hybrid model. The league's and clubs' websites would be part of an integrated network, with certain elements available on the clubs' websites and others only available on NHL.com (*Madison Square Garden, L.P. et al. v. National Hockey League et al.*, 2007, 5). The commissioner's plan restricted a portion of each team's website for NHL content and reserved 35% of each club's website for NHL-controlled advertising and required that all merchandise sales were to be made through the NHL store.

In 2007, the league and Rangers met to discuss their differences, with one of them being the internet regulation. They failed to reach agreement on any of the issues. Thus, the Rangers decided to set up an "internet store" to sell Ranger merchandise, use virtual advertising and signage in Ranger home game broadcasts, and stream broadcasts of Ranger games on the internet. All were illegal according to league rules (*Madison Square Garden, L.P. et al. v. National Hockey League et al.*, 2007, 10). Deputy Commissioner Daly sent them a letter instructing them to stop or be fined for the ongoing violation. The Rangers remained in violation for two days and were fined $200,000. Both groups met to resolve the differences. Negotiations broke down, and the league said they would begin fines the first day of the season if the Rangers did not agree to a common internet site. The Rangers went to court for an injunction against the league, alleging the league had "become an 'illegal cartel' in its attempts to prevent competition between and among NHL member clubs" (14). The Rangers' motion for a preliminary injunction was denied and the Second Circuit affirmed the decision.

Collegiate Sports

The National Collegiate Athletic Association's acquisition of women's collegiate sports was a hostile takeover of a business or agency where the plaintiff's only chance for survival was to rely upon antitrust law. This decision is discussed in detail in Chapter 5, Fourteenth Amendment and Title IX (*AIAW v. NCAA*, 1984; Hult, 1980). The decisions freed the NCAA to become "big business" and college athletics became more similar to professional team sports. It was seen as the day that higher education traded the academic sport model, now widely known as "amateurism," for a semi-professional model of sport. Since that time and that shift in legal and business strategy toward defending the principles of amateurism at all (legal and reputational) costs, the NCAA has been plagued with ongoing litigation for many years. Meanwhile, NCAA-created content such as March Madness continues to command exorbitant television rights fees, while maintaining the amateur status of of these athletes.

Electronic Arts, the creator and marketer of sport video games, was properly sued for antitrust violations by the athletes whose likenesses have been used in games (*Keller et al. v. Electronic Arts, Inc., National Collegiate Athletic Association, and Collegiate Licensing Company,* 2010; *O'Bannon et al. v. National Collegiate Athletic Association, Collegiate Licensing Company et al.,* 2009, 2010; *In re: Student-Athlete Name & Likeness Licensing Litigation,* 2011). Among Electronic Arts games are Madden NFL 10, Madden NFL 11, NCAA Football 10, and NCAA Football 11. The athletes have sued and continue to sue Electronic Arts under "the Right of Publicity" as described in Chapter 10, Intellectual Property.

Their antitrust claim is that in signing the forms required to play sports under NCAA rules, they had to agree to release their rights to their personal image, likeness, and/or name for use by NCAA on merchandise and licenses. When the athletes signed the release, they were not informed that the release was forever, not just for the four years of NCAA play. Specifically, the defendants, the National Collegiate Athletic Association (NCAA) and the Collegiate Licensing Company (CLC), have "engaged in anticompetitive conduct in two ways. First, they ... conspired to fix the prices they received for the use and sale of their images, likenesses and/or names at zero dollars.... Second, ... defendants engaged in a group boycott/refusal to deal conspiracy that required all current student athletes to sign forms ... to relinquish all rights in perpetuity for use of their images, likenesses, and/or names and to deny Antitrust Class Members compensation in the form of royalties for the continued use of their images, likenesses, and/or names for profit" (*In re: NCAA Student-Athlete Name and Likeness Litigation,* 2011[2], 10). The athletes' legal complaints are in violation of the Sherman Act for unreasonable restraint of trade, group boycott, refusal to deal, unjust enrichment, and a financial accounting.

Early complaints were filed by Keller and O'Bannon. Both cases were filed as representing themselves and all other affected athletes. Sam Keller was a starting quarterback for Arizona State University and the University of Nebraska football teams. Among the charges in his complaint was that Electronic Arts was using his likeness without consent; misconduct on the part of the NCAA and Collegiate Licensing Company (CLC) for violating one of the NCAA's bylaws; civil conspiracy; and breach of contract. A purpose in filing the claim was to request the permission of the court for a class action suit (*Keller et al. v. Electronic Arts, Inc., NCAA, and CLC,* 2010). In 2009, O'Bannon, a Nevada resident who had played basketball for UCLA, submitted a similar claim against the NCAA and CLC to the United States District Court for the Northern District of California. The NCAA, in response to the suit, requested a change of venue to Southern Indiana. The court denied the request (*O'Bannon et al. v. NCAA and CLC,* 2009). O'Bannon made the following claims, first under the Sherman Act and later under common law.

Violation of Section I of the Sherman Act:

A. Existence of a contract, combination, or conspiracy. Contract was proved through NCAA's requirement that athletes sign Form 083a, which gives away their personal rights. Arrangements between the NCAA, CLC, and Electronic Arts created a second contract. Thus, O'Bannon satisfied prong one of the Sherman Act.

B. Unreasonable restraint of trade (Rule of Reason). Conduct constituted price-fixing and a group boycott. The complaint is that the NCAA has fixed the price of former athletes' image at zero and has created a boycott of former student-athletes in the collegiate licensing market.

C. Under the statute of limitations, his plea for a continuing violation was accepted.

D. Standing must be accomplished when "(1) he or she suffers a concrete, particularized injury; (2) there is a causal connection between the injury and the conduct complained of; and (3) the injury will likely be redressed by a favorable decision" (*O'Bannon et al. v. NCAA, CLC et al.*, 2009, 16).

E. Standing was established, and he succeeded under the common law claim of unjust enrichment (*O'Bannon et al. v. NCAA et al.*, 2009, 22).

The court order, as of January 15, 2010, was for the Keller and O'Bannon actions to file a consolidated amended complaint and to attend a case management conference. The athletes joined together, and the case name became *In re: Student-Athlete Name and Likeness Litigation*. There were 17 named plaintiffs in the action. In 2011, the action for a change in venue was denied again. In May of 2011 litigation, Electronic Art's motion to dismiss the Sherman Act claims was granted; NCAA and CLC motions to dismiss similar claims were denied. On July 28, 2011, EA's motion for dismissal of common law claims was denied. No further actions are in print as of this publication.

Sport Organizations

Antitrust claims have played a role in disputes over eligibility rules and re-organization of sport competitions. Maurice Clarett, an outstanding sophomore football player at Ohio State University, decided to join the National Football league (NFL). Clarett was denied the opportunity due to an NFL rule limiting eligibility to players three seasons following high school play, so he sued under antitrust law. He based his claim on what he perceived as an unreasonable restraint of trade, noting in his legal claims that, "[a]ntitrust law will not tolerate a contract which unreasonably forbids anyone to practice his calling" (*Clarett v. National Football League*, 2004, 382). The federal district court in New York granted Clarett's motion for summary judgment and denied the NFL's motion and Clarett was deemed eligible to participate in the 2004 NFL draft.

The Association of Tennis Professionals (ATP) sponsors the worldwide tennis circuit. A re-organization of the tour moved some events and players to top tier play while others were downgraded. The Hamburg, Germany tennis tournament was moved from first tier to second tier, prompting this lawsuit (*Deutscher Tennis Bund et al. v. APT Tour, Inc. et al.*, 2010). The suit alleged that the plan, called "Brave New World," violated Sections 1 and 2 of the Sherman Act and that the ATP Directors had breached duties owed to the Federation (824). Also, individual players had complaints concerning the number and types of tournaments in which they would be required to participate. The jury returned a verdict for ATP, stating that "the Federation failed to prove ATP entered into a contract, combination, or conspiracy with any separate entity under Section 1 of the Sherman Act, and did not establish a relevant product market under Section 2 of the Sherman Act" (824). ATP appealed the verdict, alleging it was a single entity or a single enterprise. The Third Circuit affirmed defendant's claims related to the Sherman Act and also found for defendants on the breach of duty legal claims.

A review of recent antitrust cases in sport reveals the variety and diversity of legal claims now being brought against sport organization and sport events series entities, such as the cricket league events, discussed below.

Gold Medal LLC v. USA Track & Field, 899 F.3d 712 (9th Cir. 2018) is a claim alleging that USA Track & Field and the United States Olympics Committee (USOC) engaged in an anticompetitive conspiracy in violation of antitrust law by imposing advertising restrictions during the Olympic Trials for track and field athletes. On appeal before the Ninth Circuit, the court found that the US Olympic Committee and USATF did not engage in anticompetitive practices when they "impos[ed] advertising restrictions during the Olympic Trials for track and field athletes." (713) The Ninth Circuit found that USATF/USOC met implied antitrust immunity, stating, "[to] compel the Olympic Committee and USATF under the antitrust laws to permit any would-be advertiser to sponsor individual athletes without national governing body approval would unduly interfere with the operation of the [Amateur Sports Act]" (717).

In *American Cricket Premier League, LLC v. USA Cricket*, 445 F. Supp. 3d 1167 (D. Co. 2020), a case challenging a cricket start up league, the court found the group did not have an antitrust claim where they were not selected as a sanctioned league of USA Cricket. The court denied the plaintiffs' claim because "The only prospective relief this [c]ourt might award that would certainly remedy [p]laintiff's injury is to order USA Cricket to accept [p]laintiff's bid to be recognized" (1178). Further, court opined that the only prospective relief they could award was an order for USA Cricket to redo the bidding, which the court noted they had no power to require, and plaintiffs did not request that relief.

Litigation Trends and Future Directions

Recent antitrust cases in professional and Olympic sports have begun to be more varied in challenging restrictions that athletes have long argued are ongoing violations of antitrust law. The legal challenges now represent a more nuanced way to apply antitrust laws to the unique factual and economics aspect of sports as big business, especially as it relates to NCAA athletes, professional athletes participating in sports leagues where TV rights deals have exploded in the past decade, and even Olympic athletes have argued more vocally for a fair share in marketing opportunities and revenues derived from marketing rights and televisions rights fees involving Olympic content.

Antitrust law has now become the chosen legal vehicle for athletes seeking to obtain more revenues out of the current economics of the professional models of sport, specifically in the United States. In Europe, competition laws are the legal counterpart to U.S. antitrust laws, such as the legal challenges by German Olympic athletes in 2018, who pushed back at marketing and advertising restrictions during the Olympic period created by Rule 40 of the Olympic charter as too restrictive and harmful to the earning potential as highly marketable athletes with large consumer demand. (Kapser, 2018). This legal and economic argument is ripe for a legal challenge especially during an Olympic year.

Thus, antitrust laws have moved to the legal forefront as a way for athletes to seek greater economic participation for their play, as essentially the "talent" for each team and league and for without such talent, no highly valuable live television content would exist. Antitrust laws in sport are now relied upon by professional, college, and Olympic athletes, like their legal predecessor athletes and the historical cases analyzed have demonstrated. This enables greater economic participation in the professional sport and business models that have been created, notably on the backs of predominantly minority athletes. The outcomes of these cases have begun to remedy the fairness arguments long raised by primary stakeholders in the professional leagues about how to gain a larger say and financial stake in the large business deals being made related to creating and producing live content involving sports (including via digital means), to market athletes and leagues in new ways, and to using new technologies, such as virtual reality, in order to meet increased consumer demand.

Summary

Antitrust laws promote competition by regulating against monopolies. Article 1 of the U.S. Constitution, the Sherman Act, the Clayton Act, the Norris LaGuardia Act, and the National Labor Relations Act have relevance in protecting sport organizations from potential antitrust violations. Sport is particularly vulnerable from a liability perspective to increased legal scrutiny via antitrust laws. Baseball has maintained its long-held status beyond antitrust review. However, players in other professional sports have not been as successful in using antitrust as a legal theory against owners. The most recent antitrust litigation involving college athletes, involving name, image, and likeness, seems legally unique to the United States and warrants further observation. How these cases, such as *O'Bannon v. NCAA* will shape the future marketplace for college sport-themed goods and services, such as video games featuring college (amateur) athletes, remains an open topic for much debate.

Discussion Questions

1. Could the current method for selecting the teams for the Bowl Championship Series (BCS) be challenged under antitrust law?
2. After the *O'Bannon* decision and its impact, what do you anticipate as the next major antitrust complaint involving college sports? In other words, what current practices or policies of the NCAA are now also ripe for legal challenge as an antitrust violation, given the arguments and legal claims advanced by the student plaintiffs?

Activities

1. Locate the case *In re: Student-Athlete Name and Likeness* (*O'Bannon*) *Litigation* and outline the activity in the case since the 2011 decision discussed in this chapter. What financial and practical impact(s) do these court decisions have on college sport-focused content and merchandise, such as video games involving college players?
2. Contrast the antitrust issues found in the professional sport decisions with those found in the collegiate sport decisions. What makes the cases legally different or distinct?

References

AIAW v. NCAA, 735 F. 2d 577 (1984).

American Cricket Premier League, LLC v. USA Cricket, 445 F. Supp. 3d 1167 (2020)

American Needle, Inc. v. National Football League, 538 F. 3d 736 (2008); 130 S. Ct. 2201 (2010); 391 Fed. Appx. 546 (2010).

Black's Law Dictionary. (2011). Thomson Reuters.

Brady et al. v. National Football League et al., 640 F. 3d 785 (2011).

Clarett v. National Football League, 306 F. Supp. 2d 379 (2004 [1]); 369 F. 3d 124 (2004 [2]).

Clayton Act of 1914, 15 USC 15, (4) and (6) (2021).

Curt Flood Act, 15 USCA 27a(a).

Deutscher Tennis Bund, German Tennis Federation et al. v. ATP Tours, Inc. et al., 610 F. 3d 820 (2010).

Federal Baseball Club of Baltimore v. National League of Baseball Clubs, 259 U.S. 200 (1922).

Flood v. Kuhn, 316 F. Supp. 271 (1970); 443 F. 2d 264 (1971); 407 U.S. 258 (1972).

Gold Medal LLC v. USA Track & Field, 899 F.3d 712 (2018).

Hult, J. S. (1980). The philosophical conflicts in men's and women's collegiate athletics. *Quest, 32*(1), 77–94.

In re: NCAA Student-Athlete Name and Likeness Litigation, 763 F. Supp. 2d 1379 (2011).

Jackson et al. v. National Football league, 602 F 2d 226 (1992).

Kapser, D. (2018, May 31). German athletes demand more out of the Olympic money pot. *SwimSwam Magazine*. https://swimswam.com/german-athletes-demand-more-out-of-the-olympic-money-pot/.

Keller et al. v. Electronic Arts, Inc., National Collegiate Athletic Association, and Collegiate Licensing Company, 2010 U.S. Dist. LEXIS 10719.

Mackey v. National Football League, 543 F. 2d 606 (1976); 434 U.S. 801 (1977).

Madison Square Garden, L.P. v. National Hockey League et al., 2008 U.S. Dist. LEXIS 80475.

Major League Baseball v. Crist, 331 F. 3d 1177 (2003).

McCourt v. California Sports, Inc. et al., 600 F. 2d 1193 (1979).

McNeil v. National Football League, 790 F. Supp. 871 (1992).

NBA et al. v. Williams et al., 45 F. 3d 684 (1995).

National Labor Relations Act, 29 USC 101 (2021).

Norris LaGuardia Act of 1932, 29 USCS §§ 1101 et seq. (2021).

O'Bannon et al. v. NCAA, Collegiate Licensing Company et al., 2010 U.S. Dist. LEXIS 19170.

Powell et al. v. National Football League et al., 764 F. Supp. 1351 (1991).

Radovich v. National Football League, 352 U.S. 445 (1957).

Rule 40 of the IOC Charter. https://stillmed.olympic.org/media/Document%20Library/OlympicOrg/General/EN-Olympic-Charter.pdf#_ga=1.165750334.1661404243.1482776731

Roberts, G. (1991). Professional sports and the antitrust laws. In P. D. Staudohar & J. A. Mangan (Eds.), *The business of professional sport* (pp. 135–151). University of Illinois Press.

Sherman Act of 1890, 15 USCS § 1, 2 (2021).

Silverman v. Major League Baseball, 880 F. Supp. 246 (1995).

Toolson v. New York Yankees, 346 U.S. 356 (1953).

United States v. Shubert, 348 U.S. 222 (1955).

White et al. v. National Football League et al., 766 F. Supp. 2d 941 (2011).

Recommended Reading

Baker, T., Edelman, M., & Watanabe, N. M. (2018). Debunking the NCAA's myth that amateurism conforms with antitrust law: Legal and statistical analysis. *Tennessee Law Review, 85*(3), 661–706.

Block, B. M., & Ridings, M. D. (2011). Antitrust conspiracies in franchise systems after American Needle. *Franchise Law Journal, 30*, 216.

Edelman, M. (2017). A Prelude to Jenkins v. NCAA: Amateurism, Antitrust law, and the role of consumer demand in a proper Rule of Reason analysis. *Louisiana Law Review, 78*, 227.

Feinstein, J. (2019, October 16). The NCAA is still whining about pay to play. It's too late for that, *Washington Post*. https://www.washingtonpost.com/sports/colleges/the-ncaa-is-still-whining-about-pay-to-play-its-too-late-for-that/2019/10/16/d128a2c8-f01e-11e9-8693-f487e46784aa_story.html

Grow, N. (2011). Antitrust & the Bowl Championship Series. *Harvard Journal of Sports & Entertainment Law, 2*, 53.

Recommended Reading

10

Intellectual Property

OBJECTIVES

Upon completing this chapter, you will,

- delineate the differences between copyright, trademark, and patent law, and how each influences sport;
- identify the rights of the copyright owner, including fair use;
- recognize the legal benefits of registering and licensing creative works;
- understand the system the court uses in analyzing trademark infringement under confusion, dilution, trade dress, cancellation, or abandonment;
- recognize that trademark infringement may be civil or criminal; and
- appreciate the value of intellectual property to the economics and business of sport.

Introduction

Chapter 9 discussed the importance of competition in the marketplace and the protection provided entrepreneurs by the United States government. The free enterprise economy of the United States is based on competition. Intellectual property laws such as copyright, trademark, right of publicity, and patent law protect those engaging in marketplace competition and reward the creators of such materials for the fruits of their labor with ownership rights. These rights are treated by the law as personal property; they can be contracted to others through traditional agreements. Copyrights and trademarks can be licensed, sold, loaned, or given to others. Patents receive the same treatment with some restrictions. Intellectual property laws include federal, state, and common law, which are the results of court decisions. In recent years, criminal laws have been added to the civil law enforcement.

Copyright

Copyright is a system for protecting the "original works of authorship fixed in any tangible medium" (Copyright Act, 17 USC 102). Required elements of copyright are that the work is original and that it is fixed in a tangible medium, such as in print, motion pictures, or sculpture. Works of authorship:

- literary works;
- musical works, including any accompanying words;
- dramatic works, including any accompanying music;
- pantomimes and choreographic works;
- pictorial, graphic, and sculptural works;
- motion pictures and other audiovisual works;
- sound recordings; and
- architectural works. (17 USC 102)

With the fixation requirement for copyright protection, it is important to recognize that copyright protection for an original work of authorship does not extend to an "idea, procedure, process, system, method of operation, concept, principle, or discovery, regardless of the form in which it is described, explained, illustrated, or embodied in such work" (17 USC 102). Copyright can be obtained for compilations and derivative works; however, the copyright covers only the materials attributed to the new author. The original materials continue to belong to the first author (17 USC 103).

While the Copyright Act of 1790 covered books and maps, technological changes necessitated an expansion of copyright protection to include electronics, films, computer programs, and choreography. In 1971, the law was extended to sound recordings. The Sonny Bono Copyright Term Extension Fairness in Music Licensing Act of 1998 extended copyright protection to the life of the author and 70 years beyond the life of the author. Works made for hire or commissioned by an employer are protected for 95 years following publication or for 120 years after their creation (17 USC 302). The Sensenbrenner Amendment to the law provides an exemption that permits music to be played, without royalty, in restaurants and malls.

The area of choreography is fully covered under the statute but not always recognized by the public. For example, when a broadcast of a "football game covered by four television cameras, with a director guiding the activities of the four cameramen and choosing which of their electronic images are sent out to the public and in what order, there is little doubt that what that cameramen and the director are doing constitutes authorship" (Copyright Law Revision, H.R. Rep. No. 94–1476, 1976). However, courts have recognized that the underlying sporting event itself is not copyrightable since there is no authorship of the spontaneous event (*NBA v. Motorola,* 1997). Another avenue for copyright in sport, golf courses and unique sport venues usually involve architectural plans and drawings. When these fix plans are unique or custom designed, copyright protection is warranted.

Prior to 1976, all copyrighted materials had to contain a copyright notice such as the following: ©2010 Susan Jones. The 1989 Berne Convention, an international agreement, required participating nations to give copyright protection without formalities. This makes notice optional in the United States. To encourage the registration of copyrights in the United States the statute notes that the "certificate of registration is prima facie evidence that the copyright is valid" (Copyright Act, 17 USC 410).

Rights of Copyright Owners

The owner of a copyright has the exclusive right to do and to authorize any of the following:

- to reproduce the copyrighted work in copies or phonorecords;
- to prepare derivative works based upon the copyrighted work;
- to distribute copies or phonorecords of the copyrighted work to the public for sale or other transfer of ownership, or by rental, lease, or lending;
- in the case of literary, musical, dramatic, and choreographic works, pantomimes, and motion pictures and other audiovisual works, to perform the copyrighted work publicly;
- in the case of literary, musical, dramatic, and choreographic works, pantomimes, and pictorial, graphic, or sculptural works, including the individual images of a motion picture or other audiovisual work, to display the copyrighted work publicly; and
- in the case of sound recordings, to perform the copyrighted work publicly by means of a digital audio transmission. (17 USC 106)

The owner of a computer program may make a copy as an essential step in the utilization of the machine or for archival purposes. The owner of the computer program may not make a copy for another person (17 USC 117). Ownership of copyright passes at death as personal property.

Rights of Copyright Consumers—Fair Use

The fair use doctrine enables the public, under specific circumstances, to make use of a copyrighted work without infringing on the rights of the owner. Fair use is often associated with educational settings, and it has been applied from classroom materials to performances since 2002. For example, written materials, plays, and choreography may be used, without permission, by an "instructor in the course of face-to-face teaching activities of a nonprofit educational institution, in a classroom or similar place devoted to instruction" (17 USC 110). Also, copyrighted work may be reproduced "for purposes such as criticism, comment, news reporting, teaching (including multiple copies for classroom use), scholarship, or research" (17 USC 107).

Infringement

In determining liability for infringement, courts look at the following:

1) the purpose and character of the use, including whether such use is of a commercial nature or is for nonprofit educational purposes;
2) the nature of the copyrighted work;
3) the amount and the substantiality of the portion used in relation to the copyrighted work as a whole; and
4) the effect of the use upon the potential market for or value of the copyrighted work. (17 USC 107)

Adapting a work into a different form is prohibited. Adapting a book into a play without permission, for example, is infringement. Remedies for infringement are injunctive relief (e.g., stopping the infringer's use of the copyrighted materials), monetary or compensatory damages, destruction of infringing articles, and criminal penalties. Monetary or compensatory damages are assessed to make the injured party whole. The copyright owner may elect to receive statutory damages rather than compensatory damages. Statutory damages, determined by the court, will not be less than $30,000.00 or more than $750,000.00 (17 USC 504).

Work for Hire

Section 101 of the Copyright Act defines a "work for hire" as the following:

1) a work prepared by an employee within the scope of his or her employment; or
2) a work specially ordered or commissioned for use as a contribution to a collective work ... if the parties expressly agree in a written document, signed by them, that the work will be considered a work for hire. (17 USC 101)

Work made under an independent contractor agreement is not considered work for hire unless it has been identified as a "work for hire" within the agreement.

Licensing

The owner of a copyright may license others to use or make copies of the copyrighted materials. These licenses are to be legal, written contracts. A license should state the protected rights of the owner and of the person receiving the license. Topics such as date of agreement, form in which the materials will appear, and other details are to be included. Failure to carry out the license as agreed constitutes breach of contract and infringement of copyright.

Copyright Cases

Definition

Copyright, by definition, is the right of an owner to a registered, original, and fixed document. *Curtis v. Benson et al.* (1997) and *Bouchat v. Baltimore Ravens Limited Partnership et al.* (2008) are examples of court decisions addressing the definition of copyright. Curtis, the original architect for the Superdome, sued the owner of the building and recent building architects for reproducing and using his original drawings, without permission, for future work. Defendants claimed that when Curtis gave his registered architectural plans to Tulane University Architectural Archives, including the 1967 Superdome original drawing and the 1987 drawings for the renovation/modification of the Dome, all plans became part of the public domain. The issues before the court:

1) whether plaintiff's state law claims are preempted by the Federal Copyright Act;
2) whether plaintiff's claim for statutory damages and attorney's fees pursuant to the Federal Copyright Act should be dismissed as a matter of law; and
3) whether Tulane University must be joined in these proceedings as a necessary or indispensable party. (*Curtis v. Benson et al.*, 1997, 2)

The Court dismissed the plaintiff's state law claims and struck the request for statutory damages and attorney fees. This case highlights the need for both a technical and legal understanding and awareness of ownership of architectural drawings and other copyrighted materials when drafting building contracts.

A more recent case involving complex copyright issues and architectural renderings of sport facilities is *Longhorn Locker Company v. Hollman* (2020), claiming that defendant stole their plans to remodel the New Orleans Saints' locker room from a failed bid. The court initially seemed to rule in plaintiff's favor, but a pending copyright application limited the potential legal impact.

The *Bouchat v. Baltimore Ravens et al.* (2008) case has an interesting historical background. When the Cleveland Browns moved to Baltimore in 1995, they were forced to leave their logo and brand in Cleveland. Upon settling in Baltimore, the team began to explore a new team name and brands (i.e., team logos) that might accompany the new name. Bouchat, a security guard and amateur artist, took a real interest in the team and began to draw various logos for the names the team was exploring, including a wing shield for the name "Ravens." A few months later, when the team elected that name, Bouchat sent his shield drawing to the Maryland Stadium Authority, asking the authority to pass the drawing on to the Ravens' president. If the president decided to use the shield, Bouchat wanted a letter of recognition and a signed helmet. Bouchat received no response. "Through a series of misunderstandings, Bouchat's Shield Drawing was sent to the Stadium Authority Chairman's law office, forwarded to the Ravens' temporary headquarters, forwarded to the NFL in New York, and then to the commercial artists working on the Ravens project. There is no reason to believe that the Ravens or NFL intentionally caused the Shield Drawing to be provided to the artists. Nevertheless, the Shield Drawing was provided to the artists who eventually used Bouchat's drawing as the basis for the 'Flying B logo'" (*Bouchat v. Baltimore Ravens et al.*, 2008).

The Ravens' new logo, the "Flying B," created by the NFL Properties (NFLP), looked very similar, if not exactly identical, to Bouchat's submission. The Ravens were unaware that the NFLP had taken the work from a third party. Bouchat sued the Ravens and the NFLP for infringing his copyright on the shield drawing and asked for ten million dollars (*Bouchat v. Baltimore Ravens Football Club, Inc.*, 2003). A jury found for Bouchat because his shield drawing had been copied.

The Copyright Act (17 USC 504) entitled him to actual damages and any profits that were not taken into account in computing the actual damages. The jury had difficulty in arriving at the appropriate damage award and did not decide a damages award. Bouchat appealed the decision not to award him any damages. He stated that he should at least get the statutory damage allocated in federal copyright law. Bouchat was again not clear in his pleadings to establish with some specificity the direct economic losses he actually sustained from the copyright infringement, so the court denied his request. In 2007, Bouchat brought suit against all licensees of the NFLP. The Fourth Circuit affirmed no statutory damages since the artist "failed to register his copyright before the infringement began" (*Bouchat v. Bon-Ton Department Stores, Inc. et al.*, 2007, 315).

In *Spinelli v NFL* (2018), a case involving the Associated Press sports photographers where the NFL sold their images in the online store, the appeals court reversed the lower court's dismissals of copyright infringement against Associated Press and the NFL over breach of good faith and fair dealing and fraud. Regarding the copyright claims, the Second Circuit held that a licensee with a sublicense right may not retroactively grant a sublicense to serve as a defense in an action for copyright infringement (Thomson Reuters, 2018).

Key Defenses to Rights of Copyright Owners: Fair Use

Fair use enables the public to use materials under copyright, particularly library holdings and music files, for research and education without a formal agreement and to escape any liability for copyright infringement. In *Author's Guild, Inc. v. HathiTrust*, 755 F.3d 87 (2d Cir. 2014), the 2nd circuit found fair use where the universities worked with Google to digitize their works and make them text searchable. The court employed a four-factor analysis to test fair use. The court found the use was transformative; downplayed the second factor; said the third factor, even though they used the entire work, was not excessive because they needed to use the whole work (98); and found that the text searchable documents did not count as economic harm because they are not replacements for the original works (99).

Broadcast Rights

Two sport situations in which broadcast rights were questioned were *J&J Sport Productions, Inc. v. Live Oak Country Post No. 6119 Veterans of Foreign Wars et al.* (2009) where the owner of an exclusive license for closed-circuit television fights filed a complaint against a VFW veterans' lounge/bar that intercepted the program without authorization. The court denied summary judgment "because there existed an issue of fact as to whether or not the lounge acted willfully" (1). A situation where broadcast rights were questioned was a copyright infringement issue related to the exclusive distribution rights to the Floyd Mayweather v. Conor McGregor fight program. *Joe Hand Promotions, Inc. v. Amos* (2019), handed a slam dunk finding to the plaintiffs after the defendant sports bar allowed an unauthorized broadcast of the fight in blatant violation of the copyright law issues related to the exclusive nationwide television rights within the United States, as well as violation of the Communications Act of 1934, generally referred to as "satellite piracy."

Trademarks

Trademarks are governed by the Trademark Act of 1946, more commonly known as the Lanham Act (2021), and the United States Code. Three distinct categories exist under the umbrella term trademark: trademark, service mark, and collective mark. They are distinguished by what they represent.

> **Trademark** – "Any word, name, symbol, or design or any combination thereof, adopted and used by a manufacturer or merchant to identify his goods, and distinguish them from those manufactured or sold by others." (Lanham Act, 15 USC 1052)
>
> *Ex: Nike (trademark for sport clothing and equipment)*
>
> **Service Mark** – "A mark used in the sale of advertising of service to identify the services of one person and distinguish them from the services of others." (15 USC 1053)
>
> *Ex: International Management Group* (IMG)
>
> **Collective Mark** – Either a trademark or a service mark or both used by the "members of a cooperative, an association, or other collective group or organization and includes marks used to indicate membership in a union, an association, or other organization." (15 USC 1054)
>
> *Ex: The North American Society for Sport Management* (NASSM)

A party wishing to obtain a trademark must file a formal application with the Patent and Trademark Office. The application is to include the dates of the first use of the mark and the first use of the mark in commerce, goods, or services. It should also include a drawing of the mark or an explanation of the service, an attestation that the mark is original, and areas in which the mark will be used (Lanham Act, 1051–1054). A certificate of registration is returned to the owner and is published in the Official Gazette of the Patent and Trademark Office (15 USC 1051). The certificate is valid and prima facie evidence of the mark's existence (15 USC 1057). Registration is for 10 years (15 USC 1058), and re-registration should occur prior to the end of the 10-year period. A registered mark may be assigned to another; however, the assignment must be in writing (15 USC 1060), be recorded with the U.S. Patent and Trademark Office, and be published in the Official Gazette, the United States Patent and Trademark Office's official journal (15 USC 1060).

A registration may be refused by the Patent and Trademark Office for the following reasons:

> a) consists of or comprises immoral, deceptive, or scandalous matter, or matter that may disparage or falsely suggests a connection with persons, living or dead, institutions, beliefs, or national symbols, or brings them into contempt, or disrepute; ...
>
> b) consists of or comprises the flag or coat of arms or other insignia of the United States, or of any state or municipality, or of any foreign nation, or any simulation thereof;
>
> c) consists of or comprises a name, portrait, or signature identifying a particular living individual, except by written consent; or
>
> d) consists of or comprises a mark that so resembles a mark registered in the Patent and Trademark Office. (15 USC 1052)

Trademark owners are cautioned to monitor the Official Gazette for new applications for marks that could damage or infringe the owners' registered marks. If such a registration appears in the Gazette, the owner should file an opposition to the registration of the proposed mark in the Patent and Trademark Office. A hearing will be held by the Trademark Trials and Appeals Board (TTAB), and a decision will be made by the board. The decision can be appealed to a federal court. If the mark is successfully opposed, the applicant is denied registration. A registered mark may be challenged in court because it was obtained fraudulently, was abandoned (i.e., not used for a significant period of time), misrepresented goods or services, or violated antitrust law (15 USC 1115). Courts will analyze the mark for the elements of confusion, dilution, trade dress, cancellation, or abandonment.

Confusion

Confusion is usually the result of either false designation of origin or false description of a product or program. The law states that

1) any person who, on or in connection with any goods or services, or any container for goods, uses in commerce any word, term, name, symbol, or device, or any combination thereof or false designation of origin, false or misleading description of fact, or false or misleading representation of fact that

    a) is likely to cause confusion, or to cause mistake, or to deceive as to the affiliation, connection, or association of such person with another person, or as to origin, sponsorship, or approval of his or her goods, services, or commercial activities by another person, or

    b) in commercial advertising or promotion, misrepresents the nature, characteristics, qualities, or geographic origin of his or her or another person's goods, services, or commercial activities shall be liable in a civil action by any person who believes that he or she is likely to be damaged by such act. (15 USC 1125)

Dilution

Congress passed the Federal Trademark Dilution Act (FTDA) of 1995, creating a federal cause of action for dilution. Dilution is a claim brought by owners of famous marks who believe that another party's use of a similar mark will diminish or weaken the association that consumers have between their marks and their products or services. The claim is based on the likelihood that the public will become confused over common elements of two different marks. The major factor in the court's decision is whether the public will be harmed as a result of the confusion. Owners of marks used by others in parody have requested injunctions or sued for infringement; often, these sales involve altered forms of trademarks on t-shirts, caps, towels, and similar merchandise. Defenses to dilution are that the mark is confusingly similar but not the same, or that the element of distinctiveness cannot be satisfied (15 USC 1125).

Trade Dress

Trade dress is the overall appearance of a product, including the color, shape, size, logo, and other characteristics. The décor of vendors, ball parks, fitness chains, restaurants, stores, and other places of business may be trade dress. For example, the consistent exterior and interior of building designs may be protected under trade dress. While trademark law has not always been specific on trade dress, the case *Abercrombie & Fitch Company v. Hunting World Incorporated* (1976) identified the components of trade dress as generic, descriptive, suggestive, arbitrary, or fanciful (8). Generic marks are common descriptive names of objects. The mark is or becomes generic when it is the common name of the object. For example, the word "Kleenex" is routinely used in the English language to refer to a tissue; however, the manufacturers of Kleenex prevent the mark from becoming generic by running advertisements to reinforce in consumers' minds that they are the leading brand of this type of consumer product. Thus, this is a distinctive mark and is considered a strong mark. Other types of distinctive marks include suggestive, arbitrary, and fanciful marks. A suggestive mark "requires imagination, thought, and perception to reach a conclusion as to the nature of the goods" (*Abercrombie & Fitch Company v. Hunting World Incorporated*, 1976, 8). For example, Greyhound bus lines suggest speed. A fanciful mark is not a real word in the English language but is invented to be used as a mark, such as Kodak or Clorox. An arbitrary mark applies a common word in an unfamiliar way. Puma is an arbitrary mark used to identify one source of athletic gear.

Descriptive marks, on the other hand, are considered weak marks because they lack secondary meaning. Since the mark is descriptive, it does not cause mental recognition in the buyer's mind about the source of the product. A mark is descriptive if it describes the product's features, qualities, or ingredients in ordinary language or describes the use to which the product is put. For example, onion rings describe the product, rather than identify the source of the product, whereas Ball Park Franks identify a unique source and brand of hot dogs rather than the general product category.

Cancellation

A registered mark can be canceled:

- by petition by the owner of a similar mark within five years of the registration of the mark;
- if the registered mark becomes a generic name for goods or services;
- if the mark has been abandoned; or
- if the mark was obtained fraudulently.

"The primary significance of the registered mark to the relevant public rather than purchaser motivation shall be the test for determining whether the registered mark has become the generic name of the goods and services on or in connection with which it has been used" (Lanham Act, 15 USC 1064). When a party has sustained a five-year period during which the mark has not been challenged, he/she may file to make the mark incontestable (15 USC 1065). Relief can be injunctive (i.e., stopping the action) or compensatory. Compensatory relief may include recovery of defendant's profits, damage sustained by plaintiff, cost of court and appeal processes, and destruction of infringing articles. All court decisions become part of the Patent and Trademark Office records.

Abandonment

A mark is abandoned if its use has been discontinued with intent not to resume its use in regular trade. Nonuse for three years is prima facie evidence of abandonment (15 USC 1127).

Infringement

To recover for infringement of a registered mark under Section 32(1) of the Lanham Act, a plaintiff must establish first, that its mark is valid and second, that the defendant's use of the mark is likely to cause confusion. A defendant is then liable for infringement if he uses (1) any reproduction, counterfeit, copy, or colorable imitation of the mark; (2) without the registrant's consent; (3) in commerce; (4) in connection with the sale, offering for sale, distribution, or advertising of any goods; (5) where such use is likely to cause confusion or to cause mistake or to deceive (15 USC 1114 [1, a]) ... Section 43(a) of the Lanham Act provides a civil cause of action for infringement of unregistered marks. In order for an unregistered mark to be protectable under section 43(a), the mark must be capable of distinguishing the plaintiff's services from those of others (15 USC 1125[a]).

Validity and likelihood of confusion are the two criteria examined closely for service mark infringement.

Criminal Acts in Trademark

Trademark counterfeiting or pirating of memorabilia, apparel, and equipment are serious crimes affecting the sport industry. In an effort to curb these multimillion-dollar losses in sales tax revenue, the Federal Bureau of Investigation (FBI), the Internal Revenue Service (IRS), and the Department of Homeland Security have joined forces to curb, or at least control, the situation. The U.S. Border Patrol is also working with these organizations. "The Coalition to Advance the Protection of Sports Logos (CAPS), an alliance formed by the Collegiate Licensing Company (CLC), Major League Baseball Properties, NBA Properties, NFL Properties, and NHL Enterprises, works in conjunction with local law enforcement agencies to seize counterfeit property" (Grady et al., 2009).

The Lanham Act allows manufacturers, sellers, and producers of goods and services to prevent a competitor from the following:

1) using any counterfeit, copy, or imitation of their trademarks (that has been registered with the U.S. Patent and Trademark Office), in connection with the sale of any goods or services in a way that is likely to cause confusion, mistake, or deception, (15 USC 1114) or
2) using in commercial advertising any word, term, name, symbol, or device, or any false or misleading designation of origin, or false or misleading description or representation of fact, which: (a) is likely to cause confusion, mistake, or deception as to affiliation, connection, or association, or as to origin, sponsorship, or approval, of his or her goods, services, or commercial activities by another person or (b) misrepresents the nature, characteristics, qualities, or geographic origin of his or her or another person's goals, services, or commercial activities. (15 USC 1125)

Potential penalties include an injunction to stop the use of the mark, destruction of articles containing the mark, and money damages. Treble damages are fines of three times the cost of the damage. Statutory damage under the Lanham Act are also available as an alternative to seeking the defendant's profits or plaintiff's actual losses resulting from infringement in the amount of not less than $1,000 or more than $200,000 per counterfeit mark per type of goods or services sold (15 USC 1116–1118, 2010).

The Trademark Counterfeiting Act of 1984 provides that "whoever intentionally traffics or attempts to traffic in goods or services and knowingly uses a counterfeit mark on or in connection with such goods or services shall, if an individual, be fined or imprisoned" (18 USC 2320 [a], 2010). A violation of the federal counterfeiting statute requires that the following elements be established:

1) the defendant trafficked or attempted to traffic in goods and services;
2) that such trafficking, or the attempt to traffic was intentional;
3) that the defendant used a "counterfeit mark" on or in connection with such goods or services; and
4) that the defendant "knew" that the counterfeit mark was so used. (18 USC 2320 [a], 2010)

Trademark Cases

The following trademark cases will be addressed under the categories of confusion, dilution, trade dress, cancellation, and abandonment.

Confusion

The word "Olympic" and the interlocking rings associated with the Olympics have been the subject of litigation since 1982. In *United States Olympic Committee et al. v. Intelicense Corp. S.A.* (1984), exclusive ownership of the word "Olympic" was given to the United States Olympic Committee (USOC). The decision, along with the Ted Stevens Olympic and Amateur Sports Act of 1978, a federal statute, gives exclusive ownership of the word and rings to the USOC.

An example of litigation was the *United States Olympic Committee et al. v. Xclusive Leisure & Hospitality, Ltd. et al.* (2009). The United States Olympic Committee (USOC), the International Olympic Committee (IOC), and the 2008 Beijing Olympic Games Organizing Committee (BOCOG) sued beijingticketing.com for name confusion in their use of USOC and IOC marks protected under the Lanham Act (Lanham Act, 15 USC 1114) and the Ted Stevens Olympic and Amateur Sports Act. Defendants had created a website using USOC and IOC logos to sell illegal tickets for the 2008 Olympic Games. Unbeknownst to the illegal website owners was the fact that (a) many of the Beijing Official Olympic tickets, including the Opening and Closing ceremonies, contained microchips that identified the owner and that (b) ownership could only be transferred once through a complex process. Those who purchased tickets from the illegal site never received their forged tickets. The lawsuit was BOCOG's preferred method of stopping the illegal website from conducting further sales that may have been directing Olympic fans away from the official ticket website. The district court found a likelihood of confusion and granted an injunction to close the website. Plaintiffs could seek damages.

The term "March Madness" has been the subject of ongoing litigation for almost two decades. In a series of decisions beginning in 2001, the March Madness Athletic Association (MMAA), the National Collegiate Athletic Association (NCAA), and the Illinois High School Athletic Association (IHAA) sued Netfire, d/b/a Sport Marketing International (SMI), and Matthew Jones. In 2000, the Illinois High School Athletic Association sued Netfire for trademark infringement, dilution, and unfair competition. Later, the March Madness Athletic Association replaced the high school group in that suit and "amended its complaint to add a claim for cybersquatting or using a domain name in order to profit dishonestly from the reputation of someone else's trademark" (*March Madness Athletic Association, LLC. v. Netfire, Inc.*, 2005, 542).

In 2003, the Fifth Circuit found for MMAA on infringement and cybersquatting (543). The court also found that the phrase "March Madness" was a protectable trademark, not a generic term. The court found that there was a likelihood of confusion between the protected trademark and the website. Factors typically examined in determining the likelihood of confusion:

1) the type of mark allegedly infringed,
2) the similarity between the two marks,
3) the similarity of the products or services,
4) the identity of the retail outlets and purchasers,
5) the identity of the advertising media used,
6) the defendant's intent, and
7) any evidence of actual confusion. (*March Madness Athletic Association, LLC,. v. Netfire, Inc.*, 2005, 49)

Ownership of the domain name was eventually transferred from SMI to MMAA.

Other trademark lawsuits involving their marks as used for university athletic teams have run the legal gamut. On August 20, 2010, the Ohio State University (OSU) filed a motion for a temporary restraining order and preliminary injunction against Keith Antonio Thomas and GDS Marketing, LLC for trademark infringement. GDS had infringed eight of OSU's trademarks registered between 1981 and 1997 and a series of common-law trademarks, including the colors scarlet and gray, the website, and the block O (*The Ohio State University v. Keith Antonio Thomas et al.*, 2010). At the time, OSU's trademark licensing program was over 30 years old and had generated royalties of $35 million over the past five years. The defendants published two electronic magazines, "Buckeye Gameday" and "Ohio State Buckeye E-Book," freely using any and all of OSU's registered and common-law trademarks. The court found OSU owned the marks, the marks had been used in commerce, and a likelihood of confusion existed. OSU was granted a temporary restraining order and a preliminary injunction. The defendants were required to stop producing the magazines.

A 13-year trademark battle existed between the University of South Carolina and the University of Southern California over the interlocking "SC" logo used by athletic teams at both schools. The University of Southern California owns the registered mark. The University of South Carolina petitioned the TTAB to cancel Southern Cal's registration of the mark, arguing that "SC" represented the state of South Carolina and had been used prior to Southern California's use. This legal argument was succinctly summarized on a bumper sticker stating "we (S. Carolina) were a state, before they (Southern Cal) were a football team." The TTAB refused to register South Carolina's logo and also refused to cancel Southern Cal's trademark. The petition to the United States Supreme Court was denied (*University of South Carolina v. University of Southern California*, 2010).

Dilution

A recent decision that involved both confusion and dilution was *Dallas Cowboys Football Club, LTD. et al. v. America's Team Properties, Inc.* (2009). America's Team Properties (ATP), incorporated in Minnesota in 1998, took the assignment of the U.S. trademark, "America's team" to be used in selling T-shirts and other apparel. The previous owner had obtained the mark in 1990; ATP purchased the mark for $100. In 1999, the owner of ATP ran an advertisement in *USA Today* in an effort to auction the mark to the highest bidder. ATP called the Dallas Cowboys to notify the team that the registration was for sale.

The Dallas Cowboys responded by filing suit alleging common-law rights against ATP for trademark infringement. They stated that the mark "America's team" was protected and that they possessed priority over America's Team Properties. ATP filed a counterclaim against the Dallas Cowboys seeking a declaratory judgment that the registration was valid and sought cancellation of the mark on the basis that it had not been used. Two questions were raised at trial: (1) would the common marks be confused by consumers (the likelihood of confusion), and (2) if both were retained, could the value of the mark be weakened (dilution)? The court concluded that a likelihood of confusion would exist as the marks were exactly the same; however, nearly all of the remaining factors favored the plaintiffs.

Trademark dilution was identified, by the court, "as the weakening of the ability of a mark to clearly and unmistakably distinguish the source of a product" (*Dallas Cowboys Football Club, Ltd. v. America's Team Properties, Inc.*, 2009, 642). In blurring, the court considered similarity, distinctiveness, and exclusive use of the mark. Tarnishment occurs when the mark represents poor-quality products or some other event such as an inferior website. When one of two marks is weak and confusion exists, people will think of both products as weak. The Dallas Cowboys alleged both blurring and tarnishment as a result of the same mark and requested that the court cancel ATP's mark. The Court cancelled ATP's mark and ordered an injunction, as well as ordered the removal of all infringing products from the defendant's website.

In 2000, the Heisman Trophy Trust entered into a settlement with Smack Apparel, a manufacturer of humorous and occasionally irreverent T-shirts, following the company's sale of a shopping bag with a picture of a potential Heisman winner suspected of shoplifting superimposed on a picture of the Heisman Trophy. According to the agreement, Smack Apparel stated they would "cease and permanently reframe from manufacturing, displaying, selling, or offering for sale any clothing or merchandise bearing the Heisman marks" (*The Heisman Trophy Trust v. Smack Apparel Company*, 2009, 324).

Trade Dress

Golf courses may place service marks on their names and on distinguishing aspects of the course or on a particular hole on the course. *Pebble Beach Co. v. Tour 18 I, Ltd.* (1996) was an action for service mark and trade dress infringement, unfair competition, and false advertising. Confusion and dilution played an important role in the case. The legal action was brought by the owners of a number of famous golf courses against the developer of an 18-hole course in Texas. The Texas golf course consisted of replica holes from these famous courses. The developer for Tour 18 freely used the marks of Pebble Beach, Pinehurst, and Harbor Town. In response, Tour 18 asserted counterclaims under Texas law for unfair competition and interfering with an existing business. The developer claimed that the suit was a frivolous attempt to put Tour 18 out of business.

Pebble Beach and Pinehurst provided evidence of federal service mark registration for their marks; Sea Pines did not own a federal service mark for Harbor Town or the lighthouse at Harbor Town. Its exerted claim for protection was the common-law service mark under Section 43(a) of the Lanham Act. Tour 18 unsuccessfully argued a number of issues, among them the fact that Sea Pines no longer owned the lighthouse and had therefore abandoned the mark. Sea Pines continued to hold the mark after the sale of the lighthouse and had license agreements with the new owners to enable the new owners to use the mark in agreed-upon ways.

Under a likelihood of confusion analysis, the court stated that "while golfers at Tour 18 may not be confused as to the course since they will know they are playing a replica constructed by Tour 18 and not the real Pebble Beach hole 14, they may still be confused into believing Pebble Beach sponsored or approved Tour 18's use of their service marks and golf hole designs" (*Pebble Beach Co. v. Tour 18 I, Ltd*, 1998, 1542). The court found that the plaintiffs had shown the validity of their respective marks; that the defendants, without the plaintiffs' consent, copied a colorable imitation of plaintiffs' registered marks; and that Tour 18's use of plaintiffs' marks was likely to cause consumer confusion.

Trade dress was "the shapes of plaintiffs' golf holes, the length and width of the holes, the placement and shape of sand and water hazards, the size and shape of the greens, the slope and elevation of the holes, and the golf holes' surrounding vegetation" (1555). Also, the evidence indicated "that there is an unlimited number of alternative designs to plaintiffs' golf hole configurations. Additionally, while plaintiffs' design is particularly beautiful and challenging, there is no evidence to indicate that the designs are superior to the many available alternatives. Consequently, there is no need for Tour 18 to copy plaintiffs' golf hole designs to achieve the functions of a golf hole" (1556).

The issue under dilution was whether the uses of the mark would cause injury to the business reputation or dilute the distinctiveness of the owner's mark. The court found that only the 18th hole at Harbor Town and the recognizable lighthouse had the "strong, distinctive, source-identifying characteristics required for protection under the antidilution statute" (1567). Thus, the court found for Sea Pines under a dilution legal theory. The court "found Tour 18 liable for ...service mark infringement, trade dress infringement, and unfair competition in violation of the Lanham Act" (1571). The plaintiffs were given an injunction preventing Tour 18's use of a replica holes or of the Harbor Town lighthouse, Pebble Beach Golf links, Pinehurst, or Pinehurst No. 2. The defendants were also required to place a bold disclaimer of any affiliation with the original golf holes in advertising. The appeals court affirmed the finding of a likelihood of confusion.

Color schemes, such as a university's team colors, are entitled to protection as trade dress as a result of the decision in *Board of Supervisors of Louisiana State University v. Smack Apparel Co.* (2006). Smack Apparel was found by the federal district court to have intentionally infringed on the marks owned by the Collegiate Licensing Company (CLC) and those of the Ohio State, LSU, Oklahoma, and Southern California. In 2008, the Fifth Circuit affirmed, concluding that "the record established secondary meaning in the marks. Next, it found that plaintiffs possessed strong marks in their use of color schemes and other identifying indicia on college sports-themed merchandise" (*Board of Supervisors of Louisiana State University et al. v. Smack Apparel et al.*, 2009, 465). The district court eventually awarded plaintiffs around $45,000.

Cancellation

A mark can be canceled if it becomes common or generic, is offensive, or is successfully challenged by another party. It is considered to be abandoned if not used for a long period of time. In 1992, Susan Harjo petitioned the trademark trial and Appeals Board (TTAB) to cancel six Washington Redskin trademarks containing the word "Redskin(s)" on the grounds that the word was offensive, scandalous, and disparaging to Native Americans. In 1999, the TTAB ruled in favor of Harjo and the Native Americans. Pro-Football brought suit to review the TTAB decision (*Pro-Football, Inc. v. Harjo et al.*, 2000). Pro-Football argued that "the trademarks do not disparage Native Americans ... [and] do not bring Native Americans into contempt or disrepute ... [and] that the Native Americans' cancellation petition was time-barred, referred to as the defense of laches" (*Pro-Football, Inc. v. Harjo et al.*, 2000). In this case, the view was that the agency holding the mark for 25 years had continuously invested time and money into the brand, and that if one wishes to contest a mark, it should have done so in a timely manner. To counter Pro-Football's laches defense, Harjo asserted "because a laches argument requires a showing of economic prejudice, they are entitled to broad discovery of Pro-Football's financial records" (2002, 80). Pro-Football claimed the business records were confidential.

In 2003, after a lengthy trial, the federal district court found for the Washington Redskins. In 2005, the Native Americans appealed. The appeals court found that the district court applied the wrong standard in evaluating the laches time defense and returned the case to the district court. In 2008, summary judgment was granted to the Redskins organization and denied to Harjo. The court concluded the team owners had established Harjo's lack of diligence, with no valid excuse, in delaying contestation of the Redskins mark. Because the Redskins owners could establish evidence of economic prejudice showing heavy investments in marketing and developing the brand over a substantial period of time, cancellation of the marks was therefore ordered to be stopped.

A flurry of legal and business developments in 2019 and 2020 caused the Washington Redskins organization to agree to retire the Redskins name and ultimately change the team name (McGee, 2020). Now referred to as the Washington Commanders as of 2022, the name change quiets loud hackles over one of the last remaining professional sports teams with a Native American team name and offensive imagery. Subsequent steps taken by the team included the announcement that fans would no longer be allowed to wear Native American-inspired ceremonial headdresses or face paint at home games in the stadium, a decision announced ahead of the 2021 season (The Athletic staff, 2021). Despite an official legal victory by the team in front of the Trademark board (TTAB), mounting public and media pressure on team owners, and perhaps most directly internal pressure from the NFL office itself, provided a moral, if not legal victory to Harjo and the lead plaintiffs in this ongoing and entrenched litigation.

Right of Publicity

The term "right of publicity" was coined in *Haelan Laboratories, Inc. v. Topps Chewing Gum, Inc.* (1953). The right evolved principally for entertainers, celebrities, and public figures who were facing either misappropriation of name, First Amendment invasion of privacy violations, or both. Misappropriation is "the unauthorized, improper, or unlawful use of ... property for a purpose other than that for which it is intended" (*Black's Law Dictionary*, 2019). McCarthy defined the right of publicity as the "right of everyone to control the commercial use of his or her identity" (2000, p. 3:1). In 1960, Prosser organized the right of privacy into four distinct torts: "(1) unreasonable intrusion upon another's seclusion; (2) public disclosure of private facts; (3) false light invasion of privacy; and (4) appropriation of another's name or likeness" (ABA Section of Intellectual Property Law, 2004).

Right of Publicity Cases

The use of athletes' identity in fantasy sports games became an issue in professional sports in *CBC Distribution and Marketing, Inc. v. Major League Baseball Advanced Media L.P. (MLBAM) et al.* (2005). This issue was later litigated in the collegiate sports context in *Keller et al. v. Electronic Arts, Inc., NCAA, and Collegiate Licensing Company* (2010). MLBAM, the media arm of Major League Baseball and the NFL Players Association (NFLPA), alleged that CBC Distribution and Marketing, a fantasy game company, had violated their license agreement by operating a fantasy game using players' identities without permission or a license. CBC provided not only the games but also up-to-date information on players, most of which was available in newspapers. CBC entered into a license agreement with the NFLPA in 1995. The 2002 License Agreement stated "that upon termination CBC would have no right ... to use ... the rights, the trademarks, or any promotional material relating to the licensed products and that upon expiration or termination of the license agreement, CBC shall refrain from further use of the rights and/or the trademarks ..., either directly or indirectly" (*CBC Distribution and Marketing, Inc.*, 2005, 8). Between 2001 and January 2004, Advanced Media offered the fantasy baseball game on MLB.com without obtaining a license and without obtaining permission from the Players Association. With CBC anticipating a lawsuit being brought against them, they filed a complaint for declaratory judgment to state that CBC had exclusive ownership of player statistics associated with players' names and also sought injunctive relief so that Advanced Media would be enjoined from further interfering with CBC businesses. Advanced Media and the NFLPA countered with contract violations based on the 2002 license agreement and that CBC violated players' rights of publicity based on CBC's exploiting the identity of players, including their names, nicknames, likenesses, signatures, jersey numbers, pictures, player records, and biographical data. The contract issues were resolved.

On appeal, the court found a violation of the right of publicity since the players' identities had been used for commercial profit. However, the appellate court concluded the right of publicity was secondary to CBC's First Amendment right to use the players' names and statistics. The law was clear that names and statistics are facts and thus cannot be copyrighted. However, under the First Amendment, names and statistics are available to the public and are therefore in the public domain. CBC therefore succeeded in their legal arguments because preserving the First Amendment right was viewed by the court as more important than the players' publicity rights.

In *Keller et al. v. Electronic Arts, Inc., NCAA, and Collegiate Licensing Company* (2010), the same issue was litigated at the collegiate level. Sam Keller, a former star quarterback for Arizona State, filed a class action suit on behalf of collegiate football and basketball players. The claims were on the alleged use of players' identities, without permission, in NCAA football, basketball, and March Madness video games. Even though players' names were not used, sufficient information was provided so the average sports fan could easily identify the actual players represented in the video game. The plaintiff's claimed the NCAA violated

Indiana's right of publicity, a right to his likeness or image. The court disagreed and dismissed the case.

The claim against Electronic Arts was analyzed using several different balancing tests, which are, in effect, defenses, to reconcile the competing interests of the athletes' rights of publicity and the First Amendment rights of Electronic Arts. The court first used the "transformative use" balancing test. Transformative use examines whether the likeness was original or the likeness had been transformed so that it no longer represented the celebrity. Electronic Arts (EA) stated that the video game had used transformative elements in depicting the athletes. In denying EA's transformative use defense, the court noted, "these cases show that this Court's focus must be on the depiction of plaintiff in 'NCAA Football' not the game's other elements" (*Keller et al. v. Electronic Arts, Inc. et al.*, 2010, 18). Under public interest, California law states that "no cause of action will lie for the publication of matters in the public interest, which rests on the right of the public to know and the freedom of the press to tell it." The defense argued that the names and statistics were public interest and were not part of the right of publicity. The court found that EA had used more than the mere names and the statistics; it had used athletes' physical characteristics and had moved far beyond what the court had considered in the *Major League Baseball Advanced Media, L.P. et al.* case. EA lost using the public interest test. *Keller et al. v. Electronic Arts, Inc. et al.* was consolidated with other cases raising similar claims by current and former student athletes, as *In re: NCAA Student-Athlete Name and Likeness Litigation* (2010).

The most recent significant development impacting the intellectual property rights of college athletes is the *O'Bannon* litigation, which is discussed in some depth in Chapter 9 under Antitrust Law. As the case focused on those legal claims and not as much on whether college athletes have a valid right of publicity that can be licensed by them, given NCAA prohibitions on commercialism, the O'Bannon litigation opened the floodgates quite literally for cash to begin flowing to college athletes overnight, with the NCAA left standing on the sidelines still holding the ball, waiting for Congress to save them. Instead, against a strong tide of public pressure and increasing public support for college athletes to be compensated for use of their name, image, and likeness (NIL), the "NIL era of college sports" came to be. NCAA President Mark Emmert "decried the patchwork of name, image, and likeness laws" (Scharf, 2021) at the state level has now created an unequal playing field, especially when recruiting elite college athletes, while athletes rejoiced given their newfound economic freedoms.

Patent Law

Like copyright and trademark law, patent law evolved from Article I of the United States Constitution. It grants Congress the power to "promote the progress of science and useful arts, by securing for a limited time to authors and inventors the exclusive right to their respective writings and discoveries" (U.S. Constitution, Article I, Section 8, Clause 8). The Patent Act of 1952 states that a patent is obtained by "whoever invents or discovers any new and useful process, machine, manufacture, or composition of matter, or any new and useful improvement of the above" (Patent Act, 35 USC 101). A person is entitled to a patent unless:

a) the invention was known or used by others in this country ... or

b) the invention was patented or described in a printed publication in this or a foreign country ... or

c) he has abandoned the invention or ...

d) he did not himself invent the subject matter sought to be patented. (35 USC 102)

Also, "a patent may not be obtained though the invention is not identically disclosed or described as set forth in section 102 ... if the differences between the subject matter sought to be patented and the prior art are such that the subject matter as a whole would have been obvious at the time the invention was made to a person having ordinary skill in the art to which said subject matter pertains" (35 USC 103). A patent is infringed when someone "without authority makes, uses, offers to sell, or sells any patented invention, within the United States or imports into the United States any patented invention during the term of the patent" (35 USC 271). Damages for infringing on a patent are to be adequate to compensate for the infringement or a reasonable royalty. A court may increase the damage award to three times the damage assessed (35 USC 284).

Patent applications need to demonstrate that the invention or discovery is novel and non-obvious. The application is expected to describe the object of the patent in detail. Patent law does not cover laws of nature, physical phenomena, or abstract ideas (Patent Act, 35 USC 101). A patent gives the owner a monopoly on the registered object (Harkins, 2008). Currently, the life of a patent begins on the date of issue and ends 20 years from the date of application and generally cannot be renewed (Patent Act, 35 USC 154).

The majority of patents received in sport throughout the years have been for sports equipment. For example, the reader can trace the evolution of golf club and tennis racket patents as the selection of materials and the precision of mechanics changed the trajectory of the golf club swing and the sweet spot of the tennis strings. The reader who checks the patent registrar for sport equipment will be impressed with the volume of awards for sport in any one year.

Patent Law Cases

Everything Baseball v. Wilson Sporting Goods Company et al. (2009) is a sport example of a typical patent infringement case. Everything Baseball sued Wilson Sporting Goods Company and others, alleging that Wilson was infringing their patent No. 6,161,226, a baseball chest protector. Wilson and other manufacturers, including Rawlings and Riddell, moved for summary judgment. The patent was invalid as anticipated by three prior art references. The three prior art references were: No. 5,530,966, issued to Joseph West; a chest protector, manufactured and sold by Douglas under the West patent; and the "hang tag" attached to a chest protector, manufactured and sold by Wilson under the West patent. All three chest protectors were compared and found to be different from Everything Baseball's chest protector. As a result, the defendant's motion for summary judgment was denied.

Patent infringement analysis involves two steps: 1) claim construction; and 2) application of the properly construed claims to the accused device or method. The court completed the first step, a question of law, with the claim construction order. Next, the court determined if there had been patent infringement, it would have been a question of fact. To prove infringement, a patent holder must show that the accused device or method meets each claim limitation, either literally or under the doctrine of equivalents.

Process Sport Patents

Technology has had a profound impact on patent law and is directly responsible for many of the substantive changes in this area of the law. The 1998 decision in *State Street Bank and Trust Co. v. Signature Financial Group, Inc.*, however, identified a new avenue for patent registration in the sport industry. Signature Financial Group, Inc. was the assignee of a patent called the Data Processing System for hub and Spoke Financial Services Configuration. It was a data processing system (the system) for implementing an investment structure that was developed for use in Signature's business as an administrator and economic agent for mutual funds.... The system ... facilitates a structure whereby mutual funds (Spokes) pooled their assets in an investment portfolio (hub) organized as a partnership. The investment configuration provided the administrator of a mutual fund with the advantages of a partnership (*State Street Bank and Trust Co. v. Signature Financial Group, Inc.*, 1998, 1370).

The term process was defined as "a process, art or method, and includes a new use of a known process, machine, manufacture, composition of matter, or material" (Patent Act, 35 USC 100). The question was whether HUB and SPOKE could receive a patent; the court said no, it was an idea, not a process. The court of appeals reversed, holding "that the transformation of data, representing discrete dollar amounts, by a machine through a series of mathematical calculations into a final share price ... produces a useful, concrete and tangible result" (1373).

The sport industry saw the *State Street Bank and Trust* (1998) decision as a means to secure rights to strategy and skill innovations. Following the decision, a number of authors suggested that sport strategies and movements could receive not only copyright and trademarks, but protection under patent law as well. Kunstadt (1996), a law partner in a firm representing the National Basketball Association (NBA) and the United States Olympic Committee (USOC), led this bold initiative for broader intellectual property protection of sport moves with his article entitled "Are Sport Moves Next in IP Law?"

Clement and Hartman (2000) built a case for patent and/or copyright for the open/closed system of classifying human movement devised by Poulton (1957) and refined by Knapp (1963) and Robb (1972).

> Closed movements are planned sequences of movement repeated in the same manner every time. They are predetermined routines. Open movements are movements executed in response to the movement of others. they are used to react to the movements of others. Performers in open movement know many different movements and strategies; they do not, however, know the actual movement that they will execute in any event until the opponents begin to make their plays. Gymnastics, figure skating, and archery represent closed movements; basketball, fencing, and tennis favor open movements." (Clement & Hartman, 1994, p. 21)

All closed movements and original routines of such movements that are new and unique are easily fixed and thus readily suitable for copyright; some may also meet the requirements of a patent. Open movements are more difficult to copyright or patent; however, newly created strategies should still qualify.

Griffith (1998) argued for the value of patents for sport skills and techniques as a matter of economics, suggesting that as sport skills and strategies increased in monetary value while technology was making it easier to copy creative accomplishments, athletes should take steps to secure their innovations. It is not difficult for an enthusiastic synchronized swimmer to film the performance of a recent Olympic championship routine, play the stunts and sequences frame by frame, and eventually replicate the performance. These early works helped shape the current state of diverse patentable sport subject matter today.

There are a number of issues that have been discussed that may impact the future of patents as they relate to sport. With passage of the Leahy-Smith America Invents Act in 2013, the United States patent system switched from a "first to invent" to a "first to file," bringing the U.S. in line with countries who predominantly use the "first to file" system.

Summary

Intellectual property is the body of laws that (a) protect the creative aspects of the sport industry and (b) reward investment by sport properties, organizations, and manufacturers that develop a recognizable brand in their products or services. The law also protects the commercial aspects of a celebrity athlete's persona, but not facts or statistics that are already in the public domain. With innovations in technology, the ability to create digital images of star athletes will raise new concerns about how to sufficiently protect these athletes' brands. Intellectual property rights are property rights that can be licensed, sold, or transferred to others. Infringement of copyright, trademark, and patent by competitors is often the focus of litigation involving this rapidly evolving area of law.

Discussion Questions

1. Explain major differences between copyright and trademark law and define which sport context might call for using one type of intellectual property over another.
2. Explain how right of publicity concepts are evolving by examining any Name, Image, Likeness (NIL) legislation for protecting college athletes' rights in your home state.

Activities

1. Obtain a copy of one recent court decision discussed in this chapter from each of the major areas of intellectual property law: copyright, trademark, right of publicity, and patent. Summarize or "brief" each case using the information retrieved in your legal research.
2. Using Nexis Uni or Google, search and locate a patent or trademark registration involving sport, such as an professional athlete trademarking his nickname. Be ready to discuss your findings in class.

References

Abercrombie & Fitch Company v. Hunting World Incorporated, 537 F. 2d 4 (1976).

American Bar Association, Section of Intellectual Property Law. (2004). Report to the House of Delegates. http://www.abnet.org

Bambauer, K. (2005). Legal responses to the challenges of sport patents. *Harvard Journal of Law & Technology, 18*, 401.

Board of Supervisors for Louisiana State University v. Smack Apparel Co., 2009 U.S. Dist. LEXIS 27652.

Bouchat v. Baltimore Ravens Limited Partnership, 587 F. Supp. 2d 686 (2008).

Bouchat v. Bon Ton Department Stories, Inc., 506 F. 3d 315 (2007).

CBC Distribution and Marketing v. Major League Baseball Advanced Media, 505 F. 3d 818 (2007).

Clement, A. (2000). Contemporary copyright and patent law and sport. *Journal of Legal Aspects of Sport, 10*, 143.

Clement, A., & Hartman, B. G. (1994). *The Teaching of Physical Skills.* William C. Brown & Benchmark.

Communications Act of 1934, 47 U.S.C. § 553, Unauthorized reception of cable service (2021).

Copyright Act of 1976, 17 USC 101–1332 (2021).

Copyright Law Revision, House Report, No. 94–1476 (1976).

Curtis v. Benson and the New Orleans Saints Limited Partnerships, 959 F. Supp. 348 (1997).

Dallas Cowboys Football Club, LTD, v. America's Team Properties, Inc., 616 F. Supp. 2d 622 (2009).

Das, P. K. (2000). Offensive protection: The potential application of intellectual property to scripted sports plays. *Indiana Law Journal, 75*, 1073.

Everything Baseball v. Wilson Sporting Goods Company, 611 F. Supp. 2d 832 (2009).

Federal Trademark Dilution Act of 1995 (FTDFA). 15 USC 1125.

Garner, B. A. (2019). *Black's Law Dictionary* (11th edition). Thomson Reuters.

Grady, J., Clement, A., & Woishnis, J. (2009). Trademark Counterfeiting of Sport Merchandise and Criminal Law. in J. W. Lee & J. C. Lee (Eds.). *Sport and Criminal Behavior* (pp. 151–167). Carolina Academic Press.

Griffith, W. T. (1998). Beyond the perfect score: Protecting routine-oriented athletic performance with copyright law. *Connecticut Law Review, 30*, 675.

Haelan Laboratories, Inc. v. Topps Chewing Gum, Inc., 202 F. 2d 866 (1953).

Harkins, C.A. (2008). Throwing Judge Bryson's curveball: A pro patent view of process claims as patent-eligible subject matter. *John Marshall Review of Intellectual Property Law, 7*, 701.

Hawaii-Pacific Apparel Group v. Cleveland Browns Football Company, 418 F. Supp. 2d 501 (2006).

Joe Hand Promotions, Inc. v. Amos, 2019 WL 5618185 (2019).

J&J Sports Productions v. Live Oak County Post No. 6119 Veterans of Foreign Wars, 2009 U.S. Dist. LEXIS 84947.

Keller et al. v. Electronic Arts, Inc., National Collegiate Athletic Association, and Collegiate Licensing Company, 2010 U.S. Dist. LEXIS 10719; consolidated as in re: NCAA Student Athlete Name & Likeness Licensing litigation, 2010 U.S. Dist. LEXIS 139724.

Knapp, B. (1963). *Skills in Sport, The Attainment of Proficiency.* Routledge.

Kunstadt, R. M., Kieff, F. S., & Kramer, R. G. (1996, May 20). Are sport moves next in IP law? *National Law Journal*, C2.

Lanham Act, 15 USC 1051–1141 (2021).

Leahy-Smith America Invents Act, Public Law 112-29 (2011).

Longhorn Locker Company v. Hollman, 2020 WL 3963732 (2020).

Major League Baseball Advanced Media v. CBC Distribution and Marketing, 128 S. Ct. 2872 (2008).

March Madness Athletic Association v. Netfire, 2001 U.S. Dist. LEXIS 21078.

McCarthy, J. (2001). *The Right of Publicity and Privacy.* Clark Boardman Callaghan.

McGee, N. (2020, July 13). Redskins name change: Dan Snyder decides to rebrand Washington's NFL team after pressure. *The Sporting News.* https://www.sportingnews.com/us/nfl/news/redskins-name-change-dan-snyder/905uqj7tw301zmd8do3y2ney.

NBA v. Motorola, 105 F. 3d 841 (2nd Cir. 1997).

Patent Act, 35 USC 1–376 (2021).

Pebble Beach Company *et al.*, v. Tour 18, Ltd., 155 F. 3d 526 (1998).

Poulton, E. (1957). On prediction of skilled movements. *Psychological Bulletin, 54*(6), 467–478.

Pro-Football, Inc. v. Harjo et al., 565 F. 3d 880 (2009).

Prosser, W. L. (1960). Privacy. *California Law Review, 48*, 383.

Robb, M. (1972). *The Dynamics of Motor-Skill Acquisition*. Prentice Hall.

Scharf, R. (2021, September 29). NCAA president decries 'patchwork' of name, image law. *Law360 Employment Authority*. https://www.law360.com/employment-authority/articles/1426482/ncaa-president-decries-patchwork-of-name-image-laws.

Spinelli v NFL, 903 F.3d 185 (2d Cir. 2018).

State Street Bank & Trust Co. v. Signature Financial Group, 149 F. 3d 1368 (1998).

Ted Stevens Olympic and Amateur Sports Act. Exclusive right to name, seals, emblems, and badges, 36 USCS § 220506 (2021).

The Athletic staff. (2021, August 4). WFT bans fans from wearing Native American headdresses, face paint at home games. *The Athletic*. https://theathletic.com/news/wft-bans-fans-from-wearing-native-american-headdresses-face-paint-at-home-games/Ppg24y5nT6sT/

The Heisman Trophy Trust v. Smack Apparel Company, 379 Fed. Appx. 12 (2010).

The Ohio State University v. Keith Antonio Thomas, 2010 U.S. Dist. LEXIS 96478.

Thomson Reuters. (2018, September 14). Licensee cannot retroactively grant a sub-license to create license defense: Second Circuit. *Thomson Reuters, Practical Law Intellectual Property & Technology*. https://content.next.westlaw.com/Document/Iba4c1509b68611e8a5b3e3d9e23d7429/View/FullText.html?originationContext=document&transitionType=DocumentItem&contextData=(sc.Default)&firstPage=true.

Trademark Act of 1946, 15 USC 1051–1141 (2021).

United States Olympic Committee and the International Olympic Committee v. Xclusive Leisure & Hospitality, 2009 U.S. Dist. LEXIS 12698.

United States Olympic Committee v. Intelicense Corp., 737 F. 2d 263 (1984).

University of South Carolina v. University of Southern California, 367 Fed. Appx. 129 (2010).

Recommended Reading

Adams, J. M. (2013). Flag on the play: Professional sports teams calling trademark infringement on their superfans. *Jeffrey S. Moorad Sports Law Journal, 20*, 631. https://digitalcommons.law.villanova.edu/mslj/vol20/iss2/10.

Baker, T.A. (2020, March 28). NBA 2K tattoo copyright suit offers two compelling legal arguments, but only one seems practical. *Forbes*. https://www.forbes.com/sites/thomas-baker/2020/03/28/nba-2k-producer-successfully-defends-its-rim-against-tattoo-copy-right-claims-but-whats-next/?sh=1dc793f835b4

Brison, N., Baker, T., & Byon, K. (2013). Tweets and crumpets: Examining UK and US regulation of athlete endorsements and social media marketing. *Journal of Legal Aspects of Sport, 23*, 55.

Dennie, C. (2009). Tebow drops back to pass: Videogames have crossed the line but does the right of publicity protect a student-athlete's likeness when balanced against the First Amendment? *Arkansas Law Review, 62*, 645.

Epstein, A. (2017). The Ambush at Rio. *John Marshall Review of Intellectual Property Law, 16*, 350.

Gerhardt, D.M. (2017). Trademarks as entrepreneurial change agents for legal reform. *North Carolina Law Review, 95*, 1519. https://scholarship.law.unc.edu/nclr/vol95/iss5/8.

Kirshner, A. (2021, July 1). College athletes are wasting no time getting paid. *Slate*. https://slate.com/culture/2021/07/ncaa-name-image-likeness-college-athletes-endorsements-ads-pay.html.

Kline, J. (2009). Black and blue: An examination of trade marketing university color schemes. *Sports Law Journal, 16*, 47.

Saul Ewing Arnstein & Lehr LLP. (2019, November 20). With the NCAA's decision to permit amateur name, image, and likeness compensation, student-athletes and legislators score a big win, but will be a draw at the end of the season? https://www.saul.com/publications/alerts/ncaa%E2%80%99s-decision-permit-amateur-name-image-likeness-compensation-student-athletes-and-legislators

11

Risk Management

OBJECTIVES

Upon completing this chapter, you will,

- recognize the role risk management plays in business operations;
- recognize that a release is a contract;
- be conversant with the identification, evaluation, and control system in risk management, and
- understand how to create a safe and healthy environment, consistent with current CDC guidelines and in line with COVID protocols for mass gatherings and best practices in stadium management and operations.

Introduction

The goal in risk management is to avoid those dangers that one can envision. Risk management is the identification, evaluation, and control of loss to property, clients, employees, and the public. A risk management program requires a systematic examination of the environment, with the identification of potential for exposure to loss and legal liability in all facets of the organization. The purpose of risk management is to make the sport environment as safe as possible for participants and spectators and the business as efficient as possible using accepted business practices. Many people view risk management solely as a means of reducing legal liability; however, a safe, honest, and efficient environment will not only reduce liability but also will enhance the positive reputation of the business. Disaster management involves the identification of threats and vulnerabilities to natural and man-made hazards. Once the threats and vulnerabilities are identified, they are evaluated, and plans are prepared to meet, control, and survive the hazards that may occur. In recovery, the object is to return people, property, and businesses to the level at which they were before the incident. While risk management is driven by the desire to reduce accidents and possible litigation, disaster and recovery management are driven by the need for the survival of people, property, and businesses.

Persons who hold the positions of safety coordinators and committee members are to have an understanding of safety in the business of the agency. Further, staff handbooks are to contain policies and procedures relevant to safety, risk, and disaster management. An understanding of the components of a lawsuit are important to these areas (see introduction provided in Chapter 1).

Risk Management

Risk management must be a comprehensive process where all stakeholders of the sport organization participates in all components of the plan, including creation and revision of the plan. Even if an agency refuses to plan for risks or crises that may impact the business, sport professionals should create their own plans and programs. Insurance companies often demand ongoing risk management systems be present before providing coverage to a business or other agency. Other insurance companies have reduced rates when such programs are instituted.

This text has provided numerous illustrations of liability in sport and physical activity. Each of the major topics presented included an overview of the applicable law. Hypothetical examples and real cases illustrated most of the legal theories. This information, coupled with the student's practical experiences, is to be used to devise risk, disaster, and recovery management programs.

The risk management system consists of the identification, evaluation, and control of risks. The following risk management system was created for the first edition of *Law in Sport* (Clement, 1988).

Identification

The first step of risk management is to identify all areas of potential exposure to risk. Exposure means any and every event that could cause an agency to become vulnerable to a particular risk. The following is a list of elements that might be used in creating a risk management audit. This list is not meant to be comprehensive, nor has it been tailored to a specific agency or service. However, every effort has been made to demonstrate the vast array of topics a professional might consider in devising an audit. The elements include local, state, and federal codes and regulations. Professional organizations and other industry standards; policies and procedures; facilities; equipment; personnel; supervision; instruction; participant education; fiscal issues; and contracts.

Local, State, and Federal Regulations

Local, state, and federal laws, codes, and regulations that affect sport and physical activity and/or the agency under study are identified. The laws are published as health, safety, bathing, buildings, waste disposal, water pollution, medical emergency, weather, fire, crime, swimming pools, electrical, heating, refrigeration, air conditioning, industrial hygiene, and others. Agencies of importance include the Occupational Safety and Health Administration (OSHA), the Environmental Protection Agency (EPA), and the Department of Agriculture. Building codes are important. Waterslide regulations, for example, are often found in amusement park regulations, while amusement park rides are sometimes regulated by those who routinely inspect elevators! The agency's status as "for profit" or "not for profit" will, on occasion, affect its standing under a law.

All laws, codes, and regulations are to be posted, made available to employees, and reviewed with each worker whose job is impacted. They must also be retained on file, updated annually, and enforced. For example, fire safety regulations, including alarms, extinguishers, and sprinkler systems, are to be in order and must meet local codes. Enforceable provisions for electrical failure are to be made. Systems for evacuation for tornadoes, hurricanes, and severe storms are to be planned and posted, and staff must be prepared to carry them out. Employees must be educated about the differences between codes, laws, regulations, and guidelines. They should know that laws, codes, and regulations must be followed, whereas guidelines are followed on a volunteer basis. Failure to follow a code can result in civil punishment; failure to follow a *guideline* will not result in civil punishment. A court can ask why the professional ignored a guideline. Agencies choosing to ignore popular guidelines should document their knowledge of the guideline and the reason(s) for rejecting it.

Professional Organizations and Industry Standards

Managers need to know professional certificates and guidelines that affect their businesses. They are to be aware of professional organizations related to each aspect of their agencies. The literature and services of such organizations are to be evaluated and a commitment made to track the offerings of selected organizations. Records of job competencies, verifications of employee certificates and test results, and attendance at safety meetings are to be on file. Staff credentials are checked in initial employment and periodically throughout job tenure. Criminal and other background checks are conducted, and drug testing is required when appropriate. Industry standards are known and maintained. Should a professional or an agency choose to differ from industry standards, reasons for the differences are documented. Often, sport professionals adhere to standards that are higher than industry standards—such professional practice is to be encouraged.

Policies and Procedures Common to the Industry

Policies for employees, participants, facility management, and conduct of activities exist in writing and are readily available, widely known, and enforced. Employee handbooks contain all policies and procedures—including behavior, appearance, attendance, and alcohol/drug use. Policies for participants also address alcohol and drug use. Due process systems (described in Chapter 4, U.S. Constitutional Amendments) exist and are explained at time of hire to employees and volunteers.

Facilities

The sport facility is to be given major attention in any risk management program. This is because it has been a primary subject of litigation in sport contexts. The following business standards should be met as part of adhering to best practices by the organization and its employees:

1) A record of all property, including its condition and (if possible) value, exists and is readily available in the event of a fire, tornado, riot, attack by terrorists or vandals, or other loss. These lists are required for filing insurance claims and collection.

2) A detailed system for checking facilities exists and is used routinely. Hazards and cleanliness/sanitation are but two of the topics. Frequency of inspection and name of the inspector are identified for each part of the audit. Ideally, the facility audit process should be reviewed bi-yearly by the same administrators who examines the results of injuries and emergency maintenance so that the two processes align.

3) Facilities meet all code requirements, including lighting. Emergency lights for electrical failure easily lead people to exterior exits. Ground fault circuit interrupters are found in wet areas and locker rooms.

4) Verifications of building compliance with codes are on file.

5) The general condition of a facility is compared with appropriate guidelines (i.e., the American Council of Sports Medicine [ACSM], the National Intramural-Recreational Sport Association [NIRSA], etc.).

6) Protocols for repair, follow-up, and the closing of a facility in need of repair exist and are used. These protocols are reviewed at least bi-yearly.

7) Parking lots, entrances, exterior traffic patterns, and internal structures meet the Americans with Disabilities Act (ADA) requirements.

8) Facility designs that create hazards are identified and remedied.

9) Exit and entrance signs are lit and visible to all. Entrances are secure, and participants' safety is of the utmost importance.

10) A system for opening and closing the building each day is in writing, is followed, and is monitored by management.

11) Where appropriate, the facility is monitored hourly by a person with current CPR and first aid credentials.

Equipment

Equipment risk management demands that the purchaser be able to communicate with the seller. Furthermore, it requires that the purchaser comprehends the warranties and the proper uses of the equipment. Maintenance appears to be a primary cause for equipment to become part of the pattern in litigation. The following are equipment-related requirements that need to be included in any risk management plan:

1) A master list of equipment exists.
2) The equipment—permanently mounted or free standing—is cleaned and inspected routinely. Signed inspection documents are retained.
3) Any requests for equipment repair are in writing. When necessary, equipment is taken out of service if it cannot be repaired immediately.
4) The equipment is maintained as specified by manufacturers. All equipment with warranties that dictate specific repair and service are honored. Equipment is repaired and cleaned according to accepted industry practices.
5) All of the manufacturers' warnings and instructions are posted in a conspicuous place on equipment or on walls near equipment so participants can see them. The statements by manufacturers and retailers about the use of equipment are honored.
6) The staff is trained in the use of new equipment. New employees receive all necessary training before starting work for the business.
7) The equipment meets the standard established by the sport.
8) The laws of the state (i.e. statutes), with reference to equipment, are known and followed.
9) All rescue equipment meets acceptable standards and is clean and ready to use.
10) Safety equipment is provided or required of participants. When participants do not have appropriate safety equipment, they are not permitted to participate. Safety equipment fits properly to assure the safety for which it was designed.

Personnel

Audit components for personnel are organized into three categories:

- employing, evaluating, and terminating;
- employee education; and
- staff training.

Employing, Evaluating, and Terminating

1) Written procedures for advertising jobs and soliciting candidates are designed, used, and recorded.

2) Job descriptions—including tasks, appropriate experience, and credentials to carry out the tasks—exist for each position. Job descriptions explicitly identify safety responsibilities. These descriptions are used for evaluation and termination. Employees are given copies of their job description.

3) Employee records contain

    a) minimum and advanced qualifications for each employee with reference to responsibilities;

    b) contracts, references, and observations; and

    c) evaluation, performance, and attendance.

4) Employers verify that

    a) agencies licensing or certifying employees adhere to acceptable professional standards;

    b) employees know and adhere to the duty of care recommended by their profession, licensure, and certifications; and

    c) professionals know and apply the latest research, when appropriate.

5) Employee evaluation, retention, and termination policies exist and are used, and records are kept. Evaluations support quality, and a due process system is available and used.

6) Termination procedures include

    a) warnings of inadequate or poor-quality work, and evidence that these flaws are in tasks contained in the employee's job description;

    b) opportunity for rehabilitation and change; and

    c) termination, after a continued pattern of incompetence, following rehabilitation.

Employee Education

1) The employees know and understand their job descriptions.

2) The staff members understand legal liability in the tort, civil rights, and business components of this text and how each relates to their job descriptions and routine tasks.

3) The members of the staff understand the risk management system and the role they play in the system.

4) The employees know of injuries inherent in sport and physical activity and recognize the characteristics of participants who might be vulnerable to injuries.

5) The staff members understand the standard of care inherent in their jobs and how the standards would be evaluated by peers and a court of law.

6) Professionals who are engaged in the supervision or coaching of competitive athletes know they could be held for an intentional tort as a result of teaching the violation of a game rule.

7) The staff is capable of performing all safety techniques requisite to the job.

8) There are employee and participant handbooks, and these documents contain detailed information on emergency and injury protocol. Employees are asked to sign a statement that they have read and understood the information and that they will comply with the policies and procedures contained in the manual.

9) Employees and participants know the drug and alcohol rules and agree to abide by them.

10) A system for release of employee and client documents has been devised and is used. It identifies when, why, and to whom each category of document can or should be released. Employee privacy rights are secured.

11) The staff knows about the insurance coverage for the facility or organization.

12) The work environment is safe for employees and they are encouraged to report and document unsafe work conditions.

Staff Training

1) Staff training is formal, occurs during work hours, and is mandatory.

2) Orientations are provided for new personnel.

3) Evidence of the content and attendance at all meetings involving safety education and skill training are retained and available for inspection.

Supervision

The majority of the lawsuits in physical activity specifically state that there was no supervision or that the supervision was inadequate. Whether supervision should exist in a particular activity becomes part of the standard of care. When the legal standard of care demands there be supervision, the supervision must then be legally adequate.

1) Rules are prepared, reviewed, and reformulated at least yearly.

2) Rules are posted.

3) Signage meets codes and is easy to read and understand.

4) A detailed written description of the supervision process exists. It identifies the role of each employee and is contained in each employee's job description.

5) A system for crowd control exists and is rehearsed periodically.

6) Actions have been taken to eliminate horseplay.

7) Advertised standards are maintained.

8) A code of behavior exists and is in writing.

9) Penalties are established to punish participants who behave in an unsafe manner. The penalties are sufficient to deter participants from continuing unsafe behavior.

10) Control in the activity environment is maintained at all times.

Instruction and Coaching

Faulty instruction has been found in physical activity and coaching litigation. The following suggestions should be considered in the creation of a risk management plan involving coaching:

1) Instructional content is used by those prepared to use the content. Licenses, certificates, and college degrees are often required to interpret educational content. An understanding of the application of physiology and biomechanics is essential to the successful interpretation of instructional materials in sport, physical activity, and the coaching of athletics.

2) Instructional content is selected with knowledge of the client's capabilities in mind. An instructor is able to explain the physical demands placed on the performer.

3) Planning is documented. Courses of study, curricular programs, lesson plans, learning sequences, routines, and other planning materials that could be presented to a court of law, if requested, are preserved.

4) Records document the client's major learning benchmarks. Records document the learner's readiness for advanced risk-taking skills.

5) When possible, computer printouts or schedules of a participant's progress are retained.

6) The following elements are considered in program planning:

    a) Performers are matched when body contact is involved.

    b) Appropriate safety equipment is used.

    c) Athletes are properly hydrated at all times.

7) The methodologies employed for instruction meet the test of peer scrutiny.

8) Official games are played according to recognized rules and officials are used. Officials are responsible only for officiating.

Participant Education

Participants are to be informed of the risks of activities, particularly those involved in competitive sport. Warnings are to be provided to persons engaging in high-risk activities. Much of this risk management information is often provided in a waiver, warning, release, etc. The statement can be a legal document that results in a contract or merely an information sheet. Under contract law, an adult can, in many states, contract for almost anything—including contracting away his/her rights. By signing a statement and fully understanding the ramifications of the risks described, adults can contract away their rights to be reimbursed for any injury. A minor cannot contract away the minor's rights. Parents signing a statement for their child to engage in an activity cannot contract away the child's rights. Parents can, however, contract away their rights to sue and recover as a parent. Items such as information statements and waivers are often used merely to alert parents to the risks involved in physical activity and to make it known that their children are engaged in a potentially dangerous activity. In ordinary negligence situations, courts have tended to uphold a waiver when the party signing the contract was an adult and fully understood what rights he or she was releasing. Under no circumstances the courts upheld a statement absolving an agency or a person from an intentional tort. Reckless situations might pose a closer call for a court to consider.

Information statements provide an ideal method of alerting participants to the potential of catastrophic injury, as well as to the serious risks involved in various physical activities. The statements should be clear, easy to understand, specific to the activity, and describe the situation in detail. The documents should clearly outline the participant's responsibility for his/her own safety and for the safety of other participants. A note should be made that rules will be enforced and that participants are to adhere to rules or be denied entrance to the activity or event. The information statements should not only deal with the possibility of injury but should also include the personal safety required of the participant and a description of how the participant will be treated in an accident setting. These statements are to be read, understood, and agreed to by the signer. Contracts and information statements are to be reviewed by legal counsel to be sure they accomplish the objectives desired and are in conformity with state law and recent court decisions.

Fiscal Issues

As mentioned earlier, the best business practices need to be used at all times in sport and physical activity in both for-profit and nonprofit organizations. The following items provide a model to use in thinking through the risks one's agency might encounter:

1) In programs in which gate receipts or the staging of major events are essential to revenue generation, the risk of a riot, terrorist attack, or other hazard has been assessed.
2) When possible, contracts spread liability among vendors and users. All contracts are drafted by legal counsel who will be expected to defend the contracts.
3) Leases and/or contracts are required for groups using facilities.
4) State and local statutes and regulations with respect to fiscal and contract obligations are followed.

5) When transferring risks to others by contract, the transferee knows what is being signed.

6) Avoid signing hold-harmless or indemnification agreements with manufacturers or retailers of athletic equipment. A hold-harmless agreement is a contractual arrangement whereby one party assumes the liability inherent in a situation, thereby relieving the other party of responsibility. Indemnification is the process of securing another against loss or damage. Professionals need to be sure they have not assumed—by contract—the liability for a product. Should such a contract have been signed, the agency or person signing is liable for injury, loss, or damage incurred by anyone as a result of using the equipment. All contracts are to be reviewed by legal counsel before they are signed.

7) Medical examinations are recommended and, when appropriate, required. These records are examined by the staff and are used in program and participation decisions. Written medical clearance is required for injured athletes returning to play.

Evaluation

Risks are identified. Each is evaluated for probability, severity, and magnitude to determine the amount of risk that exists. The continuums shown in Figure 11.1 are used to make judgments about potential risks. A risk may have a high probability of occurring, but should it occur, only a few people will suffer minor discomfort. A risk may have a low probability of occurring, but should it occur, there is a good chance someone will die. An activity scoring high on any one of the characteristics is to be given serious thought. Even minor discomfort for large populations of people can result in a public relations disaster or situation requiring a crisis response. A single death can be devastating to an agency, especially from a public relations perspective.

Control

Control is the third essential component in successful risk management programs. At this step in the process, liability can be controlled by:

1) accepting the risk and assuming the responsibility;

2) retaining the activity and transferring the risk through contracts or insurance;

3) altering the activity to reduce the risk; or

4) eliminating the activity.

Accepting the Risk and Assuming the Responsibility

When a decision is made to retain the risk or maintain a program vulnerable to litigation or negative public image, a defense strategy is devised. The two most important components of the defense strategy are (1) a comprehensive safety or compliance check so the agency and

PROBABILITY

A...B

A. Low probability of injury or harm
B. High probability of injury or harm

SEVERITY

A...B

A. Minor discomfort
B. Serious injury or death

MAGNITUDE

A...B

A. Few people injured
B. Many people injured

FIGURE 11.1. RISK CONTINUUMS

other interested parties realize that every effort had been made to take all precautions with reference to the risk and (2) an assessment of the cost of maintaining the risk or vulnerable program.

Transferring the Risk through Insurance or Contract

When the decision is made to maintain an area that appears vulnerable to risks, risks can be transferred by insurance or contract. Insurance is obtained when the purchaser believes that there is a chance injury could occur and as a result, he is willing to pay insurance premiums to cover an injury and the need to defend, should litigation occur. The purchase of insurance is one means of transferring the risk of loss that might occur should a participant be injured. A number of different kinds of insurance are available. These include a regular policy with an insurance carrier, a regular policy with a high deductible, self-insurance, and a risk management pool where risk is shared.

Self-insurance involves a group of similarly situated professionals who put an identified sum of money in escrow in case one of them should sustain a catastrophic incident. The money is invested but easy to obtain. Should an incident occur, the money is paid to the investor involved; should none of the investors draw on the money, the money becomes an asset of the investors. Self-insurance—or small group pooling of monies for insurance—is particularly valuable when none of the parties has had a major incident in 10 or 15 years and when regular insurance rates are established by mixing high-incident-rate groups with accident-free populations.

Regular insurance policies with large deductibles combine the options of self-insurance and regular insurance. Individuals or agencies self-insure for minor losses and carry regular insurance for major disasters. Significant reduction in premiums usually accompanies these policies. A risk management insurance pool is the grouping of many like agencies in a common pool under an insurance carrier. Many agencies requiring similar insurance against common potential losses are forming groups and going to insurance brokers to obtain coverage. These groups usually keep statistics on their injury rates. Employers are also now often shifting their risks away from their own organization by contracting their risks to employees through independent contractor arrangements. They hire personnel to conduct riskier activities independent from the agency with which they are working. The independent contractor carries insurance and is liable for incidents that occur under his/her direction.

Changing the Activity to Reduce Potential Injury

An alternate program may meet the goals of the program that are considered particularly vulnerable, including vulnerable participants, employees, and/or volunteers. Consider a professional golf event in Florida that often has relied upon retirees as volunteers to staff various event roles. When these elder employees are asked to work a long shift in extreme heat, their vulnerabilities may be highlighted, and the job duties of the volunteer experience may require modification, such as working shorter shifts. When such a modification is available, the savvy manager will accept the alternate option to ensure safe operations. Sometimes, changing arbitrary components of the sport activity, such as time of day for practice to avoid extreme heat, can result in a substantially safer activity. Improving injury recordkeeping, documenting incidents when they occur, instituting safety procedures, changing or improving supervision, and training employees can all reduce the injury rate and create a safe environment. A successful sport organization would implement all of these recommendations in some way to reduce risk and liability facing the organization and its leadership team.

The International Association of Venue Managers, Inc. (IAVM), through the Academy for Venue Safety and Security, provides comprehensive risk and disaster management programs and training opportunities for persons managing and employed in sport facilities and arenas. Structures, personnel, spectators, and services are addressed in IAVM packages for facilities. IAVM works closely with Homeland Security, Health and Human Services (HHS), and numerous state and federal agencies. The National Counter Terrorism Security Office provides many publications on specific topics that will aid the protection of sport interests. Its publication for stadia and arenas was published in 2006.

The Centers for Disease Control and Prevention (CDC) and the U.S. Department of Health and Human Services Office of the Assistant Secretary for Preparedness and Response have taken over the role of the agency for health care research and quality and will provide information on bioterrorism and public health emergencies. The University of Southern Mississippi National Center for Spectator Sports Safety and Security (NCS4) provides detailed information for evacuation of spectator sport sites. Its materials, training, and advice include identifying vulnerability and threats, creation and implementation of protective systems, emergency response and recovery, evacuation capabilities, role of ushers as first responders, and evacuation drills.

Creating Emergency Action Plans

The results of litigation suggest that when liability can be found for managers of physical activity for foreseeable injuries, an emergency action plan is demanded. *Kleinknecht v. Gettysburg* (1991, 1992) was the case that brought the need for an emergency plan to the public. Since that time, health spas in at least three states have been found liable for failure to provide adequate emergency care. Emergency action plans must accommodate severe injuries, apparent drowning, heart attacks, fires, power failures, fights, robberies, vandalism, chemical discharges, bomb threats, severe weather, and other problems. Injuries that require emergency services at the scene of the accident and those that require medical service at a later date are evaluated. The emergency action system consists of research, planning, learning the system, rehearsal, and follow-up.

Research

1) Become aware of the types of injuries that might occur.
2) Simulate emergency care for each of the injuries.
3) Create an injury surveillance system. The surveillance system can classify emergency incidents as cuts and bruises, injuries that might be serious, and serious injuries. Serious injuries are those for which emergency care is required.
4) Where appropriate, medical clearance—including health histories and examinations—are analyzed in light of the incidents.
5) Litigation in the institution and in similar institutions is examined. Legal counsel and insurance representatives are invited to review injury-reporting procedures.

Planning

1) Create an emergency action plan. Put the plan in writing.
2) The plan includes three phases of response:
    a) Identification of injured person.
    b) Further identification and evaluation of injury (triage) and initiation of first aid. A decision to seek external emergency support, such as calling 911, is made quickly.
    c) External emergency support is obtained.

3) Phase one, immediate and temporary care, is handled by competently trained personnel in CPR, first aid, and when appropriate, water rescue. For example, under American Red Cross standards, the staff is to be prepared in infant and adult CPR, community first aid, and prevention of communicable diseases.

4) Phase two is the recognition of an injury requiring emergency medical assistance.

5) The emergency plan is executed by telephone. The telephone has the emergency number or the usual 911 on the phone or on a card next to the phone. When the phone is on a wall or desk, this message is posted immediately above the phone and in a position that will make it easy to read. the following information is available:

    a) Appropriate number (i.e., 911) to summon emergency medical care. If numbers differ for fire and chemical exposure, list them clearly near the other emergency information.

    b) Exact name and address of facility.

    c) Location of nearest door where emergency vehicle will be met.

    d) Number of the telephone in use. This could now often be a cell phone of the person on-site.

    e) Approximate time needed for emergency unit to reach facility.

6) The following instructions are to be used when making a call:

    a) Dial 911. Remain calm.

    b) Give your name and job title.

    c) State the emergency medical care sought, the exact address of the facility, and the location of the facility relative to highways and obvious structures. This information must be clear and concise.

    d) The injury is ... (give general description). Note to emergency responders whether the victim is conscious or unconscious. Be able to provide victim's approximate age.

    e) You are calling from (give number).

    f) Who will meet the emergency medical or fire staff?

    g) Do not hang up until the 911 dispatch operator hangs up.

Learning the System

1) Identify each employee's role in the emergency action plan.

2) Simulate various situations and identify how each will be handled.

3) First aid kits, rescue equipment, and other emergency equipment and supplies are adequate and appropriately packed for use. The equipment is checked daily and carefully repacked after each use.

4) The staff knows how to use all equipment.

5) The system is created with input from emergency medical and fire departments.

Rehearse

1) The plan is rehearsed with the staff and with the emergency medical and fire department. The approximate times required to reach the facility are determined by each of these agencies. These times will be compared to times used in an actual event to see if personnel were able to make decisions and obtain assistance in a reasonable amount of time.

2) The rehearsals are to be held periodically and whenever new staff is employed.

3) The records of all practices are retained.

Follow-up

1) Identify follow-up procedures for seriously injured persons.

2) Have on record the persons who should be contacted if a staff member or a participant sustains a serious injury.

3) Be sure that staff members are aware of workers' compensation and company insurance.

4) Parents of minors are to be notified and informed.

5) A means of working with the media exists. Often the members of the media come in response to the 911 call.

6) The entire system is known by all, rehearsed often, and periodically monitored for flaws.

Accident Reports (Incident Reports)

Accident reports become the first description of the incident and are often the most accurate description. Accident reports must be objective and accurate. Rescuers should freeze the incident in their minds, creating a snapshot of the incident in order to visualize it from start to finish. To be successful, one must practice committing routinely occurring situations to memory, knowing the steps to handle them as second nature, and being able to vividly recall all detailed aspects of an incident. Was anything observed prior to the incident? Commit the image of the incident or accident that occurred to paper as soon as possible, as memories of key witnesses and professionals on-site often change and evolve over time to no longer best reflect what actually happened. Often, this cannot happen until the emergency care vehicle door has been closed and the professional can return to the office.

1) Provide immediate and temporary care.
2) Attend to the needs of the victim. Do not make a statement.
3) If possible, contact management at once. Management needs to be contacted immediately after contacting the external emergency medical personnel.
4) Accident reports must be readily available.
5) Complete the accident report as soon as practical following the incident.
6) If possible, obtain a statement from the victim; copy that statement exactly as the victim made the statement, using quotation marks, etc.
7) Obtain the names and locations of at least three witnesses to the incident. If possible, obtain statements from these people immediately after taking care of the victim.
8) Note all emergency care on the accident report. Attend to the needs of the victim.
9) Retained attorney should be familiar with the accident report form and believe it provides the best protection. Avoid after-the-fact descriptions of the incident.
10) Contact insurance carrier. Conduct a complete investigation for insurance claim purposes.
11) Copies of completed accident reports are to be given to administrators within one hour of the incident.
12) Staff is to be debriefed as soon as possible following the incident.
13) Decisions about closing the facility or continuing the facility in use—given certain incidents—are a part of the emergency action plan. Arrangements are made to relieve staff directly involved in the incident and the rescue.

Impact of COVID 19 on Hosting Safe Sport Events

As sporting events with full attendance slowly resumed in 2021, this updated ongoing guidance reflects current knowledge and best practices about risk factors to consider, maintaining healthy environments, and maintaining (and resuming) safe operations during COVID-19. This includes recommendations about holding small and large gatherings safely, including now-full capacity stadiums of nearly 100,000 people, mask-less, during an ongoing public health crisis. Sport management students and educators should continue to refer to the CDC as the primary authority on this subject matter, and look for sport venue industry organizations, such as the International Association of Venue Managers (IAVM) to advocate about ongoing legal matters related to COVID-19, such as possible governmental immunity from liability including at the state level, as event operations fully resume, as well as the legal efficacy of posting signs or waivers acknowledging the potential risks of contracting COVID-19 in public places such as stadiums. As federal guidance is updated, seeking out information and knowledge about best practices for your particular segment of the sport industry (e.g., fitness centers) in which you intend to work may best prepare for you to responsibly manage and mitigate risks as operations resume to a "new normal" that now exists in the global sports and events sphere.

Guidance for Organizing Large Events and Gatherings Key Points

(Centers for Disease Control, updated as of May 2021):

- Avoid large events and gatherings, when possible.
- Consider the level of risk when deciding to host an event.
- Promote healthy behaviors and maintain healthy environments to reduce risk when large events and gatherings are held.
- Be prepared if someone gets sick during or after the event.

Summary

Risk management is a comprehensive system of identification, evaluation, and control of risks. The identification system consists of the examination of local, state, and federal regulations; professional organizations and industry standards; policies and procedures; facilities; equipment; personnel; supervision; instruction; participant education; fiscal issues; and contracts. Each of these risks is evaluated in light of its probability, severity, and magnitude. A system of control includes avoiding or eliminating the activity; accepting the risk and assuming responsibility; changing the activity to reduce the risk; or transferring the risk through contract or insurance.

Activities

1. You have been invited to give a thirty-minute presentation to the event staff in a high school football stadium on how to handle crowd control during a lightning event. What would you say? Where would you start in developing the training content or delivery options?
2. Prepare a risk management plan for a basketball facility that properly complies with CDC guidance and COVID best practices for social distances and proper sanitation, as well as determining eligibility to participate for all athletes, referees, coaches and game officials.

References

Clement, A. (1988). *Law in sport and physical activity.* Benchmark.

Kleinknecht v. Gettysburg College, 989 F. 2d 1360 (1991).

Recommended Reading

American College of Sports Medicine. (2018). *Health/Fitness Facility Standards and Guidelines* (5th edition). Human Kinetics.

Ammon, R., Southall, R.M., & Nagel, M. (2016). *Sport Facility Management: Organizing Events and Mitigating Risks* (3rd edition). Fitness Information Technology.

Appenzeller, H. (Ed.). (2012). *Risk Management in Sport: Issues and Strategies,* (3rd edition). Carolina Academic Press.

Baker, T. A., Connaughton, D., & Zhang, J. J. (2007). Perceived risk of terrorism and related risk management practices of NCAA Division 1A football stadium managers. *Journal of Legal Aspects of Sport, 17,* 27.

Centers for Disease Control and Prevention (2021, May 20). Guidance for organizing large events and mass gatherings. https://www.cdc.gov/coronavirus/2019-ncov/community/large-events/considerations-for-events-gatherings.html

Hall, S., Cooper, W., Marciani, L., & McGee, J. (2011). *Security Management for Sports and Special Events: An Interagency Approach to Creating Safe Facilities.* Human Kinetics.

Nicholson, W. C. (2010). Obtaining competent legal advice: Challenges for emergency managers and attorneys. *California Western Law Review, 46,* 343.

Spengler, J. O., Connaughton, D., & Pittman, A. (2006). *Risk Management in Sport and Recreation.* Human Kinetics.

Glossary

administrative law. Rules, regulations, and directives created by Acts of Congress.

affirmative action. Action designed to eliminate discrimination.

AIAW. Association for intercollegiate Athletics for Women.

amicus curiae. A brief, on a special topic, presented to the court.

answer. The defendant's first written response to the complaint.

appeal. An application to a higher court to change or modify the judgment of a lower court.

appellant. The party that takes an appeal from one court to another.

appellee. The party against whom an appeal is taken; often called a respondent.

arbitration. A binding third-party resolution.

assault. Apprehension or belief that a person will experience imminent contact. A threat; no contact occurred.

assumption of risk. The victim knew of the potential risk of the activity and voluntarily assumed the risk.

attractive nuisance. The land attracts a minor or young child.

battery. Intentional, harmful, or offensive touching or striking.

breach of contract. Failure, without legal excuse, to perform the obligations and terms of a contract.

case law. The results of a court decision; often referred to as judge-made law or common law.

cause of action. A legal right of redress against another, including the right to sue and the right to recover in a court of law.

certiorari. A writ issued by a superior court (i.e., the United States Supreme Court) directing a lower court to send up records and proceedings in a case.

***collective bargaining agreement* (*CBA*).** An agreement between an employer and a labor union; governs wages, hours, fringe benefits, and other essential working arrangements.

comparative fault. The relative degree of negligence on the part of the plaintiff and defendant, with damages awarded on a basis proportionate to each person's carelessness.

compensatory damages. Money awarded equivalent to the actual value of damage or injury.

complaint. The initial pleading in a civil action filed by the plaintiff.

consent. Failure to object to the act. See also express consent and implied consent.

contract. An agreement that includes an offer, acceptance, and consideration.

contributory negligence. The victim contributed to his/her own injuries.

defamation. holding up a person to ridicule or contempt; harming a person's reputation.

defendant. The party against whom the lawsuit is brought.

demurrer. A pleading of the defendant admitting to the plaintiff's allegation of facts but asserting that the plaintiff's claim fails to state a cause of action.

deposition. A written record of verbal testimony in the form of questions and answers made before a public officer for use in a lawsuit.

disability. A physical or mental impairment that limits one or more of the major life activities, a record of such, or being regarded as having such an impairment.

discovery. The process by which opposing parties obtain information in preparation for trial.

dismissal. An order or judgment disposing of an action or suit without trial of the issues involved.

disparate impact. A legal theory that requires an institution to show percentages of people given specific opportunities to be the same as their respective groups.

disparate treatment. Practices that appear neutral in the treatment of different groups but fall more harshly on one group than another.

due process. A legal proceeding for the enforcement of private rights; includes notice and a hearing.

duty. A legal obligation.

Establishment Clause (of freedom of religion). Separates church and state.

express consent. A signed agreement that meets the standard of a contract and relieves the provider of the activity of negligence.

fair use. Certain privileges for the use of copyright materials.

false imprisonment. Intentional confinement or restraint without consent or justified cause.

fiduciary. A person with a duty to act primarily for another's benefit; for example, a person who manages someone's money.

foreseeability. The ability to anticipate an incident.

Fourth Amendment to the United States Constitution. The right of people to be secure in their persons, houses, papers, and effects.

Free Exercise Clause (of freedom of religion). Grants the right to practice one's religion.

freedom of the press. Freedom to publish and disseminate information.

freedom of speech. The freedom to speak, remain silent, advocate, and communicate ideas.

good Samaritan law. Immunity is given to those who provide emergency care.

hostile environment. An adverse or unfriendly situation.

IAAF. international Amateur Athletic Federation.

immunity. Freedom from suit.

implied consent. A person who understands the risk of the activity consents to the risk by participating in the activity.

indemnify. To compensate a person for a loss or to reimburse a person for expenses incurred.

independent contractor. A businessperson who agrees to a specific project for a set price. The owner of the contract is responsible for his/her employees.

injunction. A court order requiring a person to act or refrain from acting in a certain manner.

injunctive relief. An order from the court to stop a person from committing an action in which he/she is currently engaging.

intentional tort. A deliberate act that results in harm. There is intent to commit the act and not always an intent to injure.

invitee. A person invited onto the land of another, usually for an economic benefit.

judgment notwithstanding the verdict (JNOV). A judgment entered by the court for legal reasons that are contrary to the verdict rendered by the jury.

jurisdiction. The authority of the court to hear and decide a lawsuit.

law in sport. The range of legal concepts found in day-to-day decisions in the sport industry.

LexisNexis Academic Universe. An electronic research system used to retrieve legal literature, including court decisions.

liability. A legal responsibility, duty, or obligation.

licensee. A person who is on the land of another for no economic benefit.

mediation. An informal dispute resolution process in which a neutral third person helps the parties reach an agreement.

motion. An application to the court or judge to direct an act in favor of the applicant; for example, a request for a directed verdict, a new trial, etc.

negligence. Conduct falling below the standard of care required of a reasonable and prudent person in the protection of others.

offer. A promise to do or to refrain from doing something.

open and obvious. An owner of land is not liable to a trespasser when the danger is obvious.

plaintiff. Person who brings an action.

pleading. Formal paper filed in a court action, including the plaintiff's complaint and the defendant's answer. it shows what is alleged by the plaintiff as well as what is admitted or denied by the defendant.

precedent. A decision considered as an example or authority for an identical or similar case arising under a similar question of law.

premise liability. Liability of the owner of property.

prima facie case. A case in which the evidence is so strong that the adverse party can overthrow the evidence only by sufficient rebutting evidence.

primary source. An original work.

product liability. The liability of the manufacturer, retailer, and seller of a dangerous or defective product.

professional relationship standard of care. The duty that exists when a body of knowledge exists and is the recognized level of performance expected.

punitive damages. Financial damages assessed to punish a party for wrongdoing. The amount assessed is based on the assets of the party causing the damage.

qualitative research. Use of non-statistical techniques to describe phenomena.

quantitative research. Research using statistics to describe phenomena.

reasonable person standard of care. What an average person would do in the situation.

release. An agreement to release someone from liability. To be effective it must meet the requirements of a contract.

remand. Action of an appellate court sending a case back to a trial court for further action.

respondeat superior. A legal rule that holds an employer liable for the negligent acts of employees.

right of publicity. The right of one to control his/her name and likeness and to prevent its use by others for commercial benefit.

secondary source. An article or book reporting the results of primary source materials.

self-defense. Enables a person under attack to defend himself/herself.

special relationship standard of care. The duty of care owed by parents and schools to children and youths.

sport law. Basic law and court decisions unique to sport.

standards of care. The attention and caution that the average person would exercise in a situation. The three standards of care are reasonable person, special relationship, and professional.

stare decisis. A court doctrine recognizing the value and use of prior court decisions in future court cases in the same jurisdiction. For example, decisions of the Supreme Court are binding on the entire United States.

statutes of limitations. Statutes of the federal and state governments setting a maximum time period for the filing of lawsuits.

summary judgment. A decision of a court on the merits of a lawsuit when the pleadings and other documents reveal that there is no genuine issue of material facts, and the party who sought the judgment is entitled to it as a matter of law.

TAC. The Athletic Congress.

Title IX. A federal statute that extends the principles articulated under the Fourteenth Amendment to public and private schools that rely upon federal or state funds.

trespasser. A person on the land of another without the owner's permission.

vacated. Set aside, canceled, or rescinded; as with a court order or judgment.

vicarious liability. Substituted or indirect responsibility for another's actions arising out of a legal responsibility. See also respondeat superior.

waiver. An intentional release of a known legal right.

warranty. Guarantee by a manufacturer, wholesaler, or retailer to a purchaser that a product will perform according to identified standards. An express warranty is in writing. An implied warranty is an unwritten understanding that the product will do what it claims to do.

writ. A written court order or a judicial process.

writ of certiorari. An order of the U.S. Supreme Court that directs a lower court to send up a case for review.

Table of Cases

Index

C

M

N

About the Author

John Grady, JD, PhD

John Grady is a professor of sport and entertainment management at the University of South Carolina. He teaches courses in sport law and risk management in sport. Dr. Grady's research interests focus on legal issues impacting sports business, including law and marketing issues in the context of the Olympic Games, as well as stadium accessibility for individuals with disabilities. His scholarship has been published in premier legal and sport management outlets, including the *Journal of Sport Management, Journal of Legal Issues in Sport,* and *Sport Management Review.*

Dr. Grady received his bachelor's degree in management with honors in finance from Penn State. He completed his JD and PhD at Florida State University. He has served as past-president of the Sport and Recreation Law Association and currently serves on the editorial board of the *Journal of Legal Aspects of Sport.* He frequently comments on legal issues involving Olympic athlete endorsement, especially as it relates to Rule 40.